GENERAL HISTORY
OF
CONNECTICUT,

THE REV. SAMUEL PETERS' LL. D.

GENERAL HISTORY

OF

CONNECTICUT,

FROM ITS FIRST SETTLEMENT UNDER GEORGE FENWICK
TO ITS LATEST PERIOD OF AMITY WITH GREAT
BRITAIN PRIOR TO THE REVOLUTION;

INCLUDING

*A DESCRIPTION OF THE COUNTRY, AND MANY CURIOUS
AND INTERESTING ANECDOTES.*

WITH AN APPENDIX, POINTING OUT THE CAUSES OF THE REBELLION IN
AMERICA; TOGETHER WITH THE PARTICULAR PART TAKEN BY
THE PEOPLE OF CONNECTICUT IN ITS PROMOTION.

BY A GENTLEMAN OF THE PROVINCE.
LONDON: 1781.

TO WHICH ARE ADDED, ADDITIONS TO APPENDIX, NOTES, AND EXTRACTS
FROM LETTERS, VERIFYING MANY IMPORTANT STATEMENTS
MADE BY THE AUTHOR.

BY

SAMUEL JARVIS McCORMICK.

Select Bibliographies Reprint Series

BOOKS FOR LIBRARIES PRESS
FREEPORT, NEW YORK

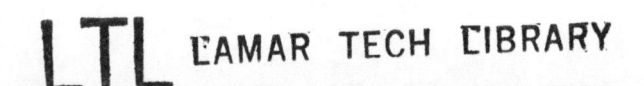

First Published 1877
Reprinted 1969

STANDARD BOOK NUMBER:
8369-5073-9

LIBRARY OF CONGRESS CATALOG CARD NUMBER:
71-95073

PRINTED IN THE UNITED STATES OF AMERICA

PREFACE.

Though Connecticut be the most flourishing, and, proportionally, the most populous, province in North America, it has hitherto found no writer to introduce it, in its own right, to the notice of the world. Slight and cursory mention in the accounts of other provinces, or of America in general, has yet only been made of it. The historians of New England have constantly endeavored to aggrandize Massachusetts Bay as the parent of the other colonies, and as comprehending all that is worthy of attention in that country. Thus Governor Hutchinson says, in the preface of his history of that province, that "there was no importation of planters from England to any part of the continent northward of Maryland, excepting to Massachusetts, for more than fifty years after the colony began;" not knowing, or willing to forget, or to conceal, that Saybrook, New Haven, and Long Island, were settled with emigrants from England within half that period. Another reason for the obscurity in which the Connectitensians have hitherto been involved is to be found among their own sinister views and purposes. Prudence dictated that their deficiency in point of right to the soil they occupied, their wanton and barbarous persecutions, illegal practices, daring usurpations, etc., had better be concealed than exposed to public view.

To dissipate this cloud of prejudice and knavery, and to bring to light truths long concealed, is the motive of my offering the following sheets to the world. I am bold to assert that Connecticut merits a fuller account than envy or ignorance has yet suffered to be given it; and that I have followed the line of truth freely, and unbiased by partiality or prejudice. The reader, therefore, will not be surprised should I have placed the New-Englanders in a different light from that in which they have yet appeared: their characterizers have not been sufficiently unprejudiced, unawed by power, or unaffected by the desire of obtaining it, always to set them in a true one. Dr. Mather and Mr. Neal were popular writers, but, at the time they extolled the prudence and piety of the colonists, they suppressed what are called in New England unnecessary truths. Governor Hutchinson, who loved fame, and feared giving offense, published a few only of those truths, which failed not to procure him a proportionate share of popular distrust and odium. For my own part, I believe my readers will give me credit for having neither the favor nor the fear of man before me in writing this history of Connecticut. I discard the one; I court not the other. My sole aim has been to represent the country, the people, and their transactions, in proper colors. Too much, however, must not be expected from me. I am very sensible of many great defects in this performance, wherein very little assistance was to be obtained from publications of others. Mr. Chambers, indeed, who is writing "Political Annals of the Present United Colonies," pursues that task with great pains and address. His researches have been of some use to me; but, as to the New England writers, error, disguise, and misrepresentations, too much abound in them to be serviceable in this undertaking, though they related more to the subject than they do. The good-natured critic, therefore, will excuse the want of a regular and connected detail of facts and events which it was impossible for me to preserve, having been deprived of papers of my ancestors which would have given my relation that and other advantages. I hope, therefore, for much indulgence, striking, as I have done, into a new and dark path, almost without a guide. If I have carried myself through it, though with some digressions, yet without incurring the danger of being accounted a deceiver, my disordered garb will, I presume, find an apology in the ruggedness of the road—my Scriptural phraseology be ascribed to the usage of my country.

For three generations my forefathers were careful observers of the proceedings of the Connecticut colonists; and if their papers and myself should continue in existence till a return of peace shall restore them to my possession, I trust the public will not be displeased with the design I have of committing them to the press. In the mean time, lest that event should never take place, I beg their acceptance of the present volume, which, whatever other historical requisite it may want, must, I think, be allowed to possess originality and truth (rare properties in modern publications), and, therefore, I hope, will not be deemed unworthy the public favor.

SECOND PREFACE.

Mr. James Hammond Trumbull, the author of the work entitled "The Blue Laws of Connecticut and New Haven, and the False Blue Laws invented by the Rev. Samuel Peters," which has just made its appearance, attempts to throw discredit on the work of Dr. Peters, and represents it as a fiction, and a calumny upon the early settlers of Connecticut.

Mr. Trumbull seems to have spared no trouble in his researches to show that no such laws as the "Blue Laws" represented by Dr. Peters were in existence, and to impress this more forcibly upon the public he gives the laws of 1639, 1650, and 1656; when, had he looked more carefully at the doctor's "History of Connecticut," he would have found he alluded to them in these words: " The laws made by the independent Dominion, and nominated the Blue Laws by the neighboring colonies, were never suffered to be printed;" nevertheless, Mr. Trumbull shows that there were laws at that time equally repugnant, though clothed in more subtile phraseology, but pointing to the same result, and that these laws were rigidly enforced.

Dr. Peters's "History of Connecticut" was published in London, in 1781, and possibly there are not twenty persons living who have ever read it. As its truthfulness was unpalatable to the Connecticut colony, the issue that came to this country, I believe, was publicly burnt, and the court prohibited the republishing of the work in the State; consequently it has become a very rare work, so much so that in March, 1877, a copy, at a sale of old works, brought the fabulous price of one hundred and fifteen dollars, demonstrating the fact that but few remained in existence.

The appearance, therefore, of Mr. Trumbull's work gives the public but one side of the case; under these circumstances I have been induced to republish the work from the original copy belonging to Dr. Peters, using notes and quotations from writers and authors of high repute, and from documents and manuscripts written before the Revolutionary War, which have come into my possession since Mr. Trumbull's work has appeared, and which, I believe, will show the unbiased public that Mr. Trumbull has not been guided solely by unselfishness in attempting to wipe out the ridicule entailed on Connecticut by the early Blue Laws; but he still retains a little of the fanaticism, bigotry, and spleen, so justly attributed to his ancestor, who was the cause of driving Dr. Peters from his native country; and he would now attempt to cast discredit upon a work that was well received in the State by the intelligent portion of the community, and indorsed as a true history.

In writing of the "Blue Laws," Prof. De Vere, of the University of Virginia, in his volume on "Americanisms," published in 1872, says, "They are confirmed without a doubt." The late Rev. A. B. Chapin, in his article published in the *Churchman* of Hartford, Connecticut, August 19, 1876, entitled "Was the History of Connecticut a Fabrication?" says, "If Dr. Peters had had my advantages he might have been a worse historian for Connecticut than he has been already." I might continue such quotations from persons of equally high standing, but my object is to let the work stand upon its merits, giving it to the public as it left the author's hands, merely adding such portions as I find in the unpublished manuscripts in my possession, relating chiefly to the doctor himself, and the cause of his having to leave the country; also to the action taken by the colony of Connecticut for the relief of the destroyers of the teas in Boston.

It has not been for the purpose of obtaining a character for the work, which it did not before possess, that I again bring it before the public; but that they may have both sides of the case for their view, joined with that of defending my ancestor, the author, a good and venerable old clergyman, who was driven from his country, and his large estates sequestrated, for obeying "the laws of his God, the laws of his country, and the dictates of his conscience, by the fanatics of Connecticut," and from the unjust and unwarrantable attacks of Mr. Trumbull.

S. J. McCormick.

GENERAL HISTORY OF CONNECTICUT.

AFTER several unsuccessful attempts to form settlements in the southern part of North America, in which little more had been done than giving the name of Virginia, in compliment to the virgin Queen Elizabeth, to the country, a patent was obtained in 1606, from James I., by Sir Thomas Gates and associates, for all lands there between the thirty-fourth and forty-fifth degrees of north latitude ; and, at the patentees' own solicitation, they were divided into two companies ;[1] to the former of which were granted all the lands between the thirty-fourth and forty-first degrees of north latitude, and to the latter all those between the thirty-eighth and forty-fifth degrees. A part of the coast of the territory last mentioned being explored in 1614, and a chart presented to the then Prince of Wales, afterward Charles I., it received from him the appellation of New England.

In the mean time, however, notwithstanding the claim of the English in general to North America, and the particular grant to Sir Thomas Gates and associates, above mentioned, the Dutch got footing on Manhattan or New York Island, pushed up Hudson's River, as high as Albany, and were beginning to spread on its

[1] Commonly denominated the London and Plymouth Companies.

banks when, in 1614, they were compelled by Sir Samuel Argal to acknowledge themselves subjects of the King of England, and submit to the authority of the Governor of Virginia.[1]

For the better enabling them to accomplish their American undertakings, the Plymouth Company, in 1620, obtained a new patent, admitting new members of rank and fortune. By this they were styled "The Council, established at Plymouth, for planting and governing the said country called New England;" and to them were now granted all the lands between the fortieth and forty-eighth degrees of north latitude, and extending east and west from the Atlantic ocean to the South Sea, except such as were then actually possessed by any Christian prince or people.[2]

[1] About two years after, he made a second voyage to the river, in the service of a number of Dutch merchants; and, some time after, made sale of his right to the Dutch. The right to the country, however, was antecedently in King James, by virtue of discovery which Hudson had made under his commission. The English protested against this sale; but the Dutch, in 1614, under the Amsterdam West India Company, built a fort, nearly on the same grounds where the city of Albany now is, which they called Fort Aurania. Sir Thomas Dale, Governor of Virginia, directly after dispatched Captain Argall to dispossess the Dutch, and they submitted to the King of England, and under him to the Governor of Virginia.

[2] November 3, 1620, just before the arrival of Mr. Robinson's people in New England, King James I., by letters-patent, under the great seal of England, incorporated the Duke of Lenox, the Marquises of Rockingham and Hamilton, the Earls of Arundel and Warwick, and others, to the number of forty noblemen, knights, and gentlemen, by the name of "the Council established at Plymouth, in the county of Devon, for the planting, ruling, and governing of New England in America . . . . and granting unto them, and their successors and assigns, all that part of America lying and being in breadth from forty degrees of north latitude, from the equinoctial line, to the forty-eighth degree of said north

DIVISION BY PATENTEES. 13

Not long afterward, the patentees came to the resolution of making a division of the country among themselves by lot, which they did in the presence of James I. The map of New England, etc., published by Purchas in 1625, which is now become scarce, and probably the only memorial extant of the result, has the following names on the following portions of the coast:

Patentees	Region
Earl of Arundel, Sir Ferdinando Gorges, Earl of Carlisle,	Between the rivers St. Croix and Penobscot.
Lord Keeper, Sir William Belassis, Sir Robert Mansell,	Between Penobscot and Sagadahoc river.
Earl of Holderness, Earl of Pembroke, Lord Sheffield, Sir Henry Spelman, Sir William Apsley, Captain Love, Duke of Buckingham, Earl of Warwick, Duke of Richmond, Mr. Jennings, Dr. Sutcliffe,	Between Sagadahoc and Charles river.
Lord Gorges, Sir Samuel Argal, Dr. Bar. Gooch,	Between Charles River and Narraganset.

In the above map, no names appear on the coast north of the river St. Croix, i. e., Nova Scotia, which was relinquished by the patentees in favor of Sir Wil-

latitude inclusively, and in length of and within all the breadth aforesaid, through the mainland from sea to sea."

The patent ordained that this tract of country should be called New England in America, and by that name have continuance forever.

14   GENERAL HISTORY OF CONNECTICUT.

liam Alexander; the coast west of Narraganset is not exhibited by Purchas, so that it is uncertain whether the division above mentioned extended to that or not. Probably, it was not then sufficiently explored. However, in 1635, the patentees, from the exigency of their affairs, thinking a surrender of their patent to the king, with reservation of their several rights with regard to the property of the land, an advisable measure, a new division of the coast was struck out, consisting of twelve lots, extending to and comprising lands on the west side of Hudson's River, and, of course, the Dutch settlement at Manhattan. The following is an account of these lots:

1. From the river St. Croix to Pemaquid.
2. From Pemaquid to Sagadahoc.
3. The land between the rivers Amarascoggin and Kenebec.
4. From Sagadahoc along the sea-coast to Piscataqua.
5. From Piscataqua to Naumkeak (or Salem).
6. From Naumkeak, round the sea-coast by Cape Cod to Narraganset.
7. From Narraganset to the half-way bound, between that and Connecticut River, and so fifty miles up into the country.
8. From the half-way bound to Connecticut River, and so fifty miles into the country.
9. From Connecticut River along the sea-coast of Hudson's River, and so up thirty miles.
10. From the thirty miles' end to cross, up forty miles eastward.
11. From the west side of Hudson's River thirty miles up the country toward the fortieth degree, where New England beginneth.
12. From the end of the thirty miles up the said river, northward thirty miles further, and from thence to cross into the land forty miles.—("Hutchinson's History of Massachusetts Bay.")

These divisions were immediately, on the above-mentioned surrender, to be confirmed by the king to the proprietors, and proposed to be erected into so many distinct provinces, under one general Governor of New England. It is certain that this plan was not then carried into execution in the whole. Several, if not all of the lots were formally conveyed to their respective owners previous to the resignation of the patent. How many were confirmed by the king is not known; there is positive evidence of but one—to Sir Ferdinando Gorges.

The eighth and ninth lots nearly form the province of Connecticut, taking its name from the great Indian king who reigned when the English made their first inroads into the country.

But before I give an account of this event, it may be proper to premise a few particulars concerning the Dutch, already spoken of as having seated themselves on New York Island and the banks of Hudson's River, and also concerning the settlements formed by the English in and near the Massachusetts Bay.

The same year which established the Council of Plymouth, established also the Dutch West India Company, to whom the States of Holland are said to have granted, the year after, all the lands between Capes Cod and Henlopen.

Under their encouragement and support the Dutch at New York were induced to look upon the act of Argal with contempt; accordingly, they revolted from the allegiance he had imposed upon them, cast off the authority of their English Governor, and proceeded in their colonizing pursuits under one of their own nation;

in which they seemed to have employed their wonted industry, having, before the year 1637, erected a fort on the spot where Hartford now stands.

A party of Brownists, who in 1619 are said to have obtained a grant of land from the Virginia Company, set sail on the 6th of September in the following year for Hudson's River; but making on the 11th of November the harbor of Cape Cod instead of the place of their destination, and finding themselves not in a fit condition to put to sea again at such a late season of the year, they ranged along the coast till a commodious situation presented itself, when they disembarked, and founded the colony of New Plymouth.

Seven years afterward a party of Puritans procured a grant of the lands from Merrimack River to the southernmost part of Massachusetts Bay. They made their first settlement at Naumkeak, by them now named Salem, and a second at Charlestown. Great numbers of the Puritans followed their brethren to New England, so that, within a few years, was laid the foundation of Boston and other towns upon the Massachusetts coast.[1]

Thus far had colonization taken place in the neighboring country when, in 1634, the first part of the English adventurers arrived in Connecticut from England[2]

[1] The same year in which the patent of Massachusetts received the royal confirmation, Mr. John Endicott was sent over with about three hundred people by the patentees, to prepare the way for the settlement of a permanent colony in that part of New England.

They arrived at Naumkeak in June, and began a settlement, which they named "Salem." This was the first town in Massachusetts, and the second in New England.

[2] Mather, Neal, Hutchinson, and other writers of New England his-

under the conduct of George Fenwick, Esq., and the Rev. Thomas Peters, and established themselves at the mouth of the Connecticut River, where they built a town, and which they called Saybrook, a church, and a fort.[1]

tory, have uniformly deviated from the truth in representing Connecticut as having been first settled by emigrants from their darling Massachusetts Bay.

[1] Nearly at the same time, October 8, 1635, Mr. John Winthrop, son of Governor Winthrop, of Massachusetts, arrived at Boston with a commission from Lord Say and Seal, Lord Brook, and other noblemen and gentlemen interested in the Connecticut patent, to erect a fort at the mouth of the Connecticut River. Their lordships sent over men, ordnance, ammunition, and two thousand pounds sterling, for the accomplishment of their design.

Mr. Winthrop was directed by his commission, immediately on his arrival, to repair to Connecticut with fifty able men, and to erect the fortifications and to build houses for the garrison, and for gentlemen who might come over into Connecticut. They were first to build houses for their own present accommodation, and after that such as should be suitable for the reception of men of quality. The latter were to be erected within the fort.

It was required that the planters at the beginning should settle themselves near the mouth of the river, and set down in bodies, that they might be in a situation for intrenching and defending themselves. The commission made provision for the reservation of a thousand or fifteen hundred acres of good land for the maintenance of the fort, as nearly adjoining it as might be with convenience.

Mr. Winthrop, having intelligence that the Dutch were preparing to take possession of the mouth of the river, as soon as he could engage twenty men and furnish them with provisions, dispatched them in a small vessel of about thirty tons, to prevent their getting command of the river, and to accomplish the service to which he had been appointed.

But a few days after the party sent by Mr. Winthrop arrived at the mouth of the river, a Dutch vessel appeared off the harbor from New Netherlands, sent on purpose to take possession of the mouth of the river and to erect fortifications. The English had by this time mounted

18   GENERAL HISTORY OF CONNECTICUT.

In 1636 another party proceeded from Boston under the conduct of Mr. John Haynes and the Rev. Thomas Hooker, and in June settled on the west bank of the

two pieces of cannon and prevented their landing; thus, providentially, was this fine tract of country preserved for our venerable ancestors and their posterity.

Mr. Winthrop was appointed Governor of the Connecticut River and the ports adjacent for the term of one year. He erected a fort, built houses, and made a settlement, according to his instructions. One David Gardiner, an expert engineer, assisted in the work, planned the fortifications, and was appointed lieutenant of the fort.

Mr. Davenport and others, who afterward settled New Haven, were active in this affair, and hired Gardiner, in behalf of their lordships, to come to New England and assist in this business.

As the settlement of the three towns on Connecticut River was begun before the arrival of Mr. Winthrop, and the design of their lordships to make plantations upon it was known, it was agreed that the settlers on the river should either remove upon full satisfaction being made by their lordships, or else sufficient room should be found for them and their companions at some other place.

While these plantations were forming in the southwestern part of Connecticut, another commenced on the west side of the mouth of the Connecticut River. A fort had been built here in 1635–'36, and preparations had been made for the reception of gentlemen of quality; but the war with the Pequots, the uncultivated state of the country, and the low condition of the colony, prevented the coming of any principal character from England to take possession of a township and make settlement in this tract.

Until this time there had been only a garrison of about twenty men in the place. They had made some small improvements in the lands, and erected a few buildings in the vicinity of the fort; but there had been no settlement of a plantation with civil privileges. But about midsummer Mr. George Fenwick, with his lady and family, arrived in a ship of two hundred and fifty tons; another ship came in company with him. They were both for Qunnipiack.

Mr. Fenwick and others came over with the view to take possession of a large tract upon the river in behalf of their lordships, the original patentees, and to plant a town at the mouth of the river. A settlement

Connecticut River, where Hartford now stands, notwithstanding the Dutch had found their way thither before them.[1]

was soon made, and named Saybrook, in honor of their lordships, Say and Seal, and Brook.

Mr. Fenwick, Mr. Thomas Peters, who was the first minister in the plantation, Captain Gardiner, Thomas Leffingwell, Thomas Tracy, and Captain John Mason, were some of the principal planters.

[1] In July, 1638, Mr. Winslow and Mr. Bradford, therefore, made a journey to Boston to confer with Governor Winthrop and his Council on the subject. Governor Winslow and Mr. Bradford proposed to them to join with Plymouth in a trade to Connecticut for hemp and beaver, and to erect a house for the purpose of commerce. It was represented as necessary to prevent the Dutch from taking possession of that fine country, who, it was reported, were about to build upon the river. But Governor Winthrop declined the motion; he considered it was not proper to make a plantation there, because there were three or four thousand warlike Indians upon the river, and small pinnaces only could enter at high water; also, because that seven months in the year no vessels could go into it, by reason of the ice and the violence of the stream.

The Plymouth people, therefore, determined to undertake the enterprise at their own risk. Preparations were made for erecting a trading-house and establishing a small company on the river. In the mean time, the master of a vessel from Massachusetts, who was trading at New Netherlands, showed to Walter Van Twiller, the Dutch Governor, the commission which the English had to trade, and settle in New England, and that his Majesty the King of England had granted all these parts to his own subjects. He, therefore, desired that the Dutch would not build at Connecticut.

This appears to have been done at the direction of Governor Winthrop, for, in consequence of it, the Dutch Governor wrote a very complaisant letter to him, in which he represented that the lords, the States-General, had granted the same country to the West India Company. He requested, therefore that the English would make no settlements in Connecticut until the affair should be determined between the court of England and the States-General.

This appears to have been a piece of policy in the Dutch Governor to keep the English still until the Dutch had got a firm footing upon the river.

Several vessels this year went to Connecticut River to trade. John

A third party of English settlers in Connecticut were headed by Mr. Theophilus Eaton and the Rev. John Davenport, who left England early in the year 1637, and, contrary to the advice of the people of Mas-

Oldham, from Dorchester, and three men with him, also traveled through the wilderness to Connecticut, to view the country and trade with the Indians. The sachem upon the river made him most welcome, and gave him a present in beaver. He found that the Indian hemp grew spontaneously in the meadows in great abundance. He purchased a quantity of it, and upon trial it appeared much to exceed the hemp which was grown in England.

William Holmes, of Portsmouth, with his company, having prepared the frame of a house, with boards, and materials for covering it immediately, put them on board of a vessel and sailed for Connecticut. Holmes had a commission from the Governor of Plymouth and a chosen company to accomplish his design.

When he came into the river he found that the Dutch had got in before him, made a light fort, and planted two pieces of cannon: this was erected at the place called Hartford.

The Dutch forbade Holmes going up the river, stood by their cannon, and ordered him to strike his colors or they would fire upon him; but he was a man of spirit, assured them that he had a commission from the Governor of Plymouth to go up the river, and that he must obey his orders. They poured out their threats, but he proceeded, and, landing on the west side of the river, erected his house a little below the mouth of the small river in Windsor. The house was covered with the utmost dispatch, and fortified with palisadoes. The sachems who were the original owners of the soil had been driven from this part of the country by the Pequots, and were now carried home on board of Holmes's vessel. Of them the Plymouth people purchased the land on which they erected their house. "This," Governor Wolcott says, "was the first house erected in Connecticut." The Dutch about the same time erected a trading-house at Hartford, which they called the "Hirse of Good Hope."

It was with great difficulty that Holmes and his company erected and fortified their house, and kept it afterward. The Indians were offended at their bringing home the original proprietors and lords of the country, and the Dutch that they had settled there, and were about to rival them in trade and in possession of these excellent lands upon the river. They

SETTLEMENT OF NEW HAVEN.

sachusetts Bay, who were very desirous of their settling in that province, fixing themselves in the July following on the north side of a small bay wherein the river Quinnipiack empties itself, forty miles southwest of Hartford, and there built the town of New Haven.[1]

were obliged, therefore, to combat both, and to keep a constant watch upon them.

The Dutch, before the Plymouth people took possession of the river, had invited them in an amicable manner to trade in Connecticut; but, when they were apprised that they were making preparations for a settlement there, they repented the invitation, and spared no exertion to prevent them.

On the 8th of June the Dutch had sent Jacob Van Curter to purchase lands upon the Connecticut. He made a purchase of about twenty acres at Hartford, of Nepuquash, a Pequot captain. Of this the Dutch took possession in October, and on the 25th of the month Curter protested against William Holmes, the builder of the Plymouth house. Some time afterward the Dutch Governor, Walter Van Twiller, of Fort Amsterdam, dispatched a reënforcement to Connecticut, designing to drive Holmes and his company from the river. A band of seventy men, under arms, with banners displayed, assaulted the Plymouth house, but they found it so well fortified, and the men who kept it so vigilant and determined, that it could not be taken without bloodshed; they therefore came to a parley, and finally returned in peace.

About the beginning of June, 1636, Mr. Hooker, Mr. Stone, and about one hundred men, women, and children, took their departure from Cambridge, and traveled more than one hundred miles through a hideous and trackless wilderness to Hartford. They had no guide but their compass; made their way over mountains, through swamps, thickets, and rivers, which were not passable but with difficulty. They had no cover but the heavens, nor any lodgings but what simple Nature afforded them. They drove with them one hundred and sixty head of cattle, and by the way subsisted upon the milk of their cows. Mrs. Hooker was borne through the wilderness upon a litter. The people generally carried their packs, arms, and utensils. They were nearly a fortnight on their journey.

[1] While the planters of Connecticut were thus exerting themselves in prosecuting and regulating the affairs of that colony, another was projected and settled at Quinnipiack, and afterward called New Haven. On

Thus, within the space of three years, was Connecticut seized upon by three distinct English parties, in three different places, forming a triangle; by what authority I will now beg leave to inquire.

the 26th of July, 1637, Mr. John Davenport, Mr. Samuel Eaton, Theophilus Eaton, and Edward Hopkins, Esquires, Mr. Thomas Gregson, and many others of good character and fortune, arrived in Boston.

Mr. Davenport had been a famous minister in the city of London, and was a distinguished character for piety, learning, and good conduct. Many of his congregation, on account of the esteem which they had for his person and ministry, followed him to New England.

Mr. Eaton and Mr. Hopkins had been merchants in London, possessed great estates, and were men of eminence for their abilities and integrity.

The fame of Davenport, and the reputation and good estates of the principal gentlemen of his company, made the people of Massachusetts exceedingly desirous of their settlement in that Commonwealth.

Great pains were taken not only by particular persons and towns, but by the General Court, to fix them in the colony.

Charlestown made them large offers, and Newbury proposed to give up the whole town to them. The General Court offered them any place which they should select. But they were determined to plant a distant colony. By the pursuit of the Pequots to the westward, the English became acquainted with that fine tract along the shore from Saybrook to Fairfield, and with its several harbors. It was represented as fruitful, and happily situated for navigation and commerce.

The company, therefore, projected a settlement in that part of the country.

In the fall of 1637 Mr. Eaton and others who were of the company made a journey to Connecticut to explore the lands and harbors on the sea-coast. They pitched upon Quinnipiack for the place of their settlement. They erected a poor hut, in which a few men subsisted through the winter.

On the 30th of March, 1638, Mr. Davenport, Mr. Prudden, Mr. Samuel Eaton, and Theophilus Eaton, Esquire, with the people of their company, sailed from Boston to Quinnipiack. In about a fortnight they arrived at their desired port.

On the 14th of April they kept their first Sabbath in the place. The people assembled under a large, spreading oak, and Mr. Daven-

TITLE OF SETTLERS. 23

In favor of the first, it is alleged that they purchased part of the lands belonging to the Lords Say and Brook, which land included the eighth and ninth lots, and had been assigned to them by the Earl of Warwick, who, about the year 1630, obtained a grant of the same from the Council of Plymouth, and a patent from the king, and that Fenwick was properly commissioned to settle and govern the colony.

Neal, Douglas, and Hutchinson, speak of the grant and assignment with the greatest confidence, but make no reference where either may be consulted.

They were very willing to believe what they said, and wished to palm it upon the credulity of their readers as a fact too well established to need proof. I shall endeavor to show the futility of their assertions; indeed, Mr. Hutchinson himself inadvertently gives reason to doubt the truth of them, writing of the transactions of 1622: " The Earl of Warwick," says he, " we are assured, had a patent for the Massachusetts Bay about the same time, but the bounds are not known." It will appear presently that a part of the territory in question was, in 1635, granted to the Marquis of Hamilton. Now, taking these several items together, the Council of Plymouth are represented to have granted not only to Massachusetts Bay in 1622, but also, in 1630, a region of vast extent, including Connecticut, to the Earl of Warwick; and then, in 1635, they have regranted the best part of the latter to the Marquis of Hamilton. There is an in-

port preached to them from Matthew v. 1. He discoursed on the temptations of man, and made such observations as were pertinent to the then present state of his hearers. He left this remark, that he enjoyed a good day.

feasibility in this supposition that, without proof, will deprive it of all credit among persons who have no particular interest in the support of it.

True it is that Fenwick and his associates were properly authorized to settle upon lands belonging to Lords Say and Brook; but that the lands they did settle upon were the property of the Earl of Warwick is not only without proof, but against it.

It seems to be generally agreed that the Lords Say and Brook were understood to have a right to lands upon Connecticut River, but that river being five hundred miles long, and running through the greatest part of New England, the situation of their property was by no means pointed out; whether it lay at the mouth, the middle, or the northern end, was equally unascertained.

The settlers, indeed, established themselves at the mouth, but without showing their right to the spot; they licentiously chose it. There never has been produced any writing of conveyance of the land in question from the Council of Plymouth to the Earl of Warwick, or from the Earl of Warwick to the Lords Say and Brook, and therefore their title to it must be deemed not good in law. By a letter from Lord Say to Mr. Vane, in 1635, it appears that he (Lord Say), Lord Brook, and others, had thought of removing to New England, but were not determined whether to join the adventurers in Boston or settle a new colony.—(Hutchinson's "History," vol. i., p. 42.)

If Connecticut had been assigned to Lords Say and Brook by the Earl of Warwick, as it is pretended was done in 1631, it is very strange that those lords should have been in doubt in 1635 where to fix themselves in New England, since interest and ambition, as well as fertility of soil, would naturally have led them to settle in Connecticut, where they had land of their own, and where a settlement was already begun, and bore a very promising appearance. Hence, it seems but reasonable to suppose that if Lords Say and Brook were entitled to any land on Connecticut River it could not lie within the province of Connecticut; and, if their claims were derived from the Earl of Warwick, it may fairly be concluded that their property lay much higher up the country, since the coast appropriated to the Earl of Warwick by Purchas is that at or about Cape Ann. Lords Say and Brook, therefore, might have a right to send Fenwick, Peters, etc., to colonize on the north parts of Connecticut River, but not southwardly, at the mouth of it; and their neglect of the colony at Saybrook may easily be accounted for, by supposing that they were sensible the settlers had fixed upon a wrong site—an idea corroborated by this circumstance, that Fenwick some years after sold his property there for a mere trifle, when he might have sold it dear if his title had been good.

But, it may be asked, who were the real proprietors of the eighth and ninth lots?

It is asserted that, on the Council of Plymouth's resignation of their patent to Charles I. in 1635, that monarch granted the latter to the Earl of Stirling.

Possibly there is not now existing any written testimony of this grant, yet it seems authenticated by the sale which the earl made in 1639, by his agent, Forrest, of the eastern part of Long Island, as appertaining to his lot, to Mr. Howell. However, though his claim is not, perhaps, clearly to be established, it is by no means liable to the many objections urged against that of Lords Say and Brook, which will in a manner be annihilated by the additional argument I am now going to adduce from the positive proof there is to whom the eighth lot really belongs.

It stands authenticated in the office of the Lords Commissioners of Colonies that, in April, 1635, was conveyed to James, Marquis of Hamilton, by a deed from the Council of Plymouth, the territory lying between Narraganset Bay and Connecticut River.[1] The right to the eighth lot, therefore, was clearly vested in the marquis; and it only remains to be shown why his descendants are not in possession of it to remove every doubt upon the matter.[2]

Unfortunately, in the civil broils of his time the marquis engaged and died fighting under the royal banners, while the king's enemies took possession of his lands in Connecticut. At the restoration of Charles II. to his crown, reason taught the children of royal sufferers to expect a restoration at least of their landed

[1] "New England Records," A., p. 201.

[2] While the colonists were thus prosecuting the business of settlement in New England, the Right Honorable James, Marquis of Hamilton, obtained a grant from the Council of Plymouth April 20, 1635, of all that tract of country which lies between Connecticut River and Narraganset River and harbor, from the mouth of each of said rivers northward sixty miles into the country.

However, by reason of its interference with the grant to Lords Say and Brook, and others, or for some other reason, the deed was never executed.

The marquis made no settlement on the land, and the claim became obsolete.

property; and the daughter of the Marquis of Hamilton petitioned Charles II. to grant her relief with respect to the land lying between Narraganset Bay and the Connecticut River—a relief she had the more reason to hope for, as "her father had died fighting for his father." But Charles had been too much polished in foreign courts to do anything effectual for his suffering friends. Afterward the Earl of Arran applied to William III. for redress in regard to the same land; but that earl having acted on the wrong side at the revolution, could not but expect as little from William as the friends of Charles II. had received from him. However, William III. ordered the Lords Commissioners of the colonies to state his title, which they fairly did; and the earl was referred to try his case in Connecticut, before the very people who had his lands in possession.

The Governor and Company of Connecticut gave a formal answer to the claims of the Earl of Arran, setting up a title under the Earl of Warwick, as is above mentioned, who, they said, disposed of the land in dispute to Lord Say and Seal and Lord Brook, and the Lords Say and Brook sold the same to Fenwick, Peters, and others. The Earl of Arran answered that, "when they produced a grant from the Plymouth Company, of those lands to the Earl of Warwick, it should have an answer;" but the colony was silent, and King William was silent also.—(*Vide* "Records of New England," A., pp. 170–201.)

Since, then, no proof of any title derived from the Earl of Warwick could be produced by the Governor and Company of Connecticut, when the question of right to the country was fairly brought into litigation, and since there is a record of the grant of the eastern part of it to the Marquis of Hamilton, it is evident that the claim of the present possessors under Lords Say and Brook is not valid. The record of the Marquis of Hamilton grant is an irrefragable proof that those lords had no right to the tract between Narraganset Bay and Connecticut River; and thence the conclusion is fair that they had no right to the tract between Connecticut and Hudson's River; for their title to both having but one and the same foundation, it follows, of course, that what destroys it in the former destroys it in the latter also.

However disputable the Earl of Stirling's claim to the land between Hudson and Connecticut Rivers may be, the Duke of Hamilton is undoubtedly the rightful owner of that between the latter and Narraganset Bay. This much I have proved, to show the errors of Mather, Neal, Douglas, and Hutchinson, who assert what the above record contradicts. I differ in opinion also with divines who say that the world grows every day worse than it was the last. I believe the world is growing better every year; and that justice will be administered to the Duke of Hamilton, and other noble proprietors of lands in New England, who have been wickedly supplanted by the emigration of Puritans, republicans, regicides, and smugglers. The time, I hope, is hastening, when the records I have quoted will be considered, and unjust possessors be ordered to give up their possessions to the right owners; for we have a king who honors his crown, and prefers justice to policy.

Hooker and Haynes, who conducted the second of

the three English parties already spoken of as making inroads into Connecticut, and who fixed their headquarters at Hertford, left Massachusets Bay for the same reason they had before left England—to avoid being persecuted, and to acquire the power to persecute. Hooker was learned, ambitious, and rigid. He lived near Boston two years, in hopes of becoming a greater favorite with the people than the celebrated Mr. Cotton; but, finding himself rather unlikely to meet with the desired success, he devised the project of flying into the wilderness of Connecticut, to get a name. Accordingly, in 1635 he applied to the General Court for leave to remove thither, but was refused. The next year, however, for reasons which will hereafter appear, he found the fanatics more compliant; and he and Haynes obtained permission to emigrate into Connecticut, carrying with them, as Mr. Neal expresses it, "a sort of commission from the government of Massachusets Bay for the administration of justice" there.

But it cannot be supposed that Hooker and his associates could derive any title to the soil, from this permission and commission granted by the Massachusets colony, who had not the least right to it themselves. The emigrants not only did not entertain any such idea, but, as soon as they had discovered a situation that pleased them, they even set at naught the commission which they took with them, the professed object of which was to secure the authority and jurisdiction claimed by the Massachusets colony over them. Knowing that they had passed the limits of that province, they voted themselves an independent people, and commenced despots, pleading the old adage, *Salus populi suprema lex*. It has never been suggested, I believe, that this party entered Connecticut with any other semblance of authority than this ridiculous permission and commission of the Massachusets dictators.[1]

[1] Such numbers were constantly emigrating to New England, in consequence of the persecution of the Puritans, that the people of Dorchester, Watertown, and Newtown, began to be much straitened by the accession of new planters.

By those who had been in Connecticut they had received intelligence of the excellent meadows on the river; they therefore determined to remove, and once more brave the dangers and hardships of making settlements in a dreary wilderness.

Upon application to the General Court for the enlargement of their boundaries, or for liberty to remove, they at first obtained consent for the latter. However, when it was afterward discovered that their determination was to plant a new colony in Connecticut, there arose a strong opposition; so that, when the Court convened, in September, there was a warm debate on the subject, and a great division between the Houses. Indeed, the whole colony was affected with the dispute.

Mr. Hooker, who was more engaged in the enterprise than the other ministers, took up the affair and pleaded for the people. He urged that they were so straitened for accommodations for their cattle, that they could not support the ministry, neither receive nor assist any more of their friends who might come over to them. He insisted that the planting of towns so near together was a fundamental error in their policy. He pleaded the fertility and happy accommodations of Connecticut; that settlements upon the river were necessary to prevent the Dutch, and others, from possessing themselves of so fruitful and important a part of the country; and that the minds of the people were strongly inclined to plant themselves there, in preference to every other place which had come to their knowledge.

On the other side, it was insisted that, in point of conscience, they ought not to depart, as they were united to Massachusetts as one body, and bound by oath to seek the good of the Commonwealth; and that, on principles of policy, it could not by any means be granted. It was pleaded that the settlement in Massachusetts was new and weak; they were in danger from an assault from their enemies; that the departure

As to the third party, headed by Eaton and Davenport, they took possession, as is already mentioned, without even pretending any purchase, grant, permission, or commission, from any one. Of these three parties, then, it appears that the last two had not the least shadow of original right to the lands they possessed themselves in Connecticut; and the claims of the first I have shown to be ill-founded. I will now consider the right they are pretended to have acquired after possession; in regard to which they seem to have been put upon the same footing, by a general war between them and the Indians, occasioned by the ambitious, oppressive, and unjust conduct of Hooker and Davenport. This war opened a door to king-killing and king-making, violence, and injustice, in America, similar to what we have of late years shuddered to hear of in India. Hence the colonies have endeavored to establish a title to the lands by purchase of the natives. Accordingly, they have produced deeds of

of Mr. Hooker, and the people of those towns, would not only draw off many from Massachusetts, but prevent others from settling in the colony. Besides, it was said that the removing of a candlestick was a great judgment; that, by suffering it, they should expose their brethren to great danger, both from the Dutch and the Indians. Indeed, it was affirmed that they might be accommodated by the enlargements offered them by other towns.

After a long and warm debate, the Governor, two assistants, and a majority of the representatives, were for granting liberty for Mr. Hooker and the people to transport themselves to Connecticut. The Deputy-Governor, however, and six of the assistants, were in the negative, and so no vote was obtained.

The next May the Newtown people determined to settle at Connecticut, renewed their application to the General Court, and obtained liberty to remove to any place which they should select, with the proviso that they should continue under the jurisdiction of Massachusetts.—Ed. Note.

sale signed by Sunksquaw, Uncas, Joshua, Moodus, and others, whom Mr. Neal and Dr. Mather call sachems, and consequently owners of the soil. Whether those gentlemen knew, or did not know, that Connecticut was owned by these sachems only, who, with their wives and families, were killed by the English, and who never would give a deed of any land to the Dutch or English, is not material; since it is a fact that not one of those Indians who have signed those famous deeds was ever a sachem or a proprietor of a single foot of land claimed by the colony.

It is true that Uncas (whom Mr. Neal calls a sachem, because the colonists declared him King of Mohegan, to reward him for deserting Sassacus, sachem of the Pequods) gave deeds of the land that he had no right or title to; and so did Sunksquaw, who, after murdering his sachem Quinnipiog, was also declared sachem by the English Dominion [1] of Newhaven. Gratitude, or pride, induced all those English-made sachems to assign deeds to their creators.

After the death of Uncas, his eldest son, Oneko, became King of Mohegan, who refused to grant any deeds of land to the colony; whereupon, vexed at his wisdom and honor, they declared him an incestuous son, deposed him, and proclaimed his natural brother, Abimeleck, to be sachem of the Mohegans. Oneko gave a deed of all his lands to Mason and Harrison, who were his friends; as did Abimeleck, of the same lands, to the colony who had made him sachem. This laid a foundation for a suit at law, which was first

[1] Dominion, in New England, signifies a sovereign, independent state, uncontrollable by any other earthly power.

tried before the judges of the colony, where Mason, of course, lost his suit. He appealed to the King in Council, who ordered a special court to sit at Norwich, in Connecticut: Mr. Dudley, a learned man, and Governor of Massachusetts Bay, was president of it. The court met, and, having heard the evidence and pleadings of both parties, gave a verdict in favor of Mason's claim. The colony appealed home to England, but never prosecuted their suit to an issue. Mason died. The colony kept possession under Abimeleck, their created King of Mohegan. About ten years ago the heirs of Mason and Harrison petitioned the government to decree that Dudley's verdict should be enforced; but the colonists found means to confound the claims of those competitors without establishing their own. The truth is, neither the colonists nor Mason and Harrison ever had any deed or title to those lands from Sassacus or his heirs; their deeds spring from Uncas, already mentioned, a rebel subject of Sassacus, without any royal blood in his veins. Nevertheless, Mr. Neal, and others, who have written histories of New England, have taken especial care to vindicate the justice of the settlers, who always, they say, conscientiously purchased their lands of the sachems. I have given the reader some idea of the purchases of the first colonizers in Connecticut, who by their iniquitous act of making Sachems have entailed lawsuits without end on their posterity; for there is not one foot of land in the whole province which is not covered by ten deeds granted by ten different nominal sachems to ten different persons; and, what aggravates the misfortune, the courts of justice differ every session concerning the true sachem, so that what a plaintiff recovers at a hearing before one jury, he loses upon a rehearing before another.

Enough, surely, has been said to nullify the colonists' plea for having bought their lands from the Indians.

As to any purchases made of the Saybrook settlers, those of Hertford totally declined them till the farcical business respecting their charter came into agitation between the two juntos who procured it, of which I shall speak hereafter; and, so far were the people of Newhaven from buying any right of Fenwick or his associates that they scorned the idea of claiming under them; nay, it was one of their principal views, in the machinations wherein they were continually employed, to reduce the Saybrook colony under the tyranny of their own dominions as having no more title to the country than possession gave them. And, upon the other supposition, it is impossible to account for the neglect of the colonizers of Hertford to secure their lands by such a purchase, seeming as they did to ransack heaven and earth for a title satisfactory even in their own eyes; they were conscious no purchase of that kind could give them firmer footing than they had already.

The truth, therefore, undoubtedly is that Fenwick and Peters had no legal right to sell the lands they occupied, whatever might be their pretensions; nor, indeed, did they pretend to the power of selling more on their own account than was granted to them severally by their patrons—the Lords Say and Brook—which cannot be supposed but an inconsiderable proportion of their American property.

A CLAIM BY CONQUEST.

No wonder, then, that we find another claim set up—a claim by conquest. This was particularly agreeable to the genius of the Hertford and Newhaven heroes, but will nevertheless appear to as little for their right as their honor, from the following considerations: 1. The invaders did not find Connecticut in a state of Nature, but cultivated and settled by its Indian inhabitants, whose numbers were thousands, and who had three kings, viz., Connecticote, Quinnipiog, and Sassacus, of whom Connecticote was the emperor, or king of kings—a dignity he and his ancestors had enjoyed, according to the Indian mode of reckoning, twenty sticks,[1] i. e., time immemorial; 2. They had no authority to invade, make war upon, and conquer the Indians, who were not at war with the King of England, nor his patentees, or their assignees; and, 3. Seizures, without legal commission, of however long standing, do not convey right or title by the English law.

Feeling the weight of these considerations, the colonists have been obliged to found their claim to the country on their charter, which was obtained in 1662—more than twenty-six years after they had taken possession. Here, again, they are destitute of support, for the king, any more than his subjects, could not give to others the property of the Duke of Hamilton unless his title had been proved to be forfeited by due course of law. But the charter created no title; it merely con-

---

[1] The Indian mode of counting is from one to twenty. Every year they cut a notch in a stick, and when the stick is full, or has twenty notches on it, they lay it up and take another. When they have thus cut twenty sticks, they reckon no more; the number of twenty times twenty with them becomes infinite, or incomprehensible.—Ed. Note.

ferred on the people the authority of a legal corporation, without conveying any title to the lands. And, indeed, the prevarications of the colonists themselves with regard to the charter-claim sufficiently explode it. Whenever they find their property affected by any duty, custom, etc., imposed by Parliament, and warranted by charter, they allege that they got the lands in possession by their own arms, without the aid of the King and Parliament of Great Britain; as Charles II. allowed in granting the charter, which conveyed no title, but was founded upon the title they possessed before the date of it. At other times, when these selfish temporizers find it convenient either for promoting their own, or preventing their neighbors' encroachments, they then plead their charter as the one only thing needful to prove their right of land even to the South Sea itself.

In short, and upon the whole, possession, begun in usurpation, is the best title the inhabitants of Connecticut ever had, or can set up, unless they can prove they hold the lands by a heavenly grant, as the Israelites did those of Canaan.

This heavenly title was, indeed, set up by Peters, Hooker, and Davenport, the first three ministers that settled Connecticut, and is generally believed through the Colony to this day. They thus syllogistically stated it: "The heathen are driven out, and we have their lands in possession; they were numerous, and we but few; therefore, the Lord hath done this great work, to give his beloved rest."

This much for the various pretensions of the occupiers of Connecticut in regard to their right to the soil. I shall now give some account of the proceedings of the first settlers with respect to their religious and civil establishments, and of their political transactions, etc.

The party which settled at Saybrook, under George Fenwick, Esquire, and the Rev. Thomas Peters, in 1634, contented themselves, in framing the polity of their civil constitution, with the laws of England and a few local regulations.

As to their ecclesiastical institutions, they voted themselves to be a church independent on lords bishops, and Mr. Peters to be their minister, whose episcopal ordination was deemed good, notwithstanding he had been silenced in England. They voted presbyters to be bishops, and possessed of power to ordain ministers when invited by a proper number of people formed into a society by a license from the Governor. They voted that a certain part of the liturgy of the Church of England might be used—the Lord's Prayer, the Apostles' Creed, together with one chapter in the Bible, to be read at morning and evening service, or omitted, at the discretion of the minister; that extempore prayers might be used at the pleasure of the minister, but that the surplice should not be worn, nor should the sign of the cross at baptisms, the ceremony of the ring at marriages, or saints'-days, etc., be observed, as in the Church of England; that every society licensed by the Governor, after having a minister ordained over it, be a complete church, and invested with the keys of discipline, dependent only upon Christ, the head of the church; that the minister should be the judge of the qualifications of church-membership, and should censure disorderly walkers; that the members in full communion should have power over the minister, and might dismiss him from his parish by a majority of voices and with the consent of the Governor; that all children were the objects of baptism, and that none should be debarred that sacrament for the sins of their parents, provided an orderly liver would engage to bring them up in the ways of Christianity; that all sober persons might partake of the Lord's Supper, provided the minister, upon examination, should find them sufficiently acquainted with their duty; that what is commonly called conversion is not absolutely necessary before receiving the Lord's Supper, because that sacrament is a converting ordinance; that all gospel ministers were upon an equality in office; and that it was the business of every one to admonish the transgressor, privately in the first place, and next, if no attention was paid to his advice, before his deacons; then, if their admonishment was disregarded, the offender should be presented to the church (that is, the minister, deacons, and communicants, united by the keys of discipline), and, upon his still continuing refractory, he should be censured and rejected by the majority of voters without any appeal; that deacons should be chosen by the minister and communicants upon a majority of voices, and ordained by the minister according to the holy practice of St. Paul; that it was the duty of the Governor and civil magistrates to protect and nurture the Church, but not to govern it, because Christ's authority, given to his Church, was above principalities and all civil powers, etc., etc.

The settlers of Hertford, having declared themselves to be an independent Colony, and that their dominions extended from sea to sea, voted Haynes to be their

Governor, and appointed six councilors to assist him in framing laws and regulating the State. The same spirit of independence dictated their church discipline. They voted Mr. Hooker to be their minister, and six of their church-members to ordain him. Mr. Hooker accepted of their vote, or call, renounced his Episcopal ordination, and was ordained by the six lay church-members, over the church of the Independents in Hertford. Thus, Mr. Hooker, who was born in Leicestershire, educated at Cambridge, ordained by a bishop, silenced by a bishop in 1630, in England, and reordained by six laymen in America, became what he wished to be—the head of the Independents in the Dominion of Hertford, where he had the honor and pleasure of exercising over all who differed from him in opinion that violent spirit of persecution which he and his friends so clamorously decried as too intolerant to be endured in England. Some of the characteristic doctrines of this persecuting fanatic were of the following purport: That Christ's Church was not universal, but a particular visible church, formed by general consent and covenant; that Christ had committed the power of binding and loosening to believers, without any distinction between clergy and laity; that ruling and preaching elders are duly ordained to their office by the election and the imposition of the hands of the people; that the tables and seals of the covenant, the offices and censures of Christ's Church, the administrations of all public worship and ordinances, are in the *cœtus fidelium*, or combination of godly, faithful men met in one congregation; that a diocesan, provincial, or national assembly, is incompatible with the nature of Christ's Church, seeing all and every member of Christ's Church are to meet every Lord's-day, in one place, for the administration of the holy ordinances of God; that a multitude of free people may elect and ordain a king over them, although they were not, prior to that act, possessed of kingly power; for the people of Israel imposed their hands on Levites, when they themselves were not Levites (Numbers viii. 10); that Nature has given virtual power to a free people to set up any Christian form of government, both in church and state, which they see best for themselves in the land; but Christ gave the power of his keys to his Church, i. e., to his believing people, and not to Peter or to Paul as ministers, but as professed believers, in conjunction with the rest of true believers; that the Church hath not absolute power to choose whom it will; it hath ministerial power only to choose whom Christ hath chosen, i. e., such as He hath gifted and fitted for the work of the ministry; that neither popes, bishops, nor presbyters, are necessary to ordain ministers of Jesus Christ, because the power of the keys are given by Christ to his Church, i. e., the people in covenant with God; that as ordination is in the power of each church, no church hath power over another, but all stand in brotherly equality; that it is unlawful for any Church of Christ to put out of its hand that power which Christ hath given it into the hands of other churches; that no one church ought to send to ministers of other churches to ordain its ministers or to censure its offenders; that baptism does not make any one a member of Christ's Church, because papists and other heretics are baptized; therefore, to be a member of Christ's Church is to own the covenant of that particular church where God has placed such members; that seven persons may form a Church of Christ, but fifteen thousand cannot, because such a number cannot meet in one place, nor hear, nor partake, nor be edified together; that no one can partake of the Lord's Supper till he be converted, and has manifested his faith and repentance before the church, etc., etc.[1]

[1] It was the opinion of the principal divines who settled in New England and Connecticut that in every church completely organized there was a pastor, teacher, ruling elder, and deacons.

Three distinct offices, they said, were clearly taught in those passages.—Romans xii. 7: "Or ministry, let us wait on our ministering; or he that teacheth on teaching." 1 Timothy v. 17: "Let the elders that rule well be counted worthy of double honor, especially they who labor in the word and doctrine." 1 Corinthians xii. 28: "And God has set some in the Church, first apostles, secondarily prophets, thirdly teachers, after that miracles, then gifts of healing, helps, governments, diversities of tongues." And Ephesians iv. 11: "And he gave some, apostles; and some, prophets; and some, evangelists; and some, pastors and teachers." From these they argued the duty of all churches which were able to be thus furnished. In this manner were the churches of Hartford, Windsor, New Haven, and other towns, organized.

The churches which were not able to support a pastor and teacher had the ruling elders and deacons.

The ruling elders were ordained with no less solemnity than their pastors and teachers. When no teacher could be obtained, the pastor performed the duty of both pastor and teacher.

It was the general opinion that the pastor's work consisted principally in exhortation, in working upon the will and affections of the people. To this the whole force of his study was to be directed, that by his judicious, powerful, and affectionate addresses he might win his hearers to the love and practice of the truth. But the teacher was *Doctor in Ecclesia*, whose business was to teach, and explain, and defend the doctrines of Christianity. He was to inform the judgment, and advance the work of illumination.

The business of the ruling elder was to assist the pastor in the gov-

The laws made by the Governor and Council of Hertford are, in general, much of the same stamp as those of the Newhaven legislators, of some of which an abstract will be given hereafter.

The fanatics at Newhaven, in like manner with those of Hertford, voted themselves to be a Dominion independent, and chose Eaton for their Governor, and Davenport for their minister. The Governor and a committee had the power of making laws for the State,

ernment of the church. He was particularly set apart to watch over all its members; to prepare and bring forward all cases of discipline; to visit and pray with the sick; and, in absence of the pastor and teacher, to pray with the congregation and expound the Scriptures.

The pastors and churches of New England maintained with the reformed churches in general that bishops and presbyters were only different names for the same office; and that all pastors regularly elected to the gospel ministry were Scripture bishops. They also insisted, agreeably to the primitive practice, that the work of every pastor was confined principally to one particular church and congregation, who could all assemble in one place, whom he could inspect, and who could all unite together in acts of worship and discipline. Indeed, the first ministers of Connecticut and New England at first maintained that all the pastor's office power was confined to his own church and congregation, and that the administering of baptism and the Lord's Supper in other churches was irregular.

With respect to ordination, they held that it did not constitute the essentials of ministerial office; but the qualifications for office were the election of the church, guided by the rule of Christ, and the acceptance of the pastor-elect. Says Mr. Hooker, "Ordination is an approbation of the officer, and solemn setting and confirmation of him in his office by prayer and laying on of hands."

It was viewed by the ministers of New England as no more than putting the pastor-elect in office, or a solemn recommending of him and his labors to the blessing of God. It was the general opinion that elders ought to lay on hands in ordination if there were a presbytery in the church, but, if there were not, the church might appoint some other elders, or a number of the brethren, to perform that service.—ED. NOTE.

THE TENETS ESTABLISHED. 43

and the minister, assisted by deacons and elders, was to rule the church. The following is a specimen of the tenets established by Davenport in the latter :

That Christ has conveyed all power to his people both in church and state; which power they are to exercise until Christ shall return on earth to reign one thousand years over his militant saints—that all other kings, besides Christ and his elected people, are pestilent usurpers, and enemies of God and man—that all vicars, rectors, deans, priests, and bishops, are of the devil; are wolves, petty popes, and antichristian tyrants; that pastors and teachers of particular congregations are of Christ and must be chosen by his people, i. e., the elect and chosen from the foundation of the world, or else their entrance and ministry are unlawful; that all things of human invention in the worship of God, such as are in the Mass-Book and Common-prayer, are unsavory in the sight of God; that ecclesiastical censures ought to be exercised by the members of particular congregations among themselves; that the people should not suffer this supreme power to be wrested out of their hands until Christ shall begin his reign; that all good people ought to pray always that God would raze the old papal foundation of the episcopal government, together with the filthy ceremonies of that antichristian church; that every particular who neglects this duty, may justly fear that curse pronounced against Meroz (Judges v. 23) : "Curse ye Meroz, because they came not to the help of the Lord against the mighty" enemies of God and his church; that every particular congregation is an absolute church, the members of it are to be all saints; those must enter into covenant among themselves, and without such covenant there can be no church; that it is a heinous sin to be present when prayers are read out of a book by a vicar or bishop; that subjects promise obedience to obtain help from the magistrates, and are discharged from their promise when the magistrates fail in their duty; that, without liberty from the prince or magistrate, the people may reform the church and state, and must not wait for the magistrate, etc., etc.

This Dominion, this tyrant of tyrants, adopted the Bible for its code of civil laws, till others should be made more suitable to its circumstances. The provision was politic. The lawgivers soon discovered that the precepts in the Old and New Testaments were insufficient to support them in their arbitrary and bloody undertakings; they, therefore, gave themselves up to their own inventions in making others, wherein, in some instances, they betrayed an extreme degree of wanton cruelty and oppression, that even the religious fanatics of Boston, and the mad zealots of Hertford, put to the blush, christened them the "Blue Laws," and the former held a day of thanksgiving, because God, in his good providence, had stationed Eaton and Davenport so far from them.[1]

[1] On the 4th of June, 1639, all the free planters at Quinnipiack convened in a large barn of Mr. Newman's, and, in a very formal and solemn manner, proceeded to lay the foundations of their civil and religious polity.

Mr. Davenport introduced the business by a sermon from the words of the royal preacher, "Wisdom has builded her house, she has hewn out seven pillars."

His design was to show that the church, the house of God, should be formed of seven pillars, or principal brethren, to whom all the other mem-

The religious system established by Peters at Saybrook was well calculated to please the moderate Puritans and zealots of all denominations; but the fanatics of the Massachusets-Bay, who hated every part of the Common Prayer-book worse than the Council of Trent,

bers of the church should be added. After a solemn invocation of the Divine Majesty, he proceeded to represent to the planters that they were met to consult respecting the settlement of civil government, according to the will of God, and for the nomination of persons who, by universal consent, were in all respects the best qualified for the foundation-work of a church. He enlarged on the great importance of the transactions before them, and desired that no man would give his voice in any matter until he fully understood it, and that all would act without respect to any man, but give their vote in the fear of God.

He then proposed a number of questions, in consequence of which the following resolutions were passed:

1. That the Scriptures hold forth a perfect rule for the direction and government of all men in all duties which they are to perform to God and man, as well in families and commonwealth as in matters of church.
2. That as in matters which concerned the gathering and ordering of a church, so likewise in all public offices which concern civil order, as the choice of magistrates and officers, making and repealing laws, dividing allotments of inheritance, and all things of like nature, they would all be governed by those rules which the Scripture held forth to them.
3. That all those who had desired to be received as free planters had settled in the plantation with a purpose, resolution, and desire, that they might be admitted into church-fellowship, according to Christ.
4. That all free planters held themselves bound to establish such civil order as might best conduce to the securing of the purity and peace of the ordinance to themselves and their posterity, according to God.

When these resolutions had been passed, and the people had bound themselves to settle civil government according to the divine word, Mr. Davenport proceeded to represent to them what men they must choose according to the divine word, that they might most effectually secure to themselves and their posterity a just, free, and peaceable government.

Time was then given to discuss and deliberate upon what had been proposed. After full discussion and deliberation, it was determined:

5. That the church-members only should be free burgesses, and that they should choose magistrates, among themselves, to have power of

and the papal power exercised over heretics, were alarmed at the conduct of the half-reformed schismatics in that colony; and, thinking that their dear Salem might be endangered by such impure worshipers, consented, in the year 1636, to give Mr. Hooker and his transacting all the public civil affairs of the plantation, of making and repealing laws, dividing inheritances, deciding of differences that may arise, and doing all things and business of a like nature.

That civil officers might be chosen and government proceed according to these resolutions, it was necessary that a church should be formed. Without this there could be neither freedmen nor magistrates. Mr. Davenport thereupon proceeded to make proposals relative to forming it, in such a manner that no blemish might be left on the "beginnings of church work." It was then resolved to this effect—

6. That twelve men should be chosen, that their fitness for the foundation-work might be tried, and that it should be in the power of those twelve men to choose seven to begin the church.

It was agreed that if seven men could not be found among the twelve qualified for the foundation-work, that such other persons should be taken into the number, upon trial, as should be judged more suitable. The form of a solemn charge, or oath, was drawn up and agreed upon at this meeting, to be given to all the freemen.

Further, it was ordered that all persons who should be received as free planters of that corporation, should submit to the fundamental agreement above related, and, in testimony of their submission, should subscribe their names among the freemen. Sixty-three subscribed on the 4th of June, and soon after fifty other names were added.

After a proper term of trial, Theophilus Eaton, Mr. John Davenport, Robert Newman, Matthew Gilbert, Thomas Fugill, John Punderson, and Jeremiah Dixon, were chosen for the seven pillars of the church.

October 25, 1639, the Court, as it is termed, consisting of these seven persons only, convened, and after a solemn address to the Supreme Majesty, they proceeded to form a body of freemen, and to elect civil officers. The manner was, indeed, singular and curious.

In the first place, all former trust for managing the public affairs of the plantation was declared to cease, and be utterly abrogated. Then all those who had been admitted to the church after the gathering of it in

associates liberty to emigrate to Hertford, notwithstanding the preceding year they had refused such liberty, seeing then no reason for Hooker's seizing the territory of other people. But when the New England vine was supposed to be threatened by the Bible, Lord's Prayer, and Ten Commandments, the pious people of

the choice of the seven pillars, and all the members of other approved churches who desired it, and offered themselves, were admitted members of the Court.

A solemn charge was then publicly given them, to the same effect as the freemen's charge, or oath, which they had previously adopted. The purport of this was nearly the same with the oath of fidelity at the present time.

Mr. Davenport expounded several scriptural texts to them, describing the character of civil magistrates given in the sacred oracles. Theophilus Eaton, Esq., was chosen Governor; Mr. Robert Newman, Matthew Gilbert, Nathaniel Turner, and Thomas Fugill, were chosen magistrates; Mr. Fugill was also chosen secretary, and Robert Seeley, marshal.

Mr. Davenport gave Governor Eaton a charge, in open Court, from Deuteronomy i. 16, 17.

It was decreed by the freemen that there should be a General Court annually in the plantation, on the first week in October. This was ordained a court of election in which all the officers of the colony were to be chosen. This Court determined that the word of God should be the only rule for ordering affairs of government in that Commonwealth.

This was the original fundamental Constitution of the government of New Haven. All government was originally in the church, and the members of the church elected the Governor, magistrates, and other officers. The magistrates at first were no more than assistants of the Governor; they might not act in any sentence or determination of the Court.

No Deputy-Governor was chosen, nor were any laws enacted, except the general resolutions which have been noticed; but as the plantation enlarged, and new towns were settled, new orders were given; the General Court received a new form, laws were enacted, and the civil polity of this jurisdiction gradually advanced, in its essential parts, to a near resemblance of the government of Connecticut.

Upon these resolutions were based the "Blue Laws" which will appear in the work.—ED. NOTE.

Massachusets-Bay permitted Hooker, in 1635, to remove into and govern Connecticut by their authority, and to impede and break up the worship of the Peterites at Saybrook. Hooker, ever faithful to his trust, excepting that, when he got to Hertford, he rejected the authority of his employers in the Massachusets-Bay, set up a new Dominion, and persecuted the Peterites under his own banner, though he called it the banner of Jesus. But for his and Davenport's tyrannical conduct, the colony of Saybrook would have lived in peace with the Indians, as they did till their artful and overbearing neighbors brought on a general war between them and the English, which ended with the death of Sassacus and the destruction of all his subjects. After that war great dissension arose among the conquerors. Fenwick was sensible, of a calm disposition, and very religious, yet not entirely void of ambition; he claimed the government of Connecticut, and insisted upon payment for such lands as were possessed by Hooker and Davenport and their associates; this, he said, was common justice, due to his constituents, the Lords Say and Brook. Hooker and Davenport, however, were not fond of his doctrine of justice, but made religion, liberty, and power, the great object of their concern, wherein they were supported by the people of Massachusets-Bay, whose spirits were congenial with their own; hence no opportunity was lost of prejudicing Saybrook, and the troubles in the mother-country furnished their enemies with many. One step they took, in particular, operated much to their disadvantage. The Massachusets colony, eager to act against Charles I., agreed with those of Hertford, Newhaven,

Newhampshire, and Rhode-Island, to send agents to England, assuring the House of Commons of their readiness to assist against the king and bishops. The Saybrook settlers, though zealous against the bishops, were not much inclined to rebellion against the king, and therefore took no part in this transaction.

As the royal cause lost ground in England, the apprehensions of this colony increased; and Fenwick, finding himself unsupported by the Lords Say and Brook, thought it prudent to dispose of his colonial property to Peters and his associates, and return to England.

Confusion being established in England, moderation became an unpardonable sin in Saybrook, which both the neighboring colonies were ready to punish by assuming the jurisdiction there: mutual jealousy alone prevented it. At length, during Cromwell's usurpation, the inhabitants, fearing the effects of his displeasure for not joining in the above-mentioned address to the Commons of England, especially lest he should put them under the power of the furious Davenport, and at the same time foreseeing no prospect of the restoration, judged it advisable, by way of preferring the lesser to the greater evil, to form a sort of alliance and junction with the people of Hertford, where Hooker now lay numbered with the dead.

The colony was not only hereby enabled to maintain its ground, but flourished greatly; and the minister, Thomas Peters, established a school in Saybrook, which his children had the satisfaction to see become a college, denominated Yale College, of which a particular account will be given in the course of this work. He was a churchman of the Puritanic order, zealous, learned, and of mild disposition, and frequently wrote to his brother Hugh at Salem to exercise more moderation, lest " overmuch zeal should ruin him and the cause they were embarked in." [1]

[1] William, Thomas, and Hugh Peters were brothers, and born in Fowery, in Cornwall, in Old England. Their father was a merchant of great property, and their mother was Elizabeth Treffry, daughter of John Treffry, Esq., of a very ancient and opulent family in Fowery. William was educated at Leyden, Thomas at Oxford, and Hugh at Cambridge Universities. About the year 1610 and 1620, Thomas and Hugh were clergymen in London, and William was a private gentleman. About 1628 Thomas and Hugh, rendered obnoxious by their popularity and Puritanism, were silenced by the Bishop of London. They then went to Holland, and remained there till 1633, when they returned to London. The three brothers sold their landed property, and went to New-England in 1634. Hugh settled at Salem, and became too popular for Mather and Cotton. He was soon appointed one of the Trustees of the College at New-Cambridge. He built a grand house, and purchased a large tract of land.—The yard before his house he paved with flint-stones from England; and, having dug a well, he paved that round with flint-stones also, for the accommodation of every inhabitant in want of water. It bears the name of Peters's Spring to this day.—He married a second wife, by whom he had one daughter named Elizabeth. The renown of this zealot increasing, he received an invitation to remove from Salem to Boston, and, complying with it, he there laid the foundation-stone of the great Meeting-House, of which the Rev. Dr. Samuel Cooper, one of the most learned of the Literati in America, is the present minister. Mather and Cotton ill brooked being out-rivalled by Hugh; yet, finding him an orthodox fanatic, and more perfect than themselves, they seemingly bowed to his superiority, at the same time that they laid a snare for his destruction. In 1641 those envious pastors conspired with the Court at Boston to convert their Bishop Hugh into a Politician, and appoint him agent to Great Britain.—The Plot succeeded; and Hugh assumed his agency under colour of petitioning for some abatement of customs and excise; but his real commission was to foment the civil discontents, jars, and wars, then prevailing between the King and Parliament.—Hugh did not see into the policy of Mather and Cotton; and he had a strong inclina-

At his death, which did not happen till after the Restoration of Charles II., he bequeathed his library to the school above mentioned.

tion to chastise the Bishops and Court, who had turned him out of the Church for his fanatical conduct. On his arrival in London, the Parliament took him into their service.—The Earls of Warwick and Essex were also his patrons.—In 1644, the Parliament gave him Archbishop Laud's library; and soon after made him Head of the Archbishop's Court, and gave him his estate and palace at Lambeth:—all of which Hugh kept till the Restoration, when he paid for his zeal, his puritanism, and rebellion, on a gibbet at Charing-Cross.—His daughter married a merchant in Newport, Rhode-Island, and lived and died with an excellent character.—Her Father having met with so tragical an end, I omit to mention her Husband's name, whose Posterity live in good reputation.— Governor Hutchinson reports, that the widow of Hugh Peters was supported, till 1671, by a collection at Salem, of 30*l*. per ann. Were this report true, it would be much to the reputation of Salem for having *once* relieved the unfortunate. Mr. Hutchinson might have pointed out the cause of the unhappy widow's necessity; but he has left that part to me, and here it follows:—After Hugh's Death, the selectmen of Salem were afraid that the King [Charles II.] would seize on his estate in Salem, as had been the case in regard to what the Parliament had given him in England. They therefore trumped up a debt, and seized and sold the said estate to the families of Lyndes and Curwin, who possess it to the present time;—and the selectmen of Salem allowed the widow 30*l*. per ann. for the wrong they had done her and her daughter. It is not likely that the widow was supported by any charitable collection; for William Peters was a man of great property, and had a deed of the whole peninsula whereon Boston stands, which he purchased of Mr. Blaxton, who bought it of the Plymouth Company; though Mr. Hutchinson says Blaxton's title arose merely from his sleeping on it the first of any Englishman.[1]—This

[1] "The Rev. Mr. Blaxton had lived on Shawmut, or the peninsula on which Boston is built, above nine years before June, 1630, when he was driven away from his possessions by the pious people of Salem, because he was not pleased with the religious system of those new-comers.—They were so generous as to vote a small lot to Mr. Blaxton, near Boston-Neck, as a compensation for the whole peninsula, and for his banishment on pain of death not to return.—Blaxton afterwards sold his right to William Peters, Esq. but who was kept out of possession of it by the supreme power of the People.—"

The religious institutions of Hooker at Hertford were not only binding on the Dutch, but even extended to the great Connecticote himself. The Sachem did was well said by Mr. Hutchinson, who wanted to justify the people of Salem in seizing the land and expelling Mr. Blaxton from his settlement in 1630, because he said he liked Lords-Brethren less than Lords-Bishops. —Moreover, Thomas Peters, at the same time, was living at Saybrook, and was not poor.—Those two Gentlemen were able and willing to support the widow of an unfortunate brother whom they loved very tenderly.—They took great care of his daughter, and left her handsome legacies.—From these considerations, I am induced to believe, that the widow of Hugh Peters never subsisted on any contributions, except what she received from her brothers William and Thomas Peters.—Mr. Hutchinson makes a curious remark, viz., If Hugh Peters had returned to his parish, he would not have suffered as he did.—He might have said, with greater propriety, that, if Hugh Peters had not been a fanatic and a rebel more zealous than wise, he never would have left his Parish for the agency of the people of New-England, who never paid him the stipulated allowance for his support in England, tho' he gave them thanksgiving-days, instead of fasting, for the space of twenty years, and procured, in 1649, from Oliver Cromwell, a charter for the Company for propagating the Gospel in New-England, which, by contributions raised in England, have supported all the missionaries among the Indians to the present time;—yet Mr. Hutchinson and Neal write largely about the vast expense the Massachusets-Bay have been at in spreading the Gospel among the poor savages!

I cannot forbear here to notice an abuse of this charter. Notwithstanding it confines the views of the Company to New-England, yet they, and their Committee of Correspondence in Boston, have of late years vouchsafed to send most of their Missionaries out of New-England, among the Six Nations, and the unsanctified episcopalians in the Southern Colonies, where was a competent number of church clergymen. Whenever this work of supererogation has met with its deserved animadversion, their answer has been, that, though Cromwell limited them to New-England, yet Christ had extended their bounds from sea to sea! With what little reason do they complain of King William's charter to the Society for the Propagation of the Gospel in Foreign Parts? This Society have sent Missionaries to New-England, where they have an undoubted right to send them, to supply episcopal Churches already estab-

not like his new neighbours; he refused to give or sell any land to them; but told them, that, as they came to trade, and to spread the Christian Religion among his subjects, which Mr. Hooker defined to consist only in peace, love, and justice, he had no objection to their building wigwams, planting corn, and hunting on his lands. The wisdom and steady temper of this great Sachem, and the vast number of subjects at his command, made Haynes and Hooker cautious in their conduct. Many people of Massachusets-Bay, hearing that Hooker had made good terms with the Sachem, left their persecutors, and fled to the fertile banks of Connecticut, that they might help Hooker spread the Gospel among the poor benighted Heathen in the wilderness. The Reverend Mr. Huet, with his disciples, fixed at Windsor, eight miles north of Hertford; and the Reverend Mr. Smith, at Weathersfield, four miles south of it. In the space of eighteen months, the Dominion of Hertford contained seven-hundred white people, and seven independent churches. Having converted over to the Christian faith some few Indians, among whom was Joshua, an ambitious captain under the great Sachem Connecticote, Hooker, Huet, Smith, and others, hereby found means to spread the *Gospel* into every

lished there; whereas the other Society send Missionaries beyond the limits of their charter, to alienate the minds of the episcopal Indians of the Six Nations, against the episcopal Missionaries and the Government of the Mother-Country.—And they have been too successful; especially since the Rev. Dr. Eleazer Wheelock, Dr. Whitaker, and the Rev. Mr. Sampson Occom, by the Charity of England, have joined in the same work.—To the General Assembly, and the Consociation of Connecticut, Dr. Wheelock and his associates are much beholden for their success in converting the poor benighted savages in the howling wilderness. Their merits are great, and their reward is pending.—Ed. Note.

Indian town, and, to the eternal infamy of christian policy, those renowned, pious fathers of this new colony, with the Gospel, spread the small-pox. This distemper raged in every corner: it swept away the great Sachem Connecticote, and laid waste his ancient kingdom. Hereupon, Haynes and his assembly proclaimed Joshua Sachem; and such as did not acknowledge his sachemic power, were compelled to suffer death, or fly the Dominion. Thus in three years time, by the Gospel and fanatic policy, was destroyed Connecticote, the greatest king in North-America. This remarkable event was considered as the work of the Lord; and the savage nations were told that the like calamities would befal them, unless they embraced the Gospel of Jesus Christ. Joshua was grateful to the English who had made him Sachem, and gave them deeds of those lands which had constantly been refused by Connecticote. But Joshua had as little honour as virtue and loyalty: he supported himself many years by signing deeds, and gulled the English through their own imprudence in neglecting to make a law for recording them.—These colonists, having driven out the Heathen, and got possession of a land which flowed with milk and honey, expelled the Dutch, as a dangerous set of heretics;—and Hooker, after doing so much for this new Dominion, expected the homage from every Church which is only due to a Bishop. This homage, however, he could not obtain, because each Minister had pretensions not much inferior to his. Disputes arose about Doctrine and Discipline. Hooker taught that there were forty-two kinds of Grace, though all of little value, except that of 'saving Grace.' As to Discipline, he held, that, as

DOCTRINES TAUGHT.

he had received his ministerial ordination from the Laity, who were members in full communion, he considered those actual communicants as *Christ's Church here on earth*, and consequently as holding the keys of discipline; and he maintained that the Minister had but a single voice, and was a subject of the Church. Other Ministers, who had received episcopal ordination, but had been silenced by their Bishops, judged themselves, notwithstanding, to be Ministers of Christ; and alleged that the installation of a Minister by prayer and imposition of hands of lay communicants, was no ordination, but a ceremony only of putting a Minister in possession of his Church, from which he might be dismissed by a majority of voters of the Members in full communion. And those Ministers taught for doctrine, that mankind were saved by Grace, and that the Gospel told us of but one Grace as necessary to Salvation; for that *he who believes that Jesus is the Son of God, is born of God, and enjoys the Grace of God which brings Salvation.* The majority of the People of course were on the side of Mr. Hooker, as his plan established their power over the Minister; and they soon determined by vote, according to their code of laws, in his favour. But the Ministers and minority were not convinced by this vote, and, to avoid an excommunication, formed themselves into separate bodies; nevertheless, they soon felt the thundering anathemas of Hooker, and the heated vengeance of the civil power. However, persecution, by her certain consequence, fixed the separatists in their schism, which continues to the present time.—Hooker reigned twelve years high-priest over Hertford; and then died above sixty years of age, to the great joy of the separatists, but, in point of populousness, to the disadvantage of the colony of Saybrook, which was the little Zoar for Hooker's heretics.

Exact in tything mint and anise, the furies of Newhaven for once affected the *weightier matters* of justice. They had no title to the land: they applied to Quinnipiog, the Sachem, for a deed or grant of it. The Sachem refused to give the lands of his ancestors to strangers. The settlers had teeming inventions, and immediately voted themselves to be the *Children of God*, and that *the wilderness in the utmost parts of the earth* was given to them. This vote became a law forever after. It is true, Davenport endeavoured to *christianize* Quinnipiog, but in vain: however, he *converted* Sunksquaw, one of his subjects, by presents and great promises; and then Sunksquaw betrayed his master, and the settlers killed him. This assassination of Quinnipiog brought on a war between the English and Indians, which never ended by treaty of peace. The Indians, having only bows and arrows, were driven back into the woods; whilst the English, with their swords and guns, kept possession of the country. But, conscious of their want of title to it, they voted Sunksquaw to be Sachem, and that whoever disputed his authority should suffer death. Sunksquaw, in return, assigned to the English those lands of which they had made him Sachem. Lo! here is all the title the settlers of the Dominion of Newhaven ever obtained.—The cruel and bloody persecutions under Eaton and Davenport in Newhaven soon gave rise to several little towns upon the sea-coast. Emigrants from England arrived every year to settle in this Dominion; but few remained in Newhaven, on account of Eaton, Davenport, the Deacons, and Elders, who possessed all power there, and were determined to keep it. The new-comers, therefore, under pretence of spreading Christ's kingdom, and shunning persecution, joined with the settlers at Stamford, Guilford, and Stratford, where, however, persecution domineered with as much fury as at Newhaven; for each town judged itself to be an independent Dominion; though, for fear of the Dutch and the Indians, they formed a political union, and swore to bear true allegiance to the capital Newhaven, whose authority was supreme. As all officers in every town were annually elected by the freemen, and as there were many candidates, some of whom must be unsuccessful, there was always room for complaints. The complainants formed schisms in the Church, which brought on persecution; and persecution drove the minority to settle new towns, in order to enjoy Liberty, Peace, and Power to persecute such as differed from them. Thus lived those ambitious people, under far worse persecutions from one another than they ever experienced or complained of in Old-England; all which they endured with some degree of patience, the persecuted one year living in hopes that the next would enable them to retaliate on their persecutors.

The laws made by this independent Dominion, and denominated *Blue-Laws* by the neighbouring Colonies, were never suffered to be printed; but the following sketch of some of them will give a tolerable idea of the spirit which pervades the whole.

"The Governor and Magistrates, convened in general Assembly, are the supreme power under God of this independent Dominion.

"From the determination of the Assembly no appeal shall be made.

"The Governor is amenable to the voice of the people.

"The Governor shall have only a single vote in determining any question; except a casting vote, when the Assembly may be equally divided.

"The Assembly of the People shall not be dismissed by the Governor, but shall dismiss itself.

"Conspiracy against this Dominion shall be punished with death.

"Whoever says there is a power and jurisdiction above and over this Dominion, shall suffer death and loss of property.

"Whoever attempts to change or overturn this Dominion shall suffer death.

"The judges shall determine controversies without a jury.

"No one shall be a freeman, or give a vote, unless he be converted, and a member in full communion of one of the Churches allowed in this Dominion.

"No man shall hold any office, who is not found in the faith, and faithful to this Dominion; and whoever gives a vote to such a person, shall pay a fine of 1*l*. for a second offence, he shall be disfranchised.

"Each freeman shall swear by the blessed God to bear true allegiance to this Dominion, and that Jesus is the only King.

"No Quaker or dissenter from the established worship of this Dominion shall be allowed to give a vote for the election of Magistrates, or any officer.

"No food or lodging shall be afforded to a Quaker, Adamite, or other Heretic.

"If any person turns Quaker, he shall be banished, and not suffered to return but upon pain of death.

"No Priest shall abide in the Dominion: he shall be banished, and suffer death on his return. Priests may be seized by any one without a warrant.

"No one to cross a river, but with an authorized ferryman.

BLUE LAWS. 59

"No one shall run on the Sabbath-day, or walk in his garden or elsewhere, except reverently to and from meeting.

"No one shall travel, cook victuals, make beds, sweep house, cut hair, or shave, on the Sabbath-day.

"No woman shall kiss her child on the Sabbath or fasting-day.

"The Sabbath shall begin at sunset on Saturday.

"To pick an ear of corn growing in a neighbour's garden, shall be deemed theft.

"A person accused of trespass in the night shall be judged guilty, unless he clear himself by his oath.

"When it appears that an accused has confederates, and he refuses to discover them, he may be racked.

"No one shall buy or sell lands without permission of the selectmen.

"A drunkard shall have a master appointed by the selectmen, who are to debar him from the liberty of buying and selling.

"Whoever publishes a lye to the prejudice of his neighbour, shall sit in the stocks, or be whipped fifteen stripes.

"No Minister shall keep a school.

"Every rateable person, who refuses to pay his proportion to the support of the Minister of the town or parish, shall be fined by the Court 2*l.* and 4*l.* every quarter, until he or she pay the rate to the Minister.

"Men-stealers shall suffer death.

"Whoever wears cloaths trimmed with gold, silver, or bone lace, above two shillings by the yard, shall be presented by the grand jurors, and the selectmen shall tax the offender at 300*l.* estate.

"A debtor in prison, swearing he has no estate, shall be let out, and sold, to make satisfaction.

"Whoever sets a fire in the woods, and it burns a house, shall suffer death ; and persons suspected of this crime shall be imprisoned, without benefit of bail.

"Whoever brings cards or dice into this Dominion shall pay a fine of 5*l.*

"No one shall read Common-Prayer, keep Christmas or Saints-days, make minced pies, dance, play cards, or play on any instrument of music, except the drum, trumpet, and jewsharp.[1]

"No Gospel Minister shall join people in marriage; the Magistrates only shall join in marriage, as they may do it with less scandal to Christ's Church.[2]

"When parents refuse their children convenient marriages, the Magistrates shall determine the point.

"The selectmen, on finding children ignorant, may take them away from their parents, and put them into better hands, at the expence of their parents.

"Fornication shall be punished by compelling marriage, or as the Court may think proper.

"Adultery shall be punished with death.

"A man that strikes his wife shall pay a fine of 10*l*.; a woman that strikes her husband shall be punished as the Court directs.

"A wife shall be deemed good evidence against her husband.

"No man shall court a maid in person, or by letter, without first obtaining consent of her parents: 5*l*. penalty for the first offence; 10*l*. for the second; and, for the third, imprisonment during the pleasure of the Court.

"Married persons must live together, or be imprisoned.

[1] As tobacco about this time was coming into use in the colony, a very curious law was made for its regulation or suppression. It was ordered that no person under twenty years of age, nor any other who had not already accustomed himself to the use of it, should take any tobacco until he had obtained a certificate, from under the hand of an approved physician, that it was useful for him, and until he had also obtained a license from the Court. All others who had addicted themselves to the use of it were prohibited from taking it in any company, or at their labors, or in traveling, unless ten miles at least from any company; and, though not in company, not more than once a day, upon pain of a fine of a sixpence for every offense. One substantial witness was to be sufficient proof of the crime.

The constables of the several towns were to make presentment to the particular Courts, and it was ordered that the fine should be paid without gainsaying.—ED. NOTE.

[2] The Savage Pawawwers, or Priests, never concern themselves with marriages, but leave them to the Paniesh, or Magistrates.

FANATICISM TURNED MAD. 61

"Every male shall have his hair cut round according to a cap."[1]

Of such sort were the laws made by the people of Newhaven, previous to their incorporation with Saybrook and Hertford colonies by the charter. They consist of a vast multitude, and were very properly termed *Blue Laws;* i. e. *bloody Laws;* for they were all sanctified with excommunication, confiscation, fines, banishment, whippings, cutting off the ears, burning the tongue, and death. Europe at this day might well say the Religion of the first settlers at Newhaven was fanaticism turned mad; and did not similar laws still prevail over New-England as the common law of the country, I would have left them in silence along with Dr. Mather's *Patres conscripti,* and the renowned Saints of Mr. Neal, to sleep to the end of time. No one, but a partial and blind bigot, can pretend to say the projectors of them were men of *Grace, Justice,* and *Liberty,* when nothing but *murders, plunders,* and *persecutions,* mark their steps. The best apology that can be made for them is, (I write in reference to those times,) that human nature is every-where the same; and that the mitred Lord and canting Puritan are both equally dangerous, or that both agree in the unchristian doctrine of persecution, and contend only which shall put it in practice. Mr. Neal says many call the first Colonizers in New-England weak men for separating from the Church of England, and suffering persecutions, rather than comply with indifferent ceremonies; and, after asserting that they were men of great learn-

[1] The Levitical law forbids cutting the hair, or rounding the head.

ing and goodness, he appeals to the world to judge, which were weak, the Bishops or the Puritans? My answer is, that those Puritans were weak men in Old England, and strong in New England, where they out-pop'd the Pope, out-king'd the King, and out-bishop'd the Bishops. Their murders and persecutions prove their strength lay in weakness, and their religion in ambition, wealth, and dominion.

Notwithstanding the perpetual jealousy and discordance between the three colonies of Connecticut, (Saybrook claiming the whole under the Lords Say and Brook, Hertford under Jehovah and Conquest, and Newhaven under King Jesus and Conquest,) they judged it necessary, for their better security against the Dutch and Indians, to strengthen each other's hands by forming a general confederacy with the Colonies of New Plymouth and the Massachusets-Bay. A measure of this kind, which they formally entered into in 1643, proved of the most salutary consequence, in a war which many years after broke out between them and Philip, sachem of the Pokanoket Indians, and which, for some time, imminently endangered the Colonies, but at length terminated in the destruction of that noted warrior and his followers.

The death of Cromwell in 1658 struck an awe throughout all New-England. Hertford and Newhaven appointed their days of fasting and prayer. Davenport prayed " the Lord to take the New-England Vine " under his immediate care, as he had removed by death " the great Protector of the protestant liberty :" nevertheless he lived to see the time when Charles II. obtained the possession of his Father's crown and kingdom, in spite of all his prayers. However, in the midst of sorrows, they were comforted by the presence of many regicides and refugees, who fled from England not so much for religion as for liberty; among whom were Whalley, Goffe, and Dixwell,[1] three of the judges and murderers of Charles I. Davenport and Leet the then Governor received them as Angels from Heaven, and blessed God that they had escaped out of the hands of " Herod the son of Barabbas." [2]

[1] *Dixwell* died and lies buried in Newhaven. His grave is visited by the *sober dissenters* with great reverence and veneration; nay, even held sacred as the tomb at Mecca. Here are buried also the children of Colonel Jones, and many other rebels.

[2] An affair had happened at New Haven, a few months before this, which now began to alarm the country, and soon gave great anxiety and trouble to the colony.

Very soon after the restoration, a large number of judges of King Charles I., commonly termed regicides, were apprehended and brought upon their trials in the Old Bailey. Thirty-nine were condemned, and ten executed as traitors. Some others, apprehensive of danger, fled out of the kingdom before King Charles II. was proclaimed. Colonels Whalley and Goffe made their escape to New England.

They were brought over by one Captain Gooking, and arrived in Boston in July, 1660. Governor Endicott, and gentlemen of character in Boston and its vicinity, treated them with peculiar respect and kindness. They were gentlemen of singular abilities, and had moved in an exalted sphere. Whalley had been a lieutenant-general, and Goffe a major-general, in Cromwell's army. Their manners and appearance commanded universal respect. They soon went from Boston to Cambridge, where they resided until February. They resorted openly to places of public worship on the Lord's-day, and at other times of public devotion. They were universally esteemed by all men of character, both civil and religious. But no sooner was it known that the judges had been condemned as traitors, and that these gentlemen were excepted from the act of pardon, than the principal gentlemen in the Massachusetts began to be alarmed.

Governor Endicott called a court of magistrates to consult measures

Newhaven Dominion being thus suddenly filled with inhabitants, saw itself enabled to support its independence, and as usual despised Hertford and Saybrook, and withal paid no attention to the King and

for apprehending them. However, their friends were so numerous that a vote could not at that time be obtained to arrest them. Some of the court declared that they would stand by them; others advised them to move out of the colony.

Finding themselves unsafe at Cambridge, they came, by the assistance of their friends, to Connecticut. They made their route by Hartford, and went directly to New Haven. They arrived about the 27th of March, and made Mr. Davenport's house the place of their residence.

They were treated with the same marks of esteem and generous friendship at New Haven which they had received in Massachusetts. The more the people became acquainted with them the more they esteemed them, not only as men of great minds, but of unfeigned piety and religion. For some time they appeared to apprehend themselves as out of danger, and happily situated among a number of pious and agreeable friends. But it was not long before the news of the king's proclamation against the regicides arrived, requiring that, wherever they might be found, they should be immediately apprehended. The Governor of Massachusetts, in consequence of the royal proclamation, issued his warrant to arrest them. As they were informed by their friends of all measures adopted respecting them, they removed to Milford. There they appeared openly in daytime, but at night often returned privately to New Haven, and were generally secreted at Mr. Davenport's, until about the last of April.

In the mean time, the Governor of Massachusetts received a royal mandate requiring him to apprehend them; and a more full circumstantial account of the condemnation and the execution of the ten regicides, and of the disposition of the Court toward them, and the republicans and Puritans in general, arrived in New England.

This gave a more general and thorough alarm to the whole country.

A feigned search had been made in the Massachusetts, in consequence of the former warrant, for the Colonels Whalley and Goffe; but now the Governor and magistrates began to view the affair in a more serious point of light, and appear to have been in earnest to secure them. They perceived that their own personal safety and the liberties and peace of the

Parliament of England.—The People of Massachusets, who were ever forward in promoting their own consequence, observing the temper and conduct of those of Newhaven, conceived an idea at once of exalting an in-country were concerned in the manner of their conduct toward these unhappy men. They therefore immediately gave a commission to Thomas Kellond and Thomas Kirk, two zealous young royalists, to go through the colonies as far as Manhadoes, and make a careful and universal search for them. They pursued the judges to Hartford, and, repairing to Governor Winthrop's, were nobly entertained.

He assured them that the colonels had made no stay in Connecticut, but went directly to New Haven. He gave them a warrant, and instructions similar to those which they had received from the Governor of Massachusetts, and transacted everything relative to the affair with dispatch. The next day they arrived at Guilford, and opened their business to Deputy-Governor Leet. They acquainted him that, according to the intelligence which they had received, the regicides were at New Haven. They desired immediately to be furnished with powers, horses, and assistance, to arrest them.

But here they were very unwelcome messengers. Governor Leet and the principal gentlemen in Guilford and New Haven had no ill opinion of the judges. If they had done wrong in the part they had acted, they viewed it as an error in judgment, and as the fault of great and good men, under peculiar and extraordinary circumstances. They were touched with compassion and sympathy, and had real scruples of conscience with respect to delivering up such men to death. They viewed them as the "excellent of the earth," and were afraid to betray them, lest they should be instrumental in shedding innocent blood. They saw no advantage in putting them to death.

They were not zealous, therefore, to assist in apprehending them. Governor Leet said he had not seen them in nine weeks, and that he did not believe they were at New Haven. He read some of the papers relative to the affair with an audible voice.

The pursuivants observed to him that their business required more secrecy than was consistent with such a reading of their instructions. He delayed furnishing them with horses until the next morning, and utterly declined giving them any powers until he had consulted his Council at New Haven.

dividual of their own province, and of attaching Hertford and Saybrook to their interest for ever. They sent Mr. John Winthrop privately to Hertford, to promote a petition to Charles II. for a charter, as a secu-

They complained that an Indian went off from Guilford to New Haven in the night, and that the Governor was so dilatory the next morning that a messenger went on to New Haven before they could obtain horses for their assistance. The judges were apprized of every transaction respecting them, and they and their friends took their measures accordingly. They changed their quarters from one place to another in the town as circumstances required, and had faithful friends to give them information, and to conceal them from their enemies.

On the 13th of March the pursuers came to New Haven, and Governor Leet arrived in town soon after them to consult his Council. They acquainted him that, from the information they had received, they were persuaded that the judges were yet in town, and pressed him and the magistrates to give them a warrant and assistance to arrest them without any further delay.

But, after the Governor and his Council had been together five or six hours, they dispersed without doing anything relative to the affair. The Governor declared that he could not act without calling a general assembly of the freedmen.

Kellond and Kirk observed to him that the other governors had not stood upon such niceties; that the honor and justice of his Majesty were concerned, and that he would highly resent the concealment and abetting of such traitors and regicides.

They demanded whether he and his Council would own and honor his Majesty? The Governor replied: "We do honor his Majesty, but have tender consciences, and wish first to know whether he will own us."— (Report of Kellond and Kirk to Governor Endicott, to which they gave oath in the presence of the Governor and Council.)

The tradition is, that the pursuers searched Mr. Davenport's house, and used him very ill. They also searched other houses where they suspected that the regicides were concealed. The report is that they went into the house of one Mrs. Eyers, where they actually were concealed, but she conducted the affair with such composure and address that they imagined that the judges had just made their escape from the house, and they went off without making any search. It is said that once, when the

rity against the ambition of Newhaven.—The Bostonians boasted of having had the honour of settling Hertford, which they therefore professed to consider in the light of a near and dear connection. The proposal was

pursuers passed a bridge, the judges were concealed under it. Several times they narrowly escaped, but never could be taken.

The zealous royalists, not finding the judges in New Haven, prosecuted their journey to the Dutch settlement, and made interest with Stuyvesant, the Dutch Governor, against them. He promised them that, if the judges should be found within his jurisdiction, he would give them immediate intelligence, and that he would prohibit all ships and vessels from transporting them.

Having thus zealously prosecuted the business of their commission, they returned to Boston, and reported the reception which they had met with at Guilford and New Haven.

Upon this report, a letter was written by Secretary Rawson, in the name of the General Court of Massachusetts, to Governor Leet and his Council, on the subject. It represented that many complaints had been exhibited in England against the colonies, and that they were in great danger. It was observed that one great source of complaint was their giving such entertainment to the regicides, and their inattention to his Majesty's warrant for their arrest. This was represented as an affair which hazarded the liberties of all the colonies, and especially those of New Haven. It was intimated that the safety of particular persons, no less than that of the colony, was in danger. It insisted that the only way to expiate their offense, and save themselves harmless, was without delay to apprehend the delinquents. Indeed, the Court urged that not only their own safety and welfare, but the essential interests of their neighbors, demanded their indefatigable exertions to exculpate themselves.

Colonels Whalley and Goffe, after the search which had been made for them at New Haven, left Mr. Davenport's, and took up their quarters at Mr. William Jones's, son-in-law to Governor Eaton, and afterward Deputy-Governor of New Haven and Connecticut. There they secreted themselves until the 11th of May.

Thence they removed to a mill in the environs of the town. For a short time they made their quarters in the woods, and then fixed them in a cave in the side of a hill, which they named Providence Hill. They had some other places of resort, to which they retired as occasion made

accepted by the few persons to whom it was communicated, but, in framing their petition, they found themselves deficient in their title to the lands. This obliged them to have recourse to a Junto at Saybrook, who claimed a title under Lords Say and Brook.—A few purchases, or rather exchanges, of land now took place between the Junto's; after which a petition was drawn up, containing an artful description of the lands claimed, "part of which they said they had purchased, and part they had conquered." They then as privately appointed Mr. Winthrop their agent to negociate the business in England, which he very willingly undertook. On his arrival here, he applied to the agents of Massachusets-Bay, and with their assistance procured from the incaution of Charles II. as ample a charter as was ever given to a

necessary, but this was generally the place of their residence until the 19th of August. When the weather was bad, they lodged at night in a neighboring house. It is not improbable that sometimes, when it could be done with safety, they made visits to their friends at New Haven.

In fact, to prevent any damage to Mr. Davenport or the colony, they once or more came into the town openly and offered to deliver up themselves to save their friends. It seems it was fully expected at that time that they would have done it voluntarily, but their friends neither desired nor advised them by any means to adopt so dangerous a measure. They hoped to save themselves and the colony harmless without such a sacrifice.

The magistrates were greatly blamed for not apprehending them at this time in particular. Secretary Rawson, in a letter of his to Governor Leet, writes: "How ill this will be taken, is not difficult to imagine—to be sure, not well. Nay, will not all men condemn you as wanting to yourselves?"

The General Court of Massachusetts further acquainted Governor Leet that the colonies were criminated by making no application to the king since his restoration, and for not proclaiming him as their king. The Court, in their letter, observed that it was highly necessary that they should send an agent to answer for them at the Court of England.—ED. NOTE.

palatinate state; it covered not only Saybrook, Hertford, and Newhaven, but half New-York, New-Jersey, and Pensylvania, and a tract of land near 100 miles wide, and extending westward to the South sea, 1400 miles from Narraganset bay. This charter, which was obtained in 1662, well pleased the people of Hertford, because it coincided with their former vote, viz. "that their dominion extended from sea to sea."[1] Newhaven Dominion too late discovered the intrigues of her artful neighbours; and, after two years opposition, submitted to the charter purely out of fear lest some of her minis-

[1] About this time, it seems, Governor Winthrop took passage for England. Upon his arrival he made application to Lord Say and Seal, and other friends of the colony, for their countenance and assistance. Lord Say and Seal appear to have been the only nobleman living who was one of the original patentees of Connecticut. He held the patent in trust, originally, for the puritanic exiles. He received the address from the colony most favorably, and gave Governor Winthrop all the assistance in his power. The Governor was a man of address, and he arrived in England at a happy time for Connecticut.

Lord Say and Seal, the great friend of the colony, had been particularly instrumental in the restoration. This had so brought him into the king's favor, that he had been made Privy Seal.

The Earl of Manchester, another friend of the Puritans and of the rights of the colonies, was chamberlain of his Majesty's household; he was an intimate friend of Lord Say and Seal, and had been united with him in defending the colonies, and pleading for their establishment and liberties. Lord Say and Seal engaged him to give Mr. Winthrop his utmost assistance.

Mr. Winthrop had an extraordinary ring, which had been given to his grandfather by King Charles I., which he presented to the king. This, it is said, exceedingly pleased his Majesty, as it had been once the property of a father most dear to him. Under these circumstances the petition for Connecticut was presented and received with uncommon grace and favor.

Upon the 20th of April, 1662, his Majesty granted the colony his

ters and magistrates should suffer ignominious deaths for aiding in the murder of their King.[1]

To the great joy of the People of Boston and Saybrook, Mr. Winthrop was appointed, by the Charter, Governor of all Connecticut. Their joy, however,

letters patent, conveying the most ample privileges, under the great seal of England. It confirmed unto it the whole tract of country granted by King Charles I. to the Earl of Warwick, and which was the next year by him consigned to Lord Say and Seal, Lord Brook, and others.

The patent granted the lands in fee and common socage. The facts stated and pleaded in the petition were recognized in the Charter, nearly in the same form of words, as reasons for the royal grant, and of the ample privileges it conveyed.

It ordained that John Winthrop, John Mason, Samuel Wyllys, Henry Clark, Matthew Allen, John Tapping, Nathan Gould, Richard Treat, Richard Lord, Henry Wolcott, John Talcott, Daniel Clark, John Ogden, Thomas Welles, Obadiah Brune, John Clark, Anthony Hawkins, John Deming, and Matthew Camfield, and all such others as there were, or should afterward be, admitted and made free of the corporation, should forever after be one body corporate and politic, in fact and name, by the name of the Governor and Company of the English Colony of Connecticut, in New England, in America; and that, by the same name, they and their successors should have perpetual succession. They were capacitated, as persons in law, to plead and be impleaded, to defend and be defended, in all suits whatsoever; to purchase, possess, lease, grant, demise, and sell lands, tenements, and goods, in as ample a manner as any of his Majesty's subjects or corporations in England. The Charter ordained that there should be, annually, two General Assemblies; one holden on the second Thursday in May, and the other on the second Thursday in October. This was to consist of the Governor, Deputy-Governor, and twelve assistants, with two deputies from every town or city. John Winthrop was appointed Governor, and John Mason Deputy-Governor, and the gentlemen named above, magistrates, until a new election should be made.—Ed. Note.

[1] Before the session of the General Assembly of Connecticut, in October, the Charter was brought over; and, as the Governors and magistrates appointed by his Majesty were not authorized to serve after this time, a general election was appointed on the 9th of October. John

sprung from different motives: Saybrook hoped for effectual protection from the insults of Hertford and the persecutions of Newhaven; and Boston expected to govern the Governor.

Winthrop, Esq., was chosen Governor, and John Mason, Esq., Deputy-Governor; the magistrates were those mentioned in the patent, and were appointed by his Majesty, with Mr. Baker and Mr. Sherman; and John Talcott, Esq., was Treasurer, and Daniel Clark, Esq., Secretary.

Upon the day of the election the Charter was publicly read to the freemen, and declared to belong to them and their successors. They then proceeded to make choice of Mr. Wyllys, Mr. Talcott, and Mr. Allen, to receive the Charter into their custody, and keep it in behalf of the colony. It was ordered that an oath should be administered by the court to the freemen, binding them to a faithful discharge of the trust committed to them.

The General Assembly established all former officers, civil and military, in their respective places of trust, and enacted that all the laws of the colony should be continued in full force, except such as should be found contrary to the tenor of the Charter. It was also enacted that the same colony seal should be continued.

The major part of the inhabitants of Southhold, several of the people of Guilford, and of the towns of Stamford and Greenwich, tendered their persons and estates to Connecticut, and, petitioning to enjoy the protection and privileges of the Commonwealth, were accepted by the Assembly, and promised the same protection and freedom which was common to the inhabitants of the colony in general. At the same time, it was enjoined on them to conduct themselves peaceably, as became Christians, toward their neighbors, who did not submit to the jurisdiction of Connecticut; and that they should pay all taxes due the ministers, with all the other public charges then due. A message was sent to the Dutch Governor, certifying him of the Charter granted to Connecticut, and desiring him by no means to trouble any of his Majesty's subjects, within its limits, with impositions or prosecutions from that jurisdiction.

The Assembly gave notice to the inhabitants of Winchester that they were comprehended within the limits of Connecticut, and ordered that, as his Majesty had thus disposed of them, they should conduct themselves as peaceable subjects.

Huntington, Setauket, Oyster Bay, and all the towns on Long Island,

Mr. Winthrop settled at New-London, in the kingdom of Sassacus, or colony of Saybrook, where he purchased lands of the claimants under Lords Say and Brook. Wisdom and moderation guided Mr. Winthrop.

were obliged to submit to the authority and govern themselves agreeably to the laws of Connecticut. A court was instituted at Southhold, consisting of Captain James Youngs, and the justices of South and East Hampton. The Assembly resolved that all the towns which should be received under their jurisdiction should bear their equal proportion of the charge of the colony in procuring the patent.

As the Charter included the colony of New Haven, Matthew Allen, Samuel Wyllys, and the Rev. Messrs. Stone and Hooker, were appointed a committee to proceed to New Haven, and treat with their friends there respecting an amicable union of the two colonies.

The committee proceeded to New Haven, and, after a conference with the Governor, magistrates, and principal gentlemen in the colony, left the following declaration to be communicated to the freemen:

"We declare that, through the providence of the Most High, a large and ample patent, and therein desirable privileges and immunities from his Majesty, being come to our hands, a copy whereof we have left with you to be considered, and yourselves, upon the sea-coast, being included and interested therein, the king having united us in one body politic, we, according to the commission wherewith we are intrusted by the General Assembly of Connecticut, do declare, in their name, that it is both their and our earnest desire, that there may be a happy and comfortable union between us and yourselves, according to the tenor of the Charter; that inconveniences and dangers may be prevented, peace and truth strengthened and established through our suitable subjection of the terms of the patent, and the blessing of God on us therein."

The authority of New Haven made the following reply:

"We have received and perused your writings, and heard the copy read of his Majesty's letters patent to the Connecticut colony; wherein, though we do not find the colony of New Haven expressly included, yet, to show our desire that matters may be issued in the conserving of peace and amity, with righteousness between them and us, we shall communicate your writings, and a copy of the patent, to the freemen, and afterward with convenient speed return their answer. Only we desire that the issuing of matters may be respited until we may receive fuller information from Mr. Winthrop, or satisfaction otherwise; and that, in the meantime, this colony may remain distinct, entire, and uninterrupted,

He was annually elected Governor till his death, which happened in 1676.

Whether it were owing to the discovery of any defect in the title of the People of Connecticut to the

as heretofore; which we hope you will see cause lovingly to assent unto, and signify the same to us with convenient speed."

On the 4th of November the freemen of the colony of New Haven convened in General Court. The Governor communicated the writings to the court, and ordered a copy of the patent to be read. After a short adjournment for consideration in an affair of so much importance, the freemen met again, and proceeded to discuss the subject.

The Rev. Mr. Davenport was entirely opposed to a union with Connecticut. He proceeded, therefore, to offer a number of reasons why the inhabitants of New Haven could not be included in the patent of that colony, and for which they ought, by no means voluntary, to form a union. He left his reasons in writing, for the consideration of the freemen. He observed that he should leave others to act, according to the light which they should receive.

It was insisted that New Haven had been owned as a distinct government, not only by her sister colonies, by Parliament, and the Protector, during their administration, but by his Majesty, King Charles II.; that it was against the express articles of confederation, by which Connecticut was no less bound than the other colonies; that New Haven had never been notified of any design as to their incorporation with Connecticut, and that they had never been heard on the subject. It was further urged that, had it been designed to unite them with Connecticut, some of their names, at least, would have been put into the patent, with the other patentees; but none of them were there. Hence it was maintained that it never could have been the design of his Majesty to comprehend them within the limits of the Charter.

It was argued, that for them to consent to a union would be inconsistent with their oath to maintain that Commonwealth, with all its privileges, civil and religious. It was also urged that it would be incompatible both with their honor and most essential interests.

After the affair had been fully debated, the freemen resolved that an answer to Connecticut should be drawn up under the following heads:

I. "Bearing a proper testimony against the great sin of Connecticut in acting so contrary to righteousness, amity, and peace.

soil, or of any undue arts practised in obtaining their charter, or whether it must be considered as an instance of Charles's fickle or arbitrary disposition, that Monarch, in the short space of two years after granting that

II. "Desiring that all future proceedings relative to the affair might be suspended until Mr. Winthrop should return, or they might otherwise obtain further information and satisfaction.

III. "To represent that they could do nothing in the affair until they had consulted the other confederates."

The magistrates and elders, with Mr. Law, of Stamford, were appointed a committee, and drew up a long letter in reply to the General Assembly of Connecticut, stating that they did not find any command in the patent to dissolve covenants and alter orderly settlements of New England, nor a prohibition against their continuance as a distinct government. They represented that the conduct of Connecticut, in acting at first without them, confirmed them in those sentiments; and that the way was still open for them to petition his Majesty, and obtain immunities similar to those of Connecticut. They declared that they must enter their appeal from the construction which Connecticut put upon the patent, and desired that they might not be interrupted in the enjoyment of their distinct privileges.

The committee also represented that these transactions were entirely inconsistent with the engagement of Governor Winthrop, contrary to his advice to Connecticut, and tended to bring injurious reflections and reproach upon him. They earnestly prayed for a copy of all which he had written to the Deputy-Governor and the Company on the subject. On the whole, they professed themselves exceedingly injured and grieved. and entreated the General Assembly of Connecticut to adopt speedy and effectual measures to repair the breaches which they had made, and to restore them to their former state, as a confederate and sister colony.

Connecticut made no reply to this letter, but, at a General Assembly held March 11, 1663, the Deputy-Governor, Matthew and John Allen, and John Talcott, were appointed a committee to treat with their friends in New Haven on the subject of a union. But the hasty measures of the General Assembly in admitting the disaffected members of the several towns under the jurisdiction of New Haven, before they had invited them to incorporate with them, had so soured their minds and

charter, comprized half Connecticut in another grant to his brother, the Duke of York, of the territory between the rivers Connecticut and Delaware, called by the Dutch New-Netherlands. This step excited much disprejudiced them, that this committee had no better success than the former.

While these affairs were transacted in the colonies, the petition and address of New Haven to his Majesty arrived in England; upon which, Governor Winthrop, who was yet there, by advice of friends of both colonies, agreed that no injury should be done to New Haven, and that the union and incorporation of the two colonies should be voluntary. Therefore, on the 3d day of March, 1663, he wrote to the Deputy-Governor and Company of Connecticut, certifying them of his engagements to the agent of New Haven, and that, before he took out the Charter, he had given assurance to their friends that their interest and privileges should not be injured by the patent. He represented that they were bound by the assurance he had given, and therefore wished them to abstain from all further injury and trouble to that colony. He imputed what they had done to their ignorance of the engagements which he had made. At the same time, he intimated his assurance that, on his return, he should be able to effect an amicable union of the colonies.

Connecticut now laid claim to Westchester, and sent one of her magistrates to lead the inhabitants to a choice of their officers, and to administer the proper oaths to such as they should elect.

The colony also extended their claim to the Narragansett country, and appointed officers for the government of the inhabitants of Wickford.

Notwithstanding the remonstrance of the court at New Haven, their appeal to King Charles II., and the engagements of Governor Winthrop, Connecticut pursued the affair of a union in the same manner in which it was begun. At a session of the General Assembly, August 19, 1663, a committee was again appointed to treat with their friends at New Haven, Milford, Guilford, and Branford, relative to their incorporation with Connecticut. Provided they could not effect a union by treaty, they were authorized to read the Charter publicly at New Haven, and to make declaration to the people there that the Assembly could not but resent their proceedings as a distinct jurisdiction, since they were evidently included within the limits of the Charter granted to the corporation of Connecticut. They were instructed to proclaim that the As-

76   GENERAL HISTORY OF CONNECTICUT.

content in Connecticut, especially when an actual defalcation of its territory was discovered to be in agitation, after Colonel Nichols had succeeded in an enterprise he was sent upon against the Dutch at New-York. Comsembly did desire, and could not but expect, that the inhabitants of the above towns would yield subjection to the government of Connecticut.

At a meeting of the commissioners in September in the same year, New Haven was owned by the colonies as a distinct confederation. Governor Leet and Mr. Fenn, who had been sent from that jurisdiction, exhibited a complaint against Connecticut for the injuries they had done, by encroaching upon their rights, receiving their members under their government, and encouraging them to disown their authority, to disregard their oath of allegiance, and to refuse all attendance on their courts. They further complained that Connecticut had appointed constables in several of their towns, to the great disquiet and injury of the colony. They prayed that effectual measures might be taken to redress their grievances, to prevent further injuries, and secure their rights as a distinct confederation.

Governor Winthrop and Mr. John Talcott, commissioners from Connecticut, replied that, in their opinion, New Haven had no just grounds of complaint; that Connecticut had never designed them any injury, but had made to them the most friendly propositions, inviting them to share with them freely in all the important and distinguishing privileges which they had obtained for themselves; that they had sent committees amicably to treat with them; that they were still treating, and would attend all just and friendly means of accommodation.

The commissioners of the other colonies, having fully heard the parties, determined that "where any act of power had been exerted against the authority of New Haven, the same ought to be recalled, and their power reserved to them entire, until such time as, in an orderly way, it shall be otherwise disposed." With respect to the particular grievances mentioned by the commissioners of New Haven, the consideration of them was referred to the next meeting of the commissioners at Hartford.

In this situation of affairs an event took place which alarmed all the New England colonies, and at once changed the opinion of the commissioners, and of New Haven, with respect to their incorporation with Connecticut.

King Charles II., on the 12th of March, 1664, gave a patent to

missioners were sent thither from Connecticut, the latter end of 1664, to defend the interests of the Colony; but, notwithstanding all the opposition they could make, they were constrained to yield up the whole of Long-

his brother, the Duke of York and Albany, of several extensive tracts of land in North America, the boundaries of which are thus described:

"All that part of the main land of New-England, beginning at a certain place called and known by the name of St. Croix, next adjoining to New-England, in America, and from thence extending along the sea-coast into a certain place called Pemaquie, or Pemaquid, and so up the river thereof to the furthest head of the same, as it tendeth northward, and from thence extending to the river Hembequin, and so upward, by the shortest course, to the river Canada northward; and also all that island or islands commonly called by the general name or names of Meitowax, or Long-Island, situate and being toward the west of Cape Cod, and the narrow Highgansets abutting on the main land, between the two rivers, these called and known by the several names of Connecticut and Hudson's Rivers; and all the land on the west side of Connecticut River, to the east side of the Delaware-Bay; and also all those several islands called or known by the names of Martin's Vineyard, or Nantucks, otherwise Nantucket: together," etc., etc.

The concern of the Duke of York for his property, and the aversion both he and his Majesty had for the Dutch, led them to dispatch an army and fleet to New England for the reduction of the Dutch settlement on the continent. Colonel Richard Nichols was chief commander of the fleet and army. Sir Robert Carr, George Cartwirth, and Samuel Maverick, Esq., were appointed commissioners with him, to determine all matters of complaint and controversy, and settling the country in peace.

Colonel Nichols arrived in Boston, with the fleet and troops under his command, on the 23d of July, 1664. He then sailed for the New Netherlands on the 20th of August, and made a demand of the town and forts upon the island of Manhadoes. Governor Winthrop, and several magistrates and principal gentlemen of Connecticut, joined him at the west end of Long Island, according to his request.

Stuyvesant, the Dutch Governor, was an old soldier, and, had he been better prepared and the people united, doubtless could have made a brave defense. But he had no intimations of the design until the 8th of July, when he received intelligence that a fleet of three or four ships of war, with three hundred and fifty soldiers on board, were about to sail from

Island and a strip of land on the east side of Hudson's river. This dismemberment is not easily to be justified; but, probably, finding it necessary to the performance of a promise he had made the Dutch of the enjoy-

England against the Dutch settlements. Upon this he immediately ordered that the forts should be put in a state of defense, and sent out spies into several parts of Connecticut for further information. It has been said that the Dutch Governor was negotiating a neutrality with Connecticut when he received the news of the fleet's arrival in Boston. Stuyvesant was extremely opposed to a surrender of the fort and town. Instead of submitting to the summons at first sent him, he drew up a long statement of the Dutch claims, and their indubitable right to the country. He insisted that, had the king of England known the justice of their claims, he never would have adopted such measures against them. He concluded by assuring Colonel Nichols that he should not submit to his demands, nor fear any evils but such as God in his providence should inflict upon him.

Colonel Nichols, in his first summons, had in his Majesty's name given assurance that the Dutch, upon their submission, should be safe as to life, liberty, and property. Governor Winthrop also wrote a letter to the Governor and Council, advising them to surrender. But they were careful to secrete the writings from the people, lest the easy terms proposed should induce them to surrender. The burgomasters and people desired to know of the Governor what was the import of the writings he had received, and especially of the letter from Governor Winthrop. The Dutch Governor and his Council giving them no intelligence, they solicited it the more earnestly. The Governor, irritated at this, in a paroxysm of anger tore the letters to pieces; upon which the people protested against his conduct and all its consequences.

While the Governor and Council were thus contending with the burgomasters and people, the English commissioners issued a proclamation to all the inhabitants who would become subject to his Majesty, "that they should be protected by his Majesty's laws and justice, and enjoy whatever God's blessing and their honest industry had furnished them with, and all the other privileges with his Majesty's English subjects."

The Dutch, therefore, on the 27th of August, submitted upon terms of capitulation. The articles secured them in the enjoyment of liberty of conscience in Divine worship, and their own mode of discipline.

ment of their possessions, Nichols might think himself at liberty of insisting upon it, furnished as he was with almost regal powers as the Duke of York's deputy. In that capacity, he assumed the government of the con-

The Dutch Governor and people became English subjects, enjoyed their estates, and all the privileges of Englishmen. Upon the surrender of the town of New Amsterdam, it was named New York, in honor of the Duke of York.

Fort Orange, or Aurania, surrendered on the 24th of September, and was named Albany, after the Duke of York and Albany. Sir Robert Carr proceeded to the Delaware, and on the 1st of October compelled the Dutch and Swedes to capitulate. Upon this day the whole of the New Netherlands became subject to the crown of England.

Mr. Whiting, who was in Boston, and learned much of the temper of the commissioners, was sent back in haste to give information of the danger in which, it was apprehended, the colonies were, to advise New Haven to incorporate with Connecticut without delay, and to make a joint exertion for the preservation of their chartered rights. This was pressed not only as absolutely necessary for New Haven, but for the general safety of the country. In consequence of this intelligence a General Court was convened at New Haven on the 11th of August, 1664. Governor Leet communicated the intelligence he had received, and acquainted them that Mr. Whiting and Mr. Bull, in their own name, and in behalf of the magistrates of Connecticut, pressed their immediate subjection to their government. The Court was certified that, after some treaty with these gentlemen, their committee had given an answer, purporting that if Connecticut would, in his Majesty's name, assert their claim to the colony of New Haven, and secure them in the full enjoyment of all the immunities which they had proposed, and engage to make a united exertion for the preservation of their chartered rights, they would make their submission. After a long debate the Court resolved that, if Connecticut should come and assist their claim, as had been agreed, they would submit until the meeting of the commissioners of the united colonies. The magistrates and principal gentlemen of the colony seem to have been sensible not only of the expediency, but of the necessity, of an incorporation with Connecticut. The opposition, however, was so general among the people that nothing further was effected. The Court of Commissioners was so near at hand that no further demands were made on New Haven

quered territory, but does not appear to have intermeddled further with that of Connecticut.

With Colonel Nichols were associated three other gentlemen, in a commission, empowering them to en-

until their advice could be known. The General Assembly met early in September, and passed a remonstrance against the sitting of Governor Leet and Deputy-Governor Jones with the commissioners. In the remonstrance they declared that New Haven was not a colony, but a part of Connecticut, and made claim to it as such. They insisted that owning that as a colony, distinct from Connecticut, after his Majesty had by his letters-patent incorporated it with that colony, was inconsistent with the king's pleasure; would endanger the right of all the colonies, and especially the charter-rights of Connecticut. The Assembly, at the same time, declared that they would have a tender regard to their honored friends and brethren at New Haven, and exert themselves to accommodate them with all the immunities and privileges which they conveyed by their Charter.

On the 1st of September the Court of Commissioners met at Hartford. The commissioners from New Haven were allowed their seats with the other confederates. The case of New Haven and Connecticut was fully heard, and though the Court did not approve of the manner in which Connecticut had proceeded, yet they earnestly pressed a speedy and amicable union of the two colonies.

To remove all obstructions on their part, the commissioners recommended it to the General Courts of Massachusetts and Plymouth, that, in case the colony of New Haven should incorporate with Connecticut, they might then be owned as one colony, and send two commissioners to each meeting; and that the determinations of any four of the six should be equally binding on the confederates as the conclusions of six out of eight had been before. It was also proposed that the meeting, which had been at New Haven, should be at Hartford.

In compliance with the advice of the commissioners, Governor Leet convened a General Court in New Haven on the 14th of September, and communicated the advice which had been given them to unite. They considered whether, if the king's commissioners should visit them, they would not be much better able to vindicate their liberty and just rights, in union with Connecticut under the royal patent, than in their present circumstances; and many insisted, notwithstanding, "that we

quire into the state of the New-England provinces, to hear and redress complaints, settle differences, and check abuses of power: but the ill humour and obstinacy of those of Connecticut and Massachusets-Bay, in a great measure frustrated their endeavours.

stand; as God had kept them to that time, was their best way." Others were intensely of the contrary opinion, and, after a full discussion of the subject, no vote for union or treaty could be obtained.

New Haven and Branford were more fixed and obstinate in their opposition to an incorporation with Connecticut than any of the other towns in that colony. Mr. Davenport and Mr. Pierson seem to have been among its chief supporters. They, with many of the inhabitants of the colony, were more rigid with respect to the terms of church-communion than the ministers and churches of Connecticut generally were. A considerable number of the churches in Connecticut were in favor of the propositions of the General Council, which met at Cambridge in 1662, relative to baptism of children whose parents were not in full communion. The ministers and churches of New Haven were universally and utterly against them. Mr. Davenport, and others in this colony, were also strong in the opinion that all government should be in the Church. No person in the colony could be a freeman unless he was a member in full communion. But, in Connecticut, all orderly persons possessing a freehold to a certain amount might be made free of the corporation. Those gentlemen who were so strong in their opposition were jealous that a union would mar the purity, order, and beauty of their churches, and have an influence on the civil administrations. Besides, it was a painful reflection that, after they had been at so much pains and expense to form and support themselves as a distinct government, and had been many years owned as one, their existence must cease and their name be obliterated. Milford at this time broke off from them, and would no more either send magistrates or deputies to the General Court. Mr. Richard Law, a principal gentleman in Stamford, also deserted them.

In this state of affairs the General Assembly of Connecticut convened on the 13th of October. This was an important crisis with the colony. Their liberties were not only in equal danger with those of the sister-colonies, from the extraordinary powers and arbitrary dispositions and measures of the king's commissioners, but the Duke of York, a powerful

82   GENERAL HISTORY OF CONNECTICUT.

By authority of the Charter, the freemen chuse annually, in May, a Governor, a Deputy-Governor, a Secretary, a Treasurer, and 12 Assistants, and, twice a year, two Representatives from each town. These, be-

antagonist, had received a patent covering Long Island and all that part of the colony west of Connecticut River. William and Anne, the Duke and Duchess of Hamilton, had petitioned his Majesty to restore to them the tract of country granted to their father, James, Marquis of Hamilton, in the year 1635; and his Majesty had, on the 6th of May, 1664, referred the case to the determination of Colonel Nichols and the other commissioners. Besides, the state of affairs with New Haven was neither comfortable nor safe.

The Legislature, to conciliate the commissioners and obtain the good graces of his Majesty, ordered a present of five hundred bushels of corn to be made to the commissioners. A large committee was appointed to settle the boundaries between Connecticut and the Duke of York. A committee, consisting of Messrs. Allen, Wyllys, Talcott, and Newburg, was appointed to settle the boundary-line between this colony and Massachusetts, and between Connecticut and Rhode Island. They were instructed not to give away any part of the lands included within the limits of the Charter.

Mr. Sherman, Mr. Allen, and the Secretary, were authorized to proceed to New Haven, and, by order of the General Assembly, "in his Majesty's name to require the inhabitants of New Haven, Milford, Branford, Guilford, and Stamford, to submit to the government established by his Majesty's most gracious grant to this colony, and to receive their answer." They were authorized to make declaration, that the Assembly did invest Messrs. Leet, Jones, Gilbert, Fenn, Crane, Treat, and Law, with the powers of magistracy, to govern their respective plantations agreeably to the laws of Connecticut, or such of their own laws as were not inconsistent with the Charter, until their session in May next.

The gentlemen appointed to this service on the 19th of November went to New Haven, and proceeded according to their instructions.

About this time Governor Winthrop, Mr. Allen, Mr. Gould, Mr. Richards, and John Winthrop, the committee appointed to settle the boundaries between Connecticut and New York, waited upon the commissioners on York Island. After they had been fully heard in behalf of Connecticut, the commissioners determined "that the southern bouning met, constitute the General Assembly, which has power to make laws, provided they are not repugnant to the laws of England, and enforce them without the consent of the King.

The General Assembly meets in May and October without summoning. By it the colony has been divided into six counties, viz. Hertford, Newhaven, New-London, Fairfield, Windham, and Litchfield; and these subdivided into 73 townships and 300 parishes.

Each town has two or more justices of peace, who hear and determine, without a jury, all causes under 2*l*.

dary of his Majesty's colony of Connecticut is the sea; and that Long Island is to be under the government of the Duke of York, as is expressed in plain words in the said patents respectively. We also order and declare, that the creek or river called Mamaroneck, which is reputed to be almost twelve miles to the east of West Chester, and a line drawn from the east point or side, where the fresh water falls into the salt, at high-water mark, north-northwest to the line of Massachusetts, be the western bounds of said colony of Connecticut; and the plantations lying westward of that creek, and a line so drawn, to be under his Royal Highness's government; and all plantations lying eastward of the creek and line to be under the government of Connecticut."

In consequence of the acts of Connecticut, and the determination of the commissioners relative to the boundaries of the colony, a General Court was called at New Haven on the 13th of December, 1664, and the following resolutions were unanimously passed:

I. "That by this act or vote we be not understood to justify Connecticut's former actings, nor anything disorderly done by their own people, on such accounts.

II. "That by it we be not apprehended to have any hand in breaking and dissolving the confederation.

III. "Yet, in loyalty to the king's Majesty, when an authentic copy of the determination of his Majesty's commissioners is published, to be recorded with us, if thereby it shall appear to our committee that we are, by his Majesty's authority, now put under Connecticut patent, we shall submit, by a necessity brought upon us by the means of Connecticut aforesaid, but with a *solvo jure* of our former rights and claims, as a people who have not yet been heard in point of plea."—ED. NOTE.

Each county has five judges, who try by a jury all causes above 2*l.*

Five judges preside over the superior court of the province, who hold two sessions in each county every year. To this court are brought appeals from the county courts when the verdict exceeds 10*l.* appeals from the courts of probate, writs of error, petitions for divorce, &c.

The General Assembly is a court of chancery, where the error or rigour of the judgments of the superior courts are corrected.

The General Assembly, and not the Governor, has the power of life and death.

The courts of probate are managed by a justice of peace appointed by the General Assembly.

Each county has its Sheriff, and each town its constables.

By charter the Governor is Captain-general of the militia. Fourteen Colonels, 14 Lieutenant-Colonels, and 14 Majors, are appointed by the General Assembly. The Captains and Subalterns are elected by the People, and commissioned by the Governor.

The ecclesiastical courts in Connecticut are: 1. The Minister and his Communicants; 2. The Association, which is composed of every minister and deacon in the county; 3. The Consociation, which consists of four ministers and their deacons, chosen from each Association; and always meets in May, at Hertford, with the General Assembly. An appeal from the Consociation will lie before the General Assembly; but the clergy have always been against it, though with less success than they wished.—The General Assembly declared "Sober Dissenters" to be the established religion of the province.

The laws of the colony enacted by the authority of the Charter are decent in comparison with the Blue Laws. They make one thin volume in folio. Yet exceptions may justly be made to many of them—equal liberty is not given to all parties—taxes are unfairly laid—the poor are oppressed.—One law is intolerable, viz. When a trespass is committed in the night, the injured person may recover damages of any-one he shall think proper to accuse, unless the accused can prove an alibi, or will clear himself by an oath; which oath, nevertheless, it is at the option of the justice either to administer or refuse. Queen Ann repealed the cruel laws respecting Quakers, Ranters, and Adamites; but the General Assembly, notwithstanding, continued the same in their law-book, maintaining that a law made in Connecticut could not be repealed by any authority but their own. It is a ruled case with them that no law or statute of England be in force in Connecticut till formally passed by the General Assembly and recorded by the Secretary.[1] Above 30 years ago, a negro castrated his master's son, and was brought to trial for it before the Superior Court at Hertford. The Court could find

[1] While the churches were thus divided, they were alarmed by the appearance of the Quakers. A number of them arrived in Boston in July and August, and had been committed to the common gaol. A great number of their books had been seized with the view to burn them. In consequence of their arrival, and the disturbance they had made in Boston, the commissioners of the united colonies, at their court in September, recommended it to the several General Courts,

"That all Quakers, Ranters, and other notorious heretics, should be prohibited coming into the united colonies; and that, if they should come

no law to punish the negro. The lawyers quoted the English statute against maiming; the Court were of opinion that statute did not reach this colony, because it had not been passed in the General Assembly; and therefore were about to remand the negro to prison till the General Assembly should meet. But an *ex-post-facto* law was objected to as an infringement upon civil liberty. At length, however, the Court were released from their difficulty by having recourse to the vote of the first settlers at Newhaven, viz. That the Bible should be their law till they could make others more suitable to their circumstances. The court were of opinion that vote was in full force, as it had not been revoked; and thereupon tried the negro upon the Jewish law, viz. Eye for Eye, and Tooth for Tooth. He suffered accordingly.

The idea fostered by the colony of independence on Great Britain was not, as might be imagined, destroyed by the royal charter, but, on the contrary, was

or arise among them, they should be forthwith secured and removed out of all the jurisdictions."

In conformity with this recommendation, the General Court of Connecticut, in October, passed the following act:

" That no town within this jurisdiction shall entertain any Quakers, Ranters, Adamites, or such like notorious heretics, or suffer them to continue in them above the space of fourteen days, upon the penalty of 5*l.* per week for any town entertaining such persons. But the townsmen shall give notice to the two next magistrates or assistants, who shall have the power to send them to prison, for securing them until they can conveniently be sent out of the jurisdiction. It is also ordered that no master of a vessel shall land any such heretics; but if they *do,* they shall be compelled to transport them again out of the colony, by any two magistrates or assistants, at their first setting sail from the port where they landed them; during which time the assistant or magistrate shall see them secured, upon the penalty of 20*l.* for any master of any vessel that shall not transport them as aforesaid."—Ed. Note.

renewed and invigorated by it. Indeed, the charter is as much in favour of Connecticut, and unfavourable to England, as if it had been drawn up in Boston or Newhaven. Had it been granted jointly by the King, Lords, and Commons, and not by the King *solus*, no one could dispute the independence of Connecticut on England, any more than they could that of Holland on Spain. The people at large did not discriminate between an act of the King *solus* and an act of the King, Lords, and Commons, conjointly; and, to prevent anyone from shewing the difference, the General Assembly made a law that " whoever should attempt to destroy the constitution of this Colony as by charter established, should suffer death." The power of a British King was held up by them much higher than the constitution allowed. The King had authority, they said, to form palatinate states without consent of Parliament. Accustomed to doctrines of this tendency, the multitude concluded the General Assembly of Connecticut to be equal to the British Parliament.

Notions of this kind did not prevail in Connecticut alone; Massachusets-Bay still more abounded with them, and Rhode Island was not uninfected. What was the consequence? Complaints against those governments poured into the British court. A reformation, therefore, became indispensable in New-England, and was begun by a disfranchisement of the Massachusets province. The death of Charles II. put a temporary stop to proceedings against the other colonies; but James II. soon found it expedient to renew them. In July, 1685, the following instances of mal-administration were formally exhibited against the Governor and

Company of Connecticut, viz., " They have made laws " contrary to the laws of England :—they impose fines " upon the inhabitants, and convert them to their own " use :—they enforce an oath of fidelity upon the inhab- " itants without administering the oath of supremacy " and allegiance, as in their charter is directed :—they " deny to the inhabitants the exercise of the religion of " the church of England, arbitrarily fining those who " refuse to come to their congregational Assemblies :— " his Majesty's subjects inhabiting there cannot obtain " justice in the courts of that colony :—they discourage " and exclude the government all gentlemen of known " loyalty, and keep it in the hands of the independent " party in the colony." (*New-Eng. Ent. vol.* ii. p. 241.) In consequence of this impeachment, James II. ordered a *Quo Warranto* to be issued against the Charter of Connecticut. The People perceived the King was in earnest; and their alarm manifested itself in humble sollicitations for favour : but, it being thought advise- able, on several accounts, particularly the extensive progress the French were making in Canada, to ap- point one general Governor over New-England, the submissive applications of the Connecticut colonists could no further be regarded than in allowing them their choice, whether to be annexed to New-York or the Massachusets. They preferred the latter; and, ac- cordingly, Sir Edmund Andros having been appointed Captain-general over all New-England, the charter of Connecticut was surrendered to him. It is very re- markable that Mr. Neal, Hutchinson, and other his- torians of New-England, have artfully passed over in silence this transaction of the surrender of Connecticut Charter to Sir Edmund Andros, the General Governor over New-England. They have represented the magistrates of Connecticut as not having resigned their charter, but by an erroneous construction put on their humble supplication to James II. by the Court of London; whereas the fact is, they resigned it, *in propria forma*, into the hands of Sir Edmund Andros, at Hertford, in October, 1687, and were annexed to the Massachusets-Bay colony, in preference to New-York, according to royal promise and their own petition.[1] But

[1] Mr. Dudley, while president of the commissioners, had written to the Governor and Company, advising them to resign the Charter into the hands of his Majesty, and promising to use his influence in favor of the colony. Mr. Dudley's commission was suspended by a commission to Sir Edmund Andros to be Governor of New England. He arrived in Boston on the 19th of December, 1686. The next day his commission was published, and he took on him the administration of the government. Soon after his arrival he wrote to the Governor and Company that he had a commission from his Majesty to receive their Charter, if they would resign it; and he pressed them, in obedience to the king, and as they would give him an opportunity to serve them, to resign it to his pleasure. At this session of the Assembly the Governor received another letter from him, acquainting him that he was assured, by the advice he had received from England, that judgment was by that time entered upon the *quo warranto* against their Charter, and that he soon expected to receive his Majesty's commands respecting them. He urged them, as he represented it, that he might not be wanting in serving their welfare, to accept his Majesty's favor, so graciously offered them, in a present compliance and surrender. But the colony insisted upon their Charter rights, and on the promise of King James, as well as of his royal brother, to defend and secure them in the enjoyment of their privileges and estates, and would not surrender their Charter to either. However, in their petition to the king, in which they prayed for the continuance of their Charter rights, they desired, if this could not be obtained, but it should be resolved to put them under another government, that it might be under Sir Edmund's, as the Massachusetts had been their former correspondents and confederates, and as they were acquainted with their principles and manners.

the very night of the surrender of it, Samuel Wadsworth, of Hertford, with the assistance of a mob, violently broke into the apartments of Sir Edmund, regained, carried off, and hid the charter in the hollow of an elm; and, in 1689, news arriving of an insurrection and overthrow of Andros at Boston, Robert Treat, who had been elected in 1687, was declared by the mob still to be Governor of Connecticut. He daringly summoned

This was construed into a resignation, though nothing could be further from the designs of the colony.

The Assembly met, as usual, in October, and the government continued according to the Charter, until the last of the month.

About this time Sir Edmund and his suite, and more than sixty regular troops, came to Hartford, where the Assembly were sitting, and demanded the Charter, and declared the government under it dissolved. The Assembly were extremely reluctant and slow with respect to any resolve to surrender the Charter, or with respect to any motion to bring it forth. The tradition is, that Governor Treat represented the great expense and hardships of the colonists in planting the country; the blood and treasure which they had expended in defending it, both against the savages and foreigners; to what hardships and dangers he himself had been exposed for that purpose; and that it was like giving up his life now to surrender the patent and privileges so dearly bought and so long enjoyed. The important affair was debated and kept in suspense until the evening, when the Charter was brought and laid upon the table where the Assembly was sitting. By this time a great number of people were assembled, and men sufficiently bold to enterprise whatever might be necessary or expedient.

The lights were instantly extinguished, and one Captain Wadsworth, of Hartford, in the most silent and secret manner, carried off the Charter and secreted it in a large, hollow tree, fronting the house of the Hon. Samuel Wyllys, then one of the magistrates of the colony. The people appeared all peaceable and orderly. The candles were relighted, but the patent was gone, and no discovery could be made of it or of the person who had conveyed it away.

It was said that the Charter was delivered up, and that same evening the apartments of Sir Edmund were entered and the patent abstracted;

his old Assembly, who, being convened, voted the charter to be valid in law, and that it could not be vacated by any power without the consent of the General-Assembly.[1] They then voted that Samuel Wadsworth should bring forth the charter; which he did in a sol-

but this does not appear to have been the case. Sir Edmund assumed the government, and the records of the colony were closed in the following words:

"At a General Court at Hertford, October 31, 1687, His Excellency Sir Edmund Andros, Knight, and Captain-General, and Governor, of his Majesty's territories and dominions in New England, by order from his Majesty James II., King of England, Scotland, France, and Ireland, the 31st of October, 1687, took into his hands the government of the Colony of Connecticut, it being by his Majesty annexed to Massachusets and other colonies under his Excellency's government.

"FINIS."

Sir Edmund appointed officers civil and military. His Council at first consisted of forty persons, and afterward of nearly fifty. Four among the number—Governor Treat, John Fitz Winthrop, Wait Winthrop, and John Allen, Esquires—were of Connecticut.—Ed. Note.

[1] Scarcely anything could be more gloomy and distressful than the state of public affairs in New England at the beginning of this year. But in the midst of darkness light arose. While the people had prayed in vain to an earthly monarch, their petition had been more successfully presented to a higher throne. Providence wrought gloriously for them and the nation's deliverance. On the 5th of November, 1688, the Prince of Orange landed at Torbay, in England. He immediately published a declaration of his design in visiting the kingdom. A copy of this was received at Boston by one Mr. Winslow, a gentleman from Virginia, in April, 1689.

Governor Andros and his Council were so much alarmed with the news, that they ordered Mr. Winslow to be arrested and committed to jail for bringing a false and traitorous libel in the country.

They also issued a proclamation commanding all the officers and people to be in readiness to prevent the landing of any forces which the Prince of Orange might send into that part of America. But the people, who sighed under their burdens, secretly wished and prayed for success to his glorious undertaking. The leaders in the country determined qui-

emn procession, attended by the High-sheriff, and delivered it to the Governor. The General Assembly voted their thanks to Wadsworth, and twenty shillings as a reward for *stealing* and hiding their charter in the elm. Thus Connecticut started from a dependent counetly to await the event; but the great body of the people had less patience. Stung with past injuries, and encouraged at the first intimations of relief, the fire of liberty rekindled, and the flame, which for a long time had been smothered in their bosoms, burst forth with irresistible violence.

On the 18th of April the inhabitants of Boston and the adjacent towns rose in arms, made themselves masters of the castle, seized Sir Edmund Andros and his Council, and persuaded the old Governor and Council at Boston to resume the government.

On the 9th of May, 1689, Governor Robert Treat, Deputy-Governor James Bishop, and the former magistrates, at the desire of the freemen, resumed the government of Connecticut. Major-General John Winthrop was at the same time chosen into the magistracy, to complete the number appointed by the Charter.

The freemen voted that, for the present safety of that part of New England called Connecticut, the necessity of its circumstances so requiring,

"They would reëstablish government as it was before and at the time Sir Edmund Andros took it, and so have it proceed, as it did before that time, according to charter, engaging themselves to submit to it accordingly, until there should be a legal establishment among them."

The Assembly, having formed, came to the following resolutions:

"That, whereas this Court hath been interrupted in the management of its government, in this Colony of Connecticut, for nineteen months past, it is now enacted, ordered, and declared, that all the laws of this colony, made according to Charter, and courts constituted for the administration of government, as they were before the late interruption, shall be of full force and virtue for the future, and until this Court shall see cause to make further and other alterations, according to the Charter."

The Assembly then confirmed all military officers in their respective posts, and proceeded to appoint their civil officers, as had been customary at the May session.—ED. NOTE.

ty into an independent province, in defiance of the authority that had lately been paid such humble submission. None should be surprized to find the People shewing more deference to Abimeleck, King of Mohegin, than to George, King of England; since a vote of men, whose legislative and even corporate capacity had been annihilated, has prevailed, for more than eighty years, over a just exertion of royal prerogative.[1] Nev-

[1] "AN ADDRESS TO KING WILLIAM, JUNE 13, 1689.

"To the King's most Excellent Majesty: The humble address of your Majesty's dutiful and loyal subjects, the Governor and Company of your Majesty's Colony of Connecticut, in New England.

"Great Sovereign: Great was that day when the Lord, who sitteth upon the floods, and sitteth King forever, did divide his and your adversaries from one another, like the waters of Jordan forced to stand upon an heap, and did begin to magnify you, like Joshua in the sight of all Israel, by those great actions that were so much for the honour of God and the deliverance of the English dominions from popery and slavery; and all this, separated from those sorrows that usually attend the introduction of a peaceable settlement in any troubled state: all which doth affect us with the sense of our duty to return the highest praise unto the King of Kings and Lord of Hosts, and bless him who hath delighted in you, to set you upon the throne of his Israel, and to say, Because the Lord loved Israel forever, therefore has he made you king, to do justice and judgment, &c.; also humble and hearty acknowledgement for the great zeal that by your Majesty has been expressed in those hazards you have put your royal person to, and in the expense of so great a treasure in the defense of the Protestant interest. In the consideration of all which, we, your Majesty's dutiful and loyal subjects of your said colony, are encouraged humbly to intimate that we, with much favour, obtained a Charter from Charles II., of happy memory, bearing date April 23, 1662, in the fourteenth year of his reign, granted to the Governor and Company of his Majesty's Colony of Connecticut, the advantages and privileges whereof made us indeed a very happy people; and, by the blessing of God upon our endeavours, we have made a considerable improvement of your dominions here, which, with the defense of ourselves from the force of both foreign and intestine enemies, has cost us much expense of treasure

ertheless, this unconstitutional Assembly, whose authority under an assumed charter has been tacitly acknowledged by the British Parliament, have not at all times been unchecked by the Corporation of Yale College. That College, by a charter received from this self-erected Government, was enabled to give Bachelors and Masters degrees; but the Corporation have presumed to give Doctors degrees. When the General Assembly

and blood; yet in the second year of the reign of his late Majesty, King James II., we had a *quo warranto* served upon us by Edward Randolph, requiring our appearance before his Majesty's court in England; and although the time of our appearance was elapsed before the serving the said *quo warranto*, yet we humbly petitioned his Majesty for his favour and the continuance of our Charter, with the privileges thereof; but we received no other favour but a second *quo warranto:* and we well observed that the Charter of London, and of other considerable cities in England, were condemned, and that the Charter of Massachusets had undergone the like fate, plainly saw what we might expect; yet as we not judged it good or lawful to be active in surrendering what had cost us so dear, nor to be altogether silent, we employed an attorney to appear in our behalf, and to prefer our humble address to his Majesty, to entreat his favour quickly upon it; but as Sir Edmund Andros informed us he was empowered by his Majesty to regain the surrender of our Charter, if we saw meet to do so, and to take ourselves under his government, we withstood all these motions, and in our reiterated addresses we petitioned his Majesty to continue us in the full and free enjoyment of our liberties and property, civil and sacred, according to our Charter. We also petitioned that if his Majesty should not see meet to continue us as we were, but was resolved to annex us to some other government, we then desired that (inasmuch as Boston had been our old correspondents, and people whose principles and manners we had been acquainted with) we might be annexed rather to Sir Edmund Andros his government than to Colonel Dungan's, which choice of ours was taken for a resignation of our government; though that was never intended by us for such, nor had it the formalities in law to make it a resignation, as we humbly conceive; yet Sir Edmund Andros was commissioned by his Majesty to take us under his government: pursuant to which, about the end of October, 1687, he,

accused them of usurping a privilege not conferred by their charter, they retorted that "to usurp upon a char-"ter was not so bad as to usurp a vacated charter." The General Assembly were obliged to be content with this answer, as it contained much truth, and came from the clergy, whose ambition and power are not to be trifled with.

Whatever might be the reason of the English Gov-
with a company of gentlemen and grenadiers to the number of sixty or upward, came to Heitford (the chief seat of this government), caused his commission to be read, and declared our government to be dissolved, and put into commission both civil and military officers through our colony, as he pleased, when he passed through the principal parts thereof.

"The good people of the colony, though they were under a great sense of injuries they sustained hereby, yet chose rather to be silent and patient than oppose, being, indeed, surprised into an involuntary submission to an arbitrary power; but when the government we were thus put under seemed to us to be determined, and we being in daily fear and hazard of those many inconveniences that will arise from a people in want of a government; being also in continual danger of our lives by reason of the natives being at war with us, with whom we had just fears of our neighbouring French to join, not receiving any order or directions what method to take for our security, we were necessitated to put ourselves into some form of government; and there being none so familiar to us as that of our Charter, nor what we could make so effectual for the gaining the universal compliance of the people, and having never received any intimation of an enrolment of that which was interpreted a resignation of our Charter, we have presumed, by the consent of the major part of the freemen assembled for that end, May 9, 1689, to resume our government according to the rules of our Charter, and this to continue till further order; yet, as we have thus presumed to dispose ourselves, not waiting orders from your Majesty, we humbly submit ourselves herein, entreating your Majesty's most gracious pardon; and that what our urgent necessity hath put upon us may no ways interrupt your Majesty's grace and favour toward us, your most humble and dutiful subjects, but that in your clemency you would be pleased to grant us such directions as to your princely wisdom may seem meet, with such ratifications and confirmations of our Charter, in the

ernment's winking at the contempt shewn to their authority by the people of Connecticut, it certainly added to their ingratitude and bias to usurpation. Having been in possession of that country one-hundred and forty years, the General Assembly, though unsupported either by law or justice, resolved to take up and settle their lands west not only of Hudson but Susquehanna river, and extending to the South-Sea. In pursuance of this resolution, they with modesty passed over New-York, and the Jerseys, because they are possessed by Mynheers and fighting christians, and seized on Pensylvania, claimed by Quakers, who fight not for either wife or daughter. They filled up their fathers iniquities, by murdering the Quakers and Indians, and taking possession of their lands; and no doubt, in another century, they will produce deeds of sale from Sunksquaw, Uncas, or some other supposititious Sachem. This is a striking instance of the use I have said the Colony sometimes make of their charter, to countenance and support their

full and free enjoyment of all our properties, privileges, and liberties, both civil and sacred, as therein granted to us by your royal predecessor, King Charles II., which may yet further insure it an inheritance to us and our posterities after us, with what further grace and favour your royal and enlarged heart may be moved to confer upon us; which, we trust, we shall not forget nor be unprofitable under; but as we have this day, with the greatest expressions of joy, proclaimed your Majesty and Royal Consort King and Queen of England, France, and Ireland, with the dominions hereto belonging, so we shall ever pray that God would grant your Majesties long life, and prosperously to reign over all your dominions, and that the great and happy work you have begun may be prospered here, and graciously rewarded with a crown of glory hereafter.

"ROBERT TREAT, *Governor.*

"Per order of the General Court of Connecticut.

"[Signed]   JOHN ALLEN, *Secretary.*"

adventurous spirit of enterprize. They plead that their charter bounds them on the west by the South-Sea; but they seem to have forgotten that their charter was surreptitiously obtained; and that the clause on which they dwell is rendered nugatory, by the petitioners having described their lands as lying upon Connecticut river, and obtained partly by purchase and partly by conquest. Now, it being a fact beyond all controversy, that they then had not conquered, nor even pretended to have purchased, any lands west of Hudson's-River, it is evident that their westernmost boundary never did or ought to extend further than to that river. Not that Mr. Pen has any just title to those lands on Susquehanna river which are the bone of contention, and which lie north of his patent: they belong to the assigns of the Plymouth Company, or to the Crown of England.

Republicanism, schisms, and persecutions, have ever prevailed in this Colony.—The religion of "*Sober Dissenters*" having been established by the General Assembly, each sect claimed the establishment in its favour. The true Independents denied that the Assembly had any further power over Christ's Church than to protect it. Few Magistrates of any religion are willing to yield their authority to Ecclesiastics; and few disciples of Luther or Calvin are willing to obey either civil or spiritual masters. In a Colony where the people are thus disposed, dominion will be religion, and faction conscience. Hence arose contentions between the Assembly and Independents; and both parties having been brought up under Cromwell, their battles were well fought. The independent Ministers published,

98   GENERAL HISTORY OF CONNECTICUT.

from their pulpits, that the Assembly played off one sect against another; and that Civilians were equal enemies to all parties, and acted more for their own interest than the glory of God. Those spiritual warriors, by their Associations, fasting, and prayers, voted themselves the "*Sober Dissenters*," and got the better of the General Assembly. Indeed, none disputed their vote with impunity. Whenever a Governor manifested an inclination to govern Christ's Ministers, Christ's Ministers were sure to instruct the freemen not to reëlect him. The Magistrates declared that they had rather be under Lords-Bishops than Lords-Associations. A Governor was appointed, who determined to reduce Christ's Ministers under the Civil Power; and, accordingly, the Assembly sent their Sheriff to bring before them certain leading men among the Ministers, of whom they banished some, silenced others, and fined many, for preaching sedition. The Ministers told the Assembly that curst cows had short horns; and that " they were "*Priests for ever after the order of Melchisedec.*" However, like good christians, they submitted to the sentence of the Assembly; went home, fasted, and prayed, until the Lord pointed out a perfect cure for all their sufferings. On the day of election, they told the freemen that the Lord's cause required a man of Grace to stand at the head of the Colony, and with sure confidence recommended the Moderator of the Association to be their Governor; and the Moderator was chosen. This event greatly inflamed the lay-magistrates, who were further mortified to see Ministers among the Representatives; whereupon they cried out, " This is a presbyterian popedom." Now Magistrates joined with other Churches which they had long persecuted; and the Connecticut Vine was rent more and more every day. The Ministers kept the power, but not always the office, of the Governor, whilst the weaker party paid the cost. One party was called Old Light, the other New Light: both aimed at power under pretence of religion; which-ever got the power, the other was persecuted. By this happy quarrel, the various sectarians were freed from their persecutions; because each contending party courted their votes and interest, to help to pull down its adversary. This has been the religious-political free system and practice of Connecticut since 1662.

In speaking of the religious phrenzies and persecutions in Connecticut under the sanction of the charter, I must notice the words of an eminent Quaker, who, as a blasphemer, had been whipped, branded, burnt in the tongue, set on the gallows, banished, and, upon return, sentenced to be hanged. "Dost thee not "think," said he to his Judges, "that the Jews, who "crucified the Saviour of the World, had a *Charter?*"

Many have been the disputes between Connecticut and the neighbouring Colonies concerning their several boundaries, and much blood has been spilt on those occasions. On the north and east, where lie the Massachusets and Rhode-Island, Connecticut has, in some degree, been the gainer; but has lost considerably on the west and south, to the engendering violent animosity against the *loyal* New-Yorkers, to whom it will probably prove fatal in the end. The detail is briefly as follows:

The Dutch settlers on New-York Island, Hudson's

river, and the west end of Long Island, being subdued by Colonel Nichols in September, 1664, the royal Commissioners, after hearing the Deputies from Connecticut in support of the charter granted to that province against the Duke of York's patent, ordered, in December following, that Long-Island should be annexed to the government of New-York, and that the West boundary of Connecticut should be a line drawn from the mouth of Mamaroneck river north-north-west to the line of the Massachusets. This settlement, although it infringed their charter, was peaceably acquiesced in by the people of Connecticut; and not complained of by those of New-York till 1683, when they set up a claim founded upon a Dutch grant, *said* to be made in 1621, of all the lands from Cape Cod to Cape Henlopen. In furtherance of their pretensions, they had recourse to invasion and slander. Of the latter Mr. Smith has given a specimen in his History of New-York, where he says that the agreement in 1664 "was founded in igno-"rance and fraud;" because, forsooth, "a north-north-"west line from Mamaroneck would soon intersect Hud-"son's river!" Could any one of common-sense suppose the Dutch on the banks of Hudson's river, who no doubt were consulted upon the occasion, less acquainted with the course of it, than persons residing on the banks of the Connecticut? Extraordinarily absurd as such an insinuation might be, the people of Connecticut were aware of its probable weight with the Duke of York, whose patent grasped half their country; and therefore, knowing by whom a contest must be decided, they consented to give up twenty miles of their land east of Hudson's river, hoping that would content a company of time-serving Jacobites and artful Dutchmen. But neither were they nor their Patron satisfied; and the agreement was suspended till 1700, when it was confirmed by William III. About twenty years afterwards, however, the New-Yorkers thought the times favourable to further encroachments; and at length, in 1731, they gained 60,000 acres more, called the Oblong, from Connecticut, purely because they had Dutch consciences, and for once reported in England what was true, that the New-England colonists hated Kings, whether natives or foreigners. Mr. Smith, indeed, p. 238, says, referring to Douglas's[1] Plan of the British Dominions of New-England in support of his assertion, that " Connecticut ceeded these 60,000 acres to " New-York, as an *equivalent* for lands near the Sound " *surrendered* to Connecticut, by New-York." Mr. Smith, and all the New-York cabal, know, that there never were any lands in the possession of the New-Yorkers *surrendered* to Connecticut: on the contrary, Connecticut was forced, by the partiality of sovereigns, to give up, not only Long-Island and the above-mentioned twenty miles east of Hudson's river, but also the Oblong, without any *equivalent*. How New-York

[1] Dr. Douglas was a naturalist, and a physician of considerable eminence in Boston, where he never attended any religious worship, having been educated in Scotland with such rancorous hatred against episcopacy, that, with his age, it ripened into open scepticism and deism. However, his many severities against the Episcopalians, New Lights, and Quakers, procured him a good name among the Old Lights, and the mongrel christians of New-York, whose policy and self-interest have always domineered over conscience and morality. For these reasons, his brother Smith, in his History of New-York, frequently quotes him, to prove his futile assertions against New-England, New-Jersey, and Pensylvania.

could surrender lands and tenements which they never had any right to or possession of, is only to be explained thus : whereas the people of New-York did not extend their eastern boundary to Connecticut river, they therefore *surrendered* to Connecticut what they never had ; which is like a highwayman's saying to a Gentleman, Give me ten guineas, and I will *surrender* to you your watch in your pocket.

Thus by degrees has Connecticut lost a tract of land sixty miles in length and above twenty in breadth, together with the whole of Long-Island ; and this in the first place by a stretch of royal prerogative, and afterwards by the chicanery of their competitors, who have broken through all agreements as often as a temporising conduct seemed to promise them success. Whenever, therefore, a favourable opportunity presents itself, it is probable, that Messrs. Smith and Livingston, and other patercons in New-York, will find the last determination also to have been "founded in ignorance and fraud," and will be pushing their claim to all the lands west of Connecticut river ; but the opportunity must be favourable indeed, that allows them to encroach one foot farther with impunity.

Another stroke the people of Connecticut received about 1753 has sorely galled them ever since, and contributed not a little to their thirst of revenge. The Governor of New-York was then appointed " Captain-" General and Commander in Chief of the militia, and "all the forces by sea and land, within the Colony of " Connecticut, and of all the forts and places of strength "within the same." This violation of the Charter of Connecticut by George II. was very extraordinary, as the reins of Government were then in the hands of protestant dissenters, whose *supposed* veneration for the House of Hanover operated so powerfully, that the American protestant dissenting ministers were allowed to be installed teachers, and to hold synods, without taking the oath of allegiance to the English King, at the same time that papists, and even members of the Church of England, were not excused that obligation. The aggravating appointment above mentioned added no celebrity to the name of George II. in New-England; nor, however excusable it may appear in the eyes of those who with me question the colonial pretensions of the people of Connecticut, was it, upon the ground they have been allowed to stand by the English government, justifiable in point of right, nor yet in point of policy, were the true character of the New-Yorkers fully known. This argument may be used on more occasions than the present.

But Connecticut hath not been the only sufferer from the restless ambition of New-York. Twenty miles depth of land belonging to the Massachusets and Newhampshire provinces, which formerly claimed to Hudson's river, were cut off by the line that deprived Connecticut of the same proportion of its western territory. With this acquisition, surely, the New-Yorkers might have been content; but very lately their *wisdom*, if not their "fraud," has prevailed over the "ignorance" of Newhampshire; which has sustained another amputation of its territory, eighty miles in width and two hundred miles in length; viz. all the land between the above-mentioned twenty-mile line and Connecticut river. The particulars of this transaction are interesting. Benning Wentworth, Esq. Governor of Newhampshire, by order of his present Majesty, divided, in 1762, the vast tract of land just mentioned into about 360 townships, six miles square each. These townships he granted to proprietors belonging to the four provinces of New-England, one township to sixty proprietors; and took his fees for the same, according to royal appointment. Every township was, in twelve years time, to have sixty families residing in it. In 1769 there were settled on this piece of land 30,000 souls, at a very great expence; and many townships contained 100 families. The New-Yorkers found means to deceive the King, and obtained a decree that the East boundary of New-York, after passing Connecticut and Massachusets-Bay, should be Connecticut river.[1] This decree annexed to the jurisdiction of New-York the said 360 townships; but was quietly submitted to by the proprietors, since it was his Majesty's will to put them under the jurisdiction of New-York, tho' they found themselves 150 miles farther from their new capital New-York, than they were from Portsmouth, their old one. Had the New-Yorkers rested satisfied with the jurisdiction, which alone the King had given them, they might have enjoyed their acquisition in peace; and New-England would have thought they had possessed some justice, though destitute of religious zeal. But the Gov-

---

[1] Perhaps their success was facilitated by the consideration, that the quit-rent payable to the Crown in New-York is 2s. 6d. per 100 acres, but only 9d. in Newhampshire. The same may be said, with still more reason, in regard to the lands acquired by New-York from Massachusets-Bay and Connecticut, where the quit-rent is——nothing.

ernor and General Assembly of New-York, finding their interest in Old-England stronger than the interest of the New-Englanders, determined at once, that, as the King had given them jurisdiction over those 360 townships, he had also given them the lands in fee simple. Sir Henry More, the Governor, therefore, in 1767, began the laudable work of regranting those townships to such people as lived in New-York, and were willing to pay him 600*l*. York currency for his valuable name to each patent. It is remarkable that Sir Harry made every *lawyer* in the whole province a patentee; but totally *forgot* the four public lots, viz. that for the Society for the Propagation of the Gospel, those for the church, the first clergyman, and school in each township, which had been reserved in Governor Wentworth's grants. Death stopped his career; but Colden, the Lieutenant-Governor, filled up the measure of his iniquity, by granting all the rest on the same conditions. Sir Henry More had taken care to grant to his dear self one township, settled with above 80 families, before he died. Colden did the same for himself. The virtuous William Smith, Esq. of New York, had a township also; and Sir Henry More left him his executor to drive off the New-England settlers. This, however, he attempted in vain. The polite New-Yorkers, having the jurisdiction, betook themselves to law, to get possession of the lands in question, which they called their own; and sent the posse of Albany to eject the possessors; but this mighty power was answered by Ethan Allen, and the old proprietors under Governor Wentworth, who was a King's Governor as well as Sir Henry More:—the Mynheers of Albany were glad to have liberty to return home alive.—See here the origin of Ethan Allen!—of the Verdmonts, and the Robbers of the Green Mountains; a compliment paid by the New-Yorkers to the settlers under Governor Wentworth;—who, on that amiable gentleman's death, had no friend of note left in England, and were therefore under the necessity of defending themselves, or becoming tenants to a set of people who neither *feared God* nor *honoured the King*, but when they got something by it.—The New-Yorkers had the grace, after this, to outlaw Ethan Allen, which rendered him of consequence in New-England; and it would not surprise me to hear that New-York, Albany, and all that the Dutchmen possess in houses east of Hudson's River, were consumed by fire, and the inhabitants sent to Heaven, in the style of Dr. Mather, by the way of Amsterdam. I must do the New-Englanders the justice to say, that, though they esteem not highly Kings or Lords, yet they never complained against his Majesty for what was done respecting Verdmont; on the contrary, they ever said the King would reverse the obnoxious decree, whenever he should be acquainted with the truth of the case, which the New-Yorkers artfully concealed from his knowledge.

There are in the four New-England provinces near 800,000 souls, and very few unconnected with the settlements on Verdmont; the property of which was duly vested in them by Wentworth, the King's Governor, whose predecessors and himself had jurisdiction over it also for 106 years. They say, what is very legal and just, that his Majesty had a right to annex Verdmont to the government of New-York, but could not give the fee of the land, because he had before given it to the New-Englanders. It appears very unlikely that those hardy sons of Oliver will ever give up Verdmont to the New-Yorkers by the order of Sir Henry More, or any other Governor, till compelled by the point of the sword. The Mynheers have more to fear than the New-Englanders, who will never yield to Dutch virtue. Van Tromp was brave; Oliver was brave and successful too.

Mather, Neal, and Hutchinson, represent religion to have been the cause of the first settlement of New-England; and the love of gold as the stimulus of the Spaniards in settling their colonies in the southern parts of America; but, if we should credit the Spanish historians, we must believe that their countrymen were as much influenced by religion in their colonial pursuits as were our own. However, in general, it may be said, that the conduct of both parties towards the aborigines discovered no principles but what were disgraceful to human nature. Murder, plunder, and outrage, were the means made use of to convert the benighted savages of the wilderness to the system of Him "who went about "doing good." If we may depend on Abbé Nicolle, the Spaniards killed of the Aytis, or the savage nations, in the Island of Hispaniola, 3,000,000 in seventeen years; 600,000 in Porto Rico, and twenty times these numbers on the continent of South-America, in order to propagate the Gospel in a savage and howling wilderness! The English colonists have been as industrious in spreading the Gospel in the howling wilderness of North-America. Upwards of 180,000 Indians, at least, have been slaughtered in Massachusets-Bay and Connecticut,[1] to make way for the protestant religion; and, upon a moderate computation for the rest of the colonies, on the continent and West-India Islands, I think one may venture to assert, that nearly 2,000,000 savages have been dismissed from an unpleasant world to the world of spirits, for the honour of the protestant religion and English liberty. Nevertheless, having travelled over most parts of British America, I am able to declare, with great sincerity, that this mode of converting the native Indians is godlike in comparison with that adopted by the Africans.

These miserable people are first kidnapped, and then put under saws, harrows, and axes of iron, and forced through the brick-kiln to Molock.

Nearly half a million of them are doomed to hug

[1] In 1680, the number of Indians, or aborigines, in the whole Province of Connecticut was 4000. This was allowed by the General Assembly. How much greater their number was in 1637, may be estimated from the accounts given by Dr. Mather, Mr. Neal, Mr. Penhallow, and Mr. Hutchinson, of the deaths of Englishmen in the Indian wars, for the space of forty-three years. It has been computed, that from 1637 to 1680, upon an average, one hundred Englishmen were killed yearly in those wars, and that there were killed, with sword and gun, and small-pox, twenty Indians for every one Englishman. If this calculation is just, it appears that the English killed of the Indians, during the above-mentioned period, 86,000, to which number the 4000 Indians remaining in 1680 being added, it is clear that there were 90,000 Indians in Connecticut when Hooker began his holy war upon them; not to form conjectures upon those who probably afterwards abandoned the country. This evinces the weakness of the Indian mode of fighting with bows and arrows against guns, and the impropriety of calling Connecticut an howling wilderness in 1636, when Hooker arrived in Hertford. The English in one hundred and thirty-six years have not much more than doubled the number of Indians they killed in forty-three years. In 1770 the number of Indians in Connecticut amounted not to 400 souls.

their misery in ignorance, nakedness, and hunger, among their master's upper servants in Georgia, the Carolinas, Virginia, and Maryland. The number of these wretches upon the Continent and Islands is scarce credible; about 100,000 in Jamaica alone; all toiling for the tyrant's pleasure; none seeking other happiness, than to be screened from the torture rendered necessary by that curious American maxim, that men must be willing to die before they are fit for the Kingdom of Heaven. However, what Mussleman, African, or American, would not prefer the state of a christian master, who dreads death above all things, to the state of those christian converts? Christianity has been cursed, through the insincerity of its professors; even savages despise its precepts, because they have no influence on christians themselves. Whatever religious pretensions the Spanish, French, or English may plead for depopulating and repeopling America, it is pretty clear that the desire of gold and dominion was no impotent instigation with them to seek the western continent. The British leaders in the scheme of emigration had felt the humiliating effects of the feudal system; particularly the partial distributions of fortunes and honour among children of the same venter in the Mother Country. They had seen that this inequality produced insolence and oppression, which awakened the sentiments of independence and liberty, the instinct of every man. Nature then kindled war against the oppressors, and the oppressors appealed to prescription. The event was, infelicity began her reign. Both parties invoked religion, but prostrated themselves before the insidious shrine of Superstition, the life of civil government, and the sinews of war;

that expiates crimes by prayers, uses ceremonies for good works, esteems devotion more than virtue, supports religion without probity, values honesty less than honour, generates happiness without morality, and is a glorious helmet to the ambitious.

They enlisted vassals with her bounty to fight, burn, and destroy one another, for the sake of religion. Behold the sequel! The vassals seemed more to themselves than the Egyptian masters and laws, both in the elder and younger brothers; yet, after all, Superstition told them they enjoyed liberty and the rights of human nature. Happy deception! The Spartan Magnates, tributary to the Turks, are jealous of their liberties; while the American Cansey, near Lake Superior, enjoy liberty complete without jealousy. Among the latter, the conscious independence of each individual warms his thoughts and guides his actions. He enters the sachemic dome with the same simple freedom as he enters the wigwam of his brother: neither dazzled at the splendour nor awed by the power of the possessor. Here is liberty in perfection! What christian would wish to travel 4000 miles to rob an unoffending savage of what he holds by the law of Nature? That is not the God or Dominion that any christian ever sought for. The first settlers of America had views very different from those of making it a christian country; their grand aim was to get free from the insolence of their elder brethren, and to aggrandise themselves in a new world at the expense of the life, liberty, and property of the savages. Had the invaders of New-England sown the seeds of christian benevolence, even after they had eradicated the savages and savage virtues, the world would not have reproached them for cherishing that all-grasping spirit to themselves, which in others had driven them from their parent country. But the feudal system, which they considered an abominable vice in England, became a shining virtue on the other side of the Atlantic, and would have prevailed there, had the people been as blind and tame in worldly as they were in spiritual concerns. But they had too long heard their leaders declaim against the monopoly of lands and titles, not to discover that they themselves were men, and entitled to the rights of that race of beings; and they proceeded upon the same maxims which they found also among the Indians, viz. that mankind are by nature upon an equality in point of rank and possession; that it is incompatible with freedom for any particular descriptions of men systematically to monopolise honours and property, to the exclusion of the rest; that it was a part despicable and unworthy of one freeman to stoop to the will and caprice of another on account of his wealth and titles, accruing not from his own, but from the heroism and virtue of his ancestors, &c., &c.

The *vox populi* established these maxims in New-England; and whoever did not, at least outwardly, conform to them, were not chosen into office. Nay, though not objectionable on that score, men very seldom met with reappointments, lest they should claim them by hereditary right. Thus, the levelling principle prevailing, equals were respected and superiors derided. Europeans, whose manners were haughty to inferiors and fawning to superiors, were neither loved nor esteemed. Hence an English traveller through Connecticut meets with supercilious treatment at taverns, as being too much addicted to the use of the imperative mood when speaking to the landlord. The answer is, "Command "your own servants, and not me." The traveller is not obeyed, which provokes him to some expressions, that are not legal in the Colony, about the impertinence of the landlord, who being commonly a Justice of the Peace, the delinquent is immediately ordered into custody, fined, and put in the stocks. However, after paying costs, and promising to behave well in future, he passes on with more attention to his "unruly member" than to his pleasures. Nevertheless, if a traveller softens his tone, and avoids the imperative mood, he will find every civility from those very people, whose natural temper are full of antipathy against all who affect superiority over them. This principle is, by long custom, blended with the religious doctrines of the province; and the people believe those to be heretics and Americans who assent not to their supremacy. Hence they consider the kingly Governors as the short-horns of Antichrist, and every Colony in a state of persecution which cannot choose its own Governor and magistrates.

Their aversion to New-York is inconceiveably great upon this account, as well as others I have mentioned. Their jealousies and fears of coming under its jurisdiction make them heroes in the cause of liberty, and great inquisitors into the characters and conduct of kingly Governors. They have selected Mr. Tryon as the only English Governor who has acted with justice and generosity in respect to the rights, liberties, and feelings of mankind, while, they say, avarice, plunder, and oppression have marked the footsteps of all the rest. This character Mr. Tryon possessed, even after he had subdued the regulators in North-Carolina, and was appointed Governor of New-York. Some persons assert, indeed, that he secured the good will of Connecticut by recommending, in England, the Livingstons, Schuylers, and Smiths, as the best subjects in New-York. However, Mr. Tryon was undoubtedly entitled to good report; he was humane and polite; to him the injured had access without a fee; he would hear the poor man's complaint, though it wanted the aid of a polished lawyer. Besides, Mr. Tryon did not think it beneath him to speak to a peasant in the street, or to stop his coach to give the people an opportunity to let him pass. His object was not to make his fortune, nor did he neglect the interests of the people. He embellished not his language with oaths and curses, nor spent the Sabbath at taverns. 'Tis true, Mr. Tryon went not to meeting; but he was forgiven this offence because he went to church, the people of New-England having so much candour as to believe a man may be a good sort of man if he goes to church, and is exemplary in his words and deeds. I have not the honour of being known to Mr. Tryon, but from what I know of him, I must say, without meaning to offend any other, that he was the best Governor, and the most pleasing gentleman, that I ever saw in a civil capacity in America; and that I cannot name any Briton so well calculated to govern in Connecticut, with ease and safety to himself, as he is. One reason for this assertion is, that Mr. Tryon has a punctilious regard for his word: a quality which, though treachery is the staple commodity of the four New-England provinces, the people greatly admire in a Governor, and which, they say, they have seldom found in royal Governors in America.

Of the share Connecticut has taken, in common with her sister colonies, in co-operating with the Mother Country against her natural enemies, it is superfluous to say anything here, that being already sufficiently known.

I shall therefore proceed to a description of the country, its towns, productions, &c. together with the manners, customs, commerce, &c. of the inhabitants, interspersing such historical and biographical anecdotes as may occur to me in the relation, and having a tendency to elucidate matter of fact or characterize the people.

The dimensions of Connecticut, according to the present allowed extent, are from the Sound on the south to the Massachusets line on the north, about sixty miles; and from Biram River and New-York line, on the west, to Narraganset-Bay, Rhode-Island, and Massachusets-Bay on the east, upon an average about one hundred miles. It is computed to contain 5,000,000 acres.

Many creeks and inlets, bays and rivers, intersect the coast. Three of the last, dividing the colony into as many parts, I shall particularly notice. They all run from north to south.

The eastern river is called the Thames, as far as it is navigable, which is only to Norwich, fourteen miles from its mouth. Then dividing, the greatest branch, called Quinnibaug, rolls rapidly from its source 100 miles distant through many towns and villages, to their great pleasantness and profit. On it are many mills and iron-works, and in it various kinds of fish, but no salmon, for want of proper places to nourish their spawn.

The middle river is named Connecticut, after the great Sachem to whom that part of the province through which it runs belonged. This vast river is five hundred miles long, and four miles wide at its mouth; its channel, or inner banks, in general, half a mile wide. It takes its rise from the White Hills, in the north of New-England, where also springs the river Kennebec. About five hundred rivulets, which issue from lakes, ponds, and drowned lands, fall into it; many of them are larger than the Thames at London. In March, when the rains and sun melt the snow and ice, each stream is overcharged, and kindly hastens to this great river, to overflow, fertilize, and preserve its trembling meadows. They lift enormous cakes of ice, bursting from their frozen beds, with threatening intentions of ploughing up the frighted earth, and carry them rapidly down the falls, where they are dashed in pieces and rise in mist. Except at these falls, of which there are five the first sixty miles from its mouth, the river is navigable throughout. In its northern part are three great bendings, called Cohosses, about one hundred miles asunder. Two hundred miles from the Sound is a narrow of five yards only, formed by two shelving mountains of solid rock, whose tops intercept the clouds. Through this chasm are compelled to pass all the waters which, in the time of the floods, bury the northern country.

At the upper Cohos the river spreads twenty-four miles wide. For five or six weeks ships of war might sail over the lands that afterward produce the greatest crops of hay and grain in all America. People who can bear the sight, the groans, the tremblings, and surly motion of water, trees, and ice, through this awful passage, view with astonishment one of the greatest phenomenons in Nature. Here, water consolidated without frost, by pressure, by swiftness, between the pinching, sturdy rocks, to such a degree of induration that an iron crow cannot be forced into it; here, iron, lead, and cork, have one common weight; here, steady as time, and harder than marble, the stream passes irresistible, if not swift as lightning; the electric fire rends trees in pieces with no greater ease than does this mighty water. The passage is about four hundred yards in length, and of a zigzag form, with obtuse corners.[1]

[1] Many years afterward the author's attention was called to this statement; he replied, as to the expression above, by saying, he meant that the pressure of the stream was so great that a crowbar, not having sufficient specific gravity to sink, would actually be carried down the stream upon its surface. As incredulous as this may appear, we have it substantiated by no less a person than the late eminent engineer, John A. Roebling, who built the suspension-bridge over the river at the Niagara Falls, in the following letter:

"SUSPENSION BRIDGE, *April* 28, 1855.
"SAMUEL WILKESON, Esq.
"DEAR SIR: I received a copy of *The Democrat*, with your account of my attempting to sound the river. After you left, another attempt was made, with a similar iron, of about forty pounds' weight, attached to a No. 11 wire, all freely suspended, so as not to impede the fall of the weight. I then let the weight fall from the bridge, a height of 225 feet. It struck the surface fairly, with the point down—must have sunk to some depth, but was not longer out of sight than one second, when it made its appearance again upon the surface, about 100 feet down stream, and skipped along like a chip, until it was checked by the wire. We then commenced hauling in slowly, which made the iron bounce like a ball, when a cake of ice struck it, and ended the sport.
"I am satisfied that no metal has sufficient gravity to pierce that

At high water are carried through this straight masts and other timber with incredible swiftness, and sometimes with safety; but when the water is too low, the masts, timber, and trees, strike on one side or the other, and, though of the largest size, are rent, in one moment, into shivers, and splintered like a broom, to the amazement of spectators. The meadows, for many miles below, are covered with immense quantities of wood thus torn in pieces, which compel the hardiest travellers to reflect, how feeble is man, and how great that Almighty who formed the lightnings, thunders, and the irresistible power and strength of waters!

No living creature was ever known to pass through this narrow, except an Indian woman, who was, in a canoe, attempting to cross the river above it, but carelessly suffered herself to fall within the power of the current. Perceiving her danger, she took a bottle of rum she had with her, and drank the whole of it; then lay down in her canoe, to meet her destiny. She marvellously went through safely, and was taken out of the canoe some miles below, quite intoxicated, by some Englishmen. Being asked how she could be so daringly imprudent as to drink such a quantity of rum with the

current, even with the momentum acquired by a fall of 225 feet. The velocity of the iron, when striking, must have been about equal to 124 feet per second, and, consequently, its momentum near 5,000 pounds. Its surface, opposed to the current, was about fifty superficial inches. This will give an idea of the strength of that current, and, at the same time, hint at the Titan forces that have been at work to scoop out the bed of the Niagara River.

"I am now satisfied that our friend, the English captain, was sounding in vain.
"Yours respectfully and truly,
"JOHN A. ROEBLING."
—ED. NOTE.

prospect of instant death before her, the squaw, as well as her condition would let her, replied, "Yes, it was too "much rum for once, to be sure; but I was not willing "to lose a drop of it: so I drank it, and you see I have "saved all."

Some persons assert that salmon have been caught above this narrow, while others deny it. Many have observed salmon attempt to pass in the time of floods, which certainly is the best and likeliest time, as, from the height of the water, and the shelving of the rocks, the passage is then broader; but they were always thrown back, and generally killed. It is not to be supposed that any fish could pass with the stream alive. Above this narrow there is plenty of fish both in summer and winter, which belong to the lakes or ponds that communicate with the river: below it are the greatest abundance and variety caught or known in North-America. No salmon are found in any river to the westward of this.

Except the Mississippi and St. Lawrence, the Connecticut is the largest river belonging to the English plantations in the New World. On each shore of it are two great roads leading from the mouth 200 miles up the country, lined on both sides with the best-built houses in America, if not in the world. It is computed, that the country on each bank of this river, to a depth of six miles, and a length of 300, is sufficient for the maintenance of an army of 100,000 men. In short, the neighbouring spacious and fertile meadow, arable, and other lands, combined with this noble river, are at once the beauty and main support of all New-England.

The western river is navigable and called Stratford only for ten miles, where Derby stands; and then takes the name of Osootonoc. It is 50 miles west from Connecticut River, and half a mile wide. It rises in the Verdmonts, above 200 miles from the sea, and travels 300 miles through many pleasant towns and villages. The adjacent meadows are narrow, and the country in general very hilly. With some expence it might be made navigable above 100 miles. It furnishes fish of various kinds, and serves many mills and iron-works.

Two principal bays, named Sassacus or New-London, and Quinnipiog or Newhaven, run five or six miles into the country, and are met by rivers which formerly bore the Sachems names.

It has already been observed, at Connecticut was settled under three distinct independent Governors; and that each Dominion, since their union in 1664, has been divided into two counties.

The KINGDOM OF SASSACUS, Sachem of the Pequods, a warlike nation, forms the counties of New-London and Windham, which contain about 10,000 houses, and 60,000 inhabitants. Sassacus was brave by nature. The sound of his coming would subdue nations, at the same time that Justice would unbend his bow, and Honour calm the thunder of his tongue. Dr. Mather, Mr. Neal, and others, have endeavoured to blast his fame by proving him to have been the aggressor in the bloody wars which ended in his ruin. They have instanced the murder of Captain Stone and others, to justify this war, but carefully concealed the assassination of Quinnipiog, the treachery of Mr. Elliot (the Massachusets-Bay Apostle of the Indians), and the infamous villainy of Hooker, who spread death upon the leaves of his

Bible, and struck Connecticote mad with disease. They also conceal another important truth, that the English had taken possession of lands belonging to Sassacus, without purchase or his consent. Besides, Sassacus had too much sagacity to let christian spies, under the appellation of gospel missionaries, pass through his country. He had seen the consequences of admitting such ministers of christianity from Boston, Hertford, &c. among his neighbouring nations, and generously warned them to keep their gospel of peace from his dominions. The invaders of this howling wilderness, finding their savage love detected, and that the Pequods were not likely to fall a sacrifice to their hypocrisy, proclaimed open war with sword and gun. The unfortunate Sassacus met his fate. Alas! he died, not like Connecticote, nor Quinnipiog, but in the field of battle; and the freedom of his country expired with his final groan. This mighty conquest was achieved by the colonists of Connecticut, without the aid of the Massachusets; nevertheless, Mr. Neal and others have ascribed the *honour* of it to the latter, with a view of magnifying their consequence—ever Mr. Neal's grand object.

The country of New-London abounds chiefly with wool, butter, cheese, and Indian-corn; and contains eight towns, all which I shall describe.

New-London has the river Thames on the east, and the bay of its own name on the south, and resembles Islington. Its port and harbour are the best in the colony. The church, the meeting, and court-house, are not to be boasted of; the fort is trifling. The houses in this, as in all the towns in the province, are insulated, at the distance of three, four, or five yards one from the other, to prevent the ravages of fire. That of John Winthrop, Esq. is the best in the province. The township is ten miles square, and comprizes five parishes, one of which is episcopal. Abimeleck, a descendant of the first English-made king of Mohegin, resides with his small party in this township. He is a king to whom the people pay some respect,—*because they made him so.*

The people of this town have the credit of inventing tar and feathers as a proper punishment for heresy. They first inflicted it on quakers and anabaptists.

New-London has a printing press, much exercised in the business of pamphlets, sermons, and newspapers. It is employed by the Governor and Company, and is the oldest and best in the colony. Newhaven, Hertford, and Norwich, also, have each a printing press; so that the people are plentifully supplied with news, politics, and polemical divinity.——A very extraordinary circumstance happened here in 1740. Mr. George Whitefield paid them a visit, and preached of *righteousness, temperance,* and *a judgment to come,* which roused them into the belief of an heaven and an hell. They became as *children weaned* and pliable as *melted wax,* and with great eagerness cried out, *What shall we do to be saved?* The preacher, then in the pulpit, thus answered them, "Repent—do violence to "no man—part with your self-righteousness, your silk "gowns, and laced petticoats—burn your ruffles, neck- "laces, jewels, rings, tinselled waistcoats, your morality "and bishops books, this very night, or damnation will "be your portion before the morning-dawn." The people, rather thro' fear than faith, instantly went out on the common, and prepared for heaven, by burning all the above *enumerated goods*, excepting that of self-righteousness, which was exchanged for the preacher's velvet breeches.—Vide *Dr. Chancy*.[1]

Groton, across the bay from New-London, resembles Battersea. The township is ten miles square, and forms four parishes, one of which is episcopal. This town was the residence of the valiant Sassacus, Sachem of the Pequod nation.

Stonington lies on Narraganset-Bay, is the east corner of Connecticut, and consists of three parishes. The township is 8 miles square.

[1] Of the separation from the standing churches an account has been given, and of the disorders and oppressions of those times when they commenced. Churches of this character were formed in New London, Stonington, Preston, Norwich, Lyme, Canterbury, Plainfield, Windsor, Suffield, and Middletown. Some of these churches and congregations were nearly as large as some of the standing churches. There were ten or twelve churches and congregations of this denomination, first and last, in the colony. Some of them carried their enthusiasm to a greater extent than others. In New London they carried it to such a degree that they made a large fire to burn their books, clothes, and ornaments, which they called their idols, and which they now determined to forsake, and utterly to put away.

This imaginary work of piety and self-denial they undertook on the Lord's-day, and brought their books, necklaces, and jewels, together in the main street.

They began by burning their erroneous books, dropping them, one after another, into the fire, pronouncing these words: " If the author of this book died in the same sentiments and faith in which he wrote it, as the smoke of this pile ascends, so the smoke of his torment will ascend forever and ever. Hallelujah! Amen."

But they were prevented from burning their clothes and jewels. John Lee, of Lyme, told them his idols were his wife and children, and that he could not burn them; it would be contrary to the laws of God and man; that it was impossible to destroy idolatry without a change of heart and of the affections.—ED. NOTE.

A SINGULAR CUSTOM.

Preston, on Quinnibaug river, forms three parishes, one of which is episcopal. The township is 8 miles square.

Norwich, on the Thames, 14 miles from the sea, is an half-shire with New-London. The town stands on a plain, one mile from Chelsea, or the Landing. Its best street is two miles long, and has good houses on both sides, five yards asunder from each other. In the centre is a common, of the size of Bloomsbury Square, in which stand a beautiful court-house, and a famous meeting with clocks, bells, and steeples. The township is fifteen miles square, and forms 13 parishes, one episcopal. Chelsea, or the Landing, resembles Dover. [Here land is sold at fifteen shillings sterling by the square foot.]—This town is famous for its trade; for iron-works, grist, paper, linseed, spinning and fulling mills; also for a furnace that makes stone ware.—— Some peculiarities and curiosities here attract the notice of Europeans:—1, a bridge over Quinnibaug, 60 yards long, butted on two rocks, and geometrically supported; under which pass ships with all their sails standing:—2, the steeple of the grand meeting-house stands at the east end:—3, the inhabitants bury the dead with their feet to the west.—The following couplet was written by a traveller, on the steeple:

> "They're so perverse and opposite,
> "As if they built to God in spite."

The reasons for the singular custom of burying the dead with their feet to the west, are two, and special: first, when Christ begins his millenarian reign, he will come from the west, and his saints will be in a ready posture to rise and meet him: secondly, the papists and episcopalians bury their dead with their feet to the east.

Was I to give a character of the people of Norwich, I would do it in the words of the famous Mr. George Whitefield, (who was a good judge of mankind,) in his farewel-sermon to them a short time before his death; viz. "When I first preached in this magnificent "house, above 20 years ago, I told you, that you were "part beast, part man, and part devil; at which you "were offended. I have since thought much about "that expression, and confess that for once I was mis-"taken. I therefore take this last opportunity to cor-"rect my error. Behold! I now tell you, that you are "not part man and part beast, but wholly of the devil."

Lyme stands on the east side of Connecticut River, opposite Saybrook; and resembles Lewisham. The township is 16 miles long, and 8 wide; and forms four parishes.

Saybrook is situated on the west side of Connecticut river, 20 miles west from New-London, and resembles Battersea. The township is twenty miles long and six wide, and forms four parishes. This town was named after the Lords Say and Brook, who were said to claim the country, and sent, in 1634, a Governor and a large number of people from England to build a fort and settle the colony. See p. 17. It was principally owing to this fort that Hertford and Newhaven made good their settlements: it prevented Sassacus from giving timely aid to Connecticote and Quinnipiog.

Saybrook is greatly fallen from its ancient grandeur; but is, notwithstanding, resorted to with great veneration, as the parent town of the whole colony.

The tombs of the first settlers are held sacred, and travellers seldom pass them without the compliment of a sigh or tear. On one mossy stone is written,

"Here pride is calm'd, and death is life."

In 1709, this town was honoured by a convention of contending independent divines, who were pleased with no constitution in church or state.—This multitude of sectarians, after long debates, published a book, called The Saybrook Platform, containing the doctrines and rules of the churches in Connecticut. The only novelty in this system is, that Christ has delegated his ministerial, kingly, and prophetical power, one half to the people, and the other half to the ministers. This proposition may be thought in Europe a very strange one; but, if it be recollected, that the people in the province claimed all power in heaven and on earth, and that the ministers had no other ordination than what came from the people, it will appear, that the ministers hereby gained from the people one half of their power. From this article originated the practice of the right hand of fellowship at the ordination of a minister. No one can be a minister, till he receives the right hand of the messenger who represents six deacons from six congregations. The conclusion of this reverend and venerable body is, "The Bible is our rule."

Mr. Neal says, p. 610, " That every particular so-
" ciety is a compleat church, having power to exercise
" all ecclesiastical jurisdiction, without appeal to any
" classis :—they allow of synods for council and advice,
" but not to exercise the power of the keys."

If Mr. Neal had taken the trouble to read the

History of the Church of Massachusets-Bay, written by the Reverend Mr. John Wise, a minister of that church, he would have found that the contrary to all he has advanced is the truth. The people of that province held the keys from 1620 to 1650: then the ministers got possession of them by their own vote, which was passed into a law by the General Assembly. The vote was, "There cannot be a minister, unless he is ordained "by ministers of Jesus Christ." Thus commenced ordination by ministers in New-England. The people were alarmed at the loss of the keys, and asked the ministers who had ordained them? The ministers answered, The people. Then, replied the people, we are the ministers of Jesus Christ, you are not ministers; and we will keep the power. A violent contest ensued between the people and the ministers; but the latter, by the help of the General Assembly, retained the power of the keys, and instituted three ecclesiastical courts, viz. 1, the minister and his communicants; 2, the associations; and 3, the synod. There lies an appeal from one to the other of these courts, all which exercise so much ecclesiastical power that few are easy under it. The first court suspends from communion, the second re-hears the evidence, and confirms or sets aside the suspension; the synod, after hearing the case again, excommunicates or discharges the accused. From the last judgment no appeal is allowed by the synod. The excommunicated person has no other resource than petitioning the General Assembly of the province, which sometimes grants relief, to the great grief of the synod and ministers. But the representatives commonly pay dear for overlooking the conduct of the synod at the next election.

The people of Connecticut have adopted the same mode of discipline as prevails in Massachusets-Bay, but call the synod a Consociation.

To show that the synods are not quite so harmless as Mr. Neal reports, I will give an instance of their authority exercised in Connecticut in 1758. A Mr. Merret, of Lebanon, having lost his wife, with whom he had lived childless forty years, went to Rhode-Island, and married a niece of his late wife, which was agreeable to the laws of that province. By her having a child, Mr. Merret offered the same for baptism to the minister of whose church he was a member. The minister refused, because it was an incestuous child; and cited Merret and his wife to appear before himself and his church upon an indictment of incest. Merret appeared; the verdict was, "Guilty of incest." He appealed to the Association, which also found him guilty of incest. He again appealed to the Consociation, and was again found guilty of incest. Merret and his wife were then ordered to separate, and make a public confession, on pain of excommunication. Merret refused; whereupon the minister read the act of excommunication, while the deacons shoved Merret out of the meeting-house. Being thus cast out of the synagogue, and debarred from the conversation of any one in the parish, it was well said by Mr. Merret: "If this be not to "exercise the power of the keys, I know not what it is." The poor man soon after died with a broken heart, and was buried in his own garden by such christian brethren as were not afraid of the mild puissance of the Consociation.

Mr. Neal says, also, p. 609, after evincing his

jealousy at the growth of the Church of England in New-England : " If the religious liberties of the planta- " tions are invaded by the setting up of spiritual courts, " &c., they will feel the sad effects of it." In this sentiment I agree with Mr. Neal; but, unluckily, he meant the bishops courts, and I meant the courts of synods, composed of his "meek, exemplary, and learned divines " of New-England," but who are more severe and terrible than even was the Star-Chamber under the influence of Laud, or the Inquisition of Spain. The ecclesiastical courts of New-England have, in the course of 160 years, bored the tongues with hot needles, cut off the ears, branded the foreheads of, and banished, imprisoned, and hanged more quakers, baptists, adamites, ranters, episcopalians, for what they call heresy, blasphemy, and witchcraft, than there are instances of persecution in Fox's book of Martyrology, or under the bishops of England since the death of Henry VIII. And yet Mr. Neal was afraid of spiritual courts, and admired the practice of New-England churches, who only excommunicated offenders, delivering them over to the civil magistrates to torture and ruin. If I remember right, I once saw the Inquisition of Portugal act after the same manner, when the priest said, "We deal with " the soul, and the civil magistrate with the body."

Time not having destroyed the walls of the fort at Saybrook, Mr. Whitefield, in 1740, attempted to bring them down, as Joshua brought down the walls of Jericho, to convince the gaping multitude of his divine mission. He walked several times round the fort with prayer, and rams'-horns blowing; he called on the angel of Joshua to come and do as he had done at the walls of Jericho; but the angel was deaf, or on a journey, or asleep, and therefore the walls remained. Hereupon George cried aloud: "This town is accursed "for not receiving the messenger of the Lord; there-"fore the angel is departed, and the walls shall stand "as a monument of sinful people." He shook off the dust of his feet against them, and departed, and went to Lyme.

Killingsworth is ten miles west from Saybrook, lies on the sea, and resembles Wadsworth. The town is eight miles square, and divided into two parishes. This town is noted for the residence of the Rev. Mr. Elliot, commonly known as Dr. Elliot, who discovered the art of making steel out of sand, and wrote a book on husbandry, which will secure him a place in the Temple of Fame.

Windham, the second county in the ancient kingdom of Sassacus, or colony of Saybrook, is hilly; but the soil being rich, has excellent butter, cheese, hemp, Indian-corn, and horses. Its towns are twelve.

Windham resembles Rumford, and stands on Winnomantic River. Its meeting-house is elegant, and has a steeple, bell, and clock. Its court-house is scarcely to be looked upon as an ornament. The township forms four parishes, and is ten miles square.

Strangers are very much terrified at the hideous noise made on summer evenings by the vast number of frogs in the brooks and ponds. There are about thirty different voices among them, some of which resemble the bellowing of a bull. The owls and whippoorwills complete the rough concert, which may be heard several miles. Persons accustomed to such serenades are not disturbed by them at their proper stations; but one night in July, 1758, the frogs of an artificial pond, three miles square, and about five from Windham, finding the water dried up, left the place in a body, and marched, or rather hopped, towards Winnomantic River. They were under the necessity of taking the road and going through the town, which they entered about midnight. The bull-frogs were the leaders, and the pipers followed without number. They filled the road, forty yards wide, for four miles in length, and were for several hours in passing through the town unusually clamorous.

The inhabitants were equally perplexed and frightened: some expected to find an army of French and Indians; others feared an earthquake, and dissolution of Nature. The consternation was universal. Old and young, male and female, fled naked from their beds, with worse shriekings than those of the frogs. The event was fatal to several women. The men, after a flight of half a mile, in which they met with many broken shins, finding no enemies in pursuit of them, made a hault, and summoned resolution enough to venture back to their wives and children, when they distinctly heard from the enemy's camp these words: Wight, Hilderkin, Dier, Tete. This last, they thought, meant treaty, and, plucking up courage, they sent a triumvirate to capitulate with the supposed French and Indians. These the men approached in their shirts, and begged to speak with the general; but, it being dark and no answer given, they were sorely agitated for some time betwixt hope and fear: at length, however, they discovered that the dreaded inimical army

AN ARMY OF THIRSTY FROGS. 131

was an army of thirsty frogs going to the river for a little water.

Such an incursion was never known before nor since; and yet the people of Windham have been ridiculed for their timidity on this occasion. I verily believe an army under the Duke of Marlborough would, under like circumstances, have acted no better than they did.

In 1768 the inhabitants of Connecticut River were as much alarmed by an army of caterpillars as those of Windham were at the frogs; and no one found reason to jest at their fears. Those worms came in one night and covered the earth, on both sides of the river, to an extent of three miles in front and two in depth. They marched with great speed, and eat up everything green for the space of one hundred miles, in spite of rivers, ditches, fires, and the united efforts of 1,000 men. They were, in general, two inches long, had white bodies covered with thorns, and red throats. When they had finished their work they went down to the river Connecticut, where they died, poisoning the waters, until they were washed into the sea. This calamity was imputed by some to the vast number of logs and trees lying in the creeks, and to cinders, smoke, and fires, made to consume the waste wood for three or four hundred miles up the Connecticut River; while others thought it augurated future evils, similar to those of Egypt. The inhabitants of the Verdmonts would unavoidably have perished with famine, in consequence of the devastation of these worms, had not a remarkable Providence filled the wilderness with wild pigeons, which were killed by sticks as they sat upon the branches of the trees, in such multitudes that 30,000 people lived on them for three weeks. If a natural cause may be assigned for the coming of the frogs and caterpillars, yet the visit of the pigeons to the wilderness in August has been necessarily ascribed to the interposition of infinite Power and Goodness. Happy will it be for America, if the smiling providence of Heaven produces gratitude, repentance, and obedience, amongst her children!

Lebanon lies on the west side of Winnomantic River. The best street, which has good houses on both sides, is one mile long and one hundred yards wide. An elegant meeting-house, with steeple and bell, stands in the centre. The township is ten miles square, and forms four parishes. This town was formerly famous for an Indian school, under the conduct of Rev. Eleazer Wheelock, whose great zeal for the spiritual good of the savages in the wilderness induced him to solicit a collection from England. Having met with success, his school at Lebanon became a college in the province of Newhampshire, where he has converted his godliness into gain, and promises fair to excuse government from the expense of a superintendent of Indian affairs.

Coventry lies on the same river; the houses are straggling. The township is ten miles square, and consists of two parishes. Here are two ponds, the one three and the other four miles long, and half as wide, well filled with mackerel and other fish.

Mansfield lies east of Coventry, on Winnomantic and Fundy Rivers; the houses are scattered. The township is eight miles square, and divided into two parishes.

Union and *Wilmington* lie on Winnomantic River,

forming two parishes. Each township is six miles square.

Ashford lies on the Fundy, in a township ten miles square, and forms three parishes. The people of the town have distinguished themselves by a strict enforcement of the colony-laws against heretics and episcopalians, for not attending their meeting on the Sabbath.

Woodstock lies on Quinnibaug, and resembles Finchley. The township is ten miles square, and divided into three parishes. Woodstock had the honour of giving birth to the Rev. Thomas Bradbury Chandler, D. D., a learned divine of the Church of England, and well known in the literary world.

Killingsley lies east of Woodstock. The township, twenty miles long and six wide, forms three parishes.

Pomfret stands on Quinnibaug River, and resembles Battersea. The township is twelve miles square, and forms four parishes, one of which is episcopal. Fanaticism had always prevailed in the county of Windham over christian moderation: where, about the year 1770, after many abuses, the episcopalians found a friend in Godfree Malebone, Esq. who built on his own estate an elegant church, which was patronized by the Society for the Propagation of the Gospel in Foreign Parts, who appointed a clergyman.

We read that David slew a lion and a bear, and afterwards that Saul trusted him to fight Goliath. In Pomfret lives Colonel Israel Putnam, who slew a she-bear and her two cubs with a billet of wood. The bravery of this action brought him into public notice; and it seems he is one of fortune's favourites. The story is as follows: In 1754 a large she-bear came in the night from her den, which was three miles from Mr. Putnam's house, and took a sow out of his pen. The sow, by squeaking, awoke Mr. Putnam, who hastily ran to the poor creature's relief; but, before he could reach the pen, the bear had left it, and was trotting away with the sow in her mouth. Mr. Putnam took up a billet of wood and followed the screaming of the sow, till he came to the foot of the mountain where the den was. Dauntless he entered the horrid cavern, and, after walking and crawling on his hands and knees for fifty yards, came to a roomy cell, where the bear met him with great fury. He saw nothing but the fire of her eyes, but that was sufficient for our hero; he accordingly directed his blow, which at once proved fatal to the bear, and saved his own life at a most critical moment. Putnam then discovered and killed the two cubs; and having, though in Egyptian darkness, dragged them and the dead sow, one by one, out of the cave, he went home, and calmly reported to his family what had happened. The neighbors declared, on viewing the place by torchlight, that his exploit exceeded those of Samson or David. Soon after, the General Assembly appointed Mr. Putnam a lieutenant in the army marching against Canada. His courage and good conduct raised him to the rank of Captain the next year. The third year he was made a Major, and the fourth a Colonel. Putnam and Rogers were the heroes through the last war. Putnam was so hardy, at a time when the Indians had killed all his men and completely hemmed him in upon a river, as to leap into the stream, which in a minute carried him down a stupendous falls, where no tree could pass without being torn to pieces.

The Indians reasonably concluded that Putnam, their terrible enemy, was dead, and made their report accordingly at Ticonderoga; but soon after a scouting party found their sad mistake in a bloody rencontre. Some few that got off declared that Putnam was yet living, and that he was the first son of Hobbomockow, and therefore immortal. However, at length the Indians took this terrible warrior prisoner, and tied him to a tree, where he hung three days without food or drink. They did not attempt to kill him, for fear of offending Hobbomockow; but they sold him to the French at a great price. The name of Putnam was more alarming to the Indians than cannon, and they never would fight him after his escape from the falls. He was afterwards redeemed by the English.

Plainfield and *Canterbury* lie on Quinnibaug River, opposite to one another, and have much the appearance of Lewisham. Each township is eight miles square, and forms two parishes.

Voluntown lies on a small river, and resembles Finchley Common. The township is fifteen miles long and five wide, and forms three parishes, one of which is Presbyterian. This sect has met with as little christian charity and humanity in this hair-brained country as the Anabaptists, Quakers, and Churchmen. The *Sober Dissenters* of this town, as they style themselves, will not attend the funeral of a Presbyterian.

The KINGDOM OF CONNECTICOTE forms two counties, viz. Hertford and Litchfield, which contain about 15,000 houses and 120,000 inhabitants. The county of Hertford excels the rest in tobacco, onions, grain of all sorts, hay, and cider. It contains twenty-one towns, the chief of which I shall describe, comparing the rest to the towns near London.

Hertford town is deemed the capital of the province; it stands forty miles from Saybrook, and the same distance from Newhaven, on the west bank of Connecticut River, and is formed into squares. The township is twenty miles from east to west, and six in breadth, comprising six parishes, one of which is episcopal.

The houses are partly of brick and partly of wood, well built, but, as I have observed in general of the towns in Connecticut, do not join. King's Street is two miles long and thirty yards wide, well paved, and cut in two by a small river, over which is a high bridge. The town is half a mile wide. A grand court-house, and two elegant meetings, with steeples, bells, and clocks, adorn it. In 1760 a foundation of quarry-stone was laid for an Episcopal church in this town, at the expense of nearly 300*l.*, on which occasion the episcopalians had a mortifying proof that the present inhabitants inherit the spirit of their ancestors. Samuel Talcott, Esq. one of the Judges of the County Court, with the assistance of a mob, took away the stones, and with them built a house for his son. What added to so meritorious an action, was its being justified by the General Assembly and the Consociation. In 1652 this town had the honour of executing Mrs. Greensmith, the first witch ever heard of in America. She was accused, in the indictment, of practising evil things on the body of Ann Cole, which did not appear to be true; but the Rev. Mr. Stone, and other ministers, swore that Greensmith had confessed to them that the devil had had carnal knowledge of her. The Court then ordered her to be hanged upon the indictment. Surely none of the learned divines and statesmen studied in the Temple or Lincoln's Inn! It should seem that every Dominion or township was possessed of an ambition to make itself famous in history. The same year Springfield, not to be outdone by Hertford, brought Hugh Parsons to trial for witchcraft, and the jury found him guilty. Mr. Pincheon, the Judge, had some understanding, and prevented his execution till the matter was laid before the General Court in Boston, who determined that he was not guilty of witchcraft. The truth was, Parsons was blessed with a fine person and genteel address, insomuch that the women could not help admiring him above every other man in Springfield, and the men could not help hating him; so that there were witnesses enough to swear that Parsons was a wizzard, because he made the females love and the men hate him.

In Hertford are the following curiosities: 1. A house built of American oak in 1640, the timbers of which are yet sound, nay, almost petrified; in it was born John Belcher, Esq. Governor of Massachusets-Bay, and New-Jersey. 2. An elm, esteemed sacred, for being the tree in which their Charter was concealed. 3. A wonderful well, which was dug sixty feet deep without any appearance of water, when a large rock was met with. The miners, boring this rock in order to blast it with powder, drove the auger through it, upon which the water spouted up with such great velocity that it was with difficulty the well was stoned. It soon filled and ran over, and has supported, or rather made, a brook for above one hundred years.

The tomb of Mr. Hooker is viewed with great rev-

138   GENERAL HISTORY OF CONNECTICUT.

erence by his disciples. Nathaniel, his great-grandson, a minister in Hertford, inherits more than all his virtues, without any of his vices.[1]

Weathersfield is four miles from Hertford, and more compact than any town in the colony. The meeting-house is of brick, with a steeple, bell, and clock. The inhabitants say it is much larger than Solomon's Temple. The township is ten miles square; parishes four. The people are more gay than polite, and more superstitious than religious. This town raises more onions than are consumed in all New-England. It is a rule with parents to buy annually a silk gown for each daughter above seven years old, till she is married. The young beauty is obliged, in return, to weed a patch of onions with her own hands; which she performs in the cool of the morning, before she dresses her beefsteak. This laudable and healthy custom is ridiculed by the ladies of other towns, who idle away their mornings in bed, or in gathering the pink, or catching the butterfly, to ornament their toilets; while the gentlemen, far and near, forget not the Weathersfield ladies' silken industry.

Weathersfield was settled in 1637 by the Rev. Mr. Smith and his followers, who left Watertown, near Boston, in order to get out of the power of Mr. Cotton, whose severity in New-England exceeded that of the bishops in Old-England. But Mr. Smith did not discard the spirit of persecution as the sole property of Mr. Cotton, but carried with him a sufficient quantity of it to distress and divide his little flock.

Middletown is ten miles below Weathersfield, and

[1] Mr. Hooker died while this work was in course of publication.—ED. NOTE.

beautifully situated upon the Connecticut, between two small rivers one mile asunder, which is the length of the town and grand street. Here is an elegant church, with steeple, bell, clock, and organ; and a large meeting without a steeple. The people are polite, and not much troubled with that fanatic zeal which pervades the rest of the colony. The township is ten miles square, and forms four parishes, one episcopalian. This and the two preceding towns may be compared to Chelsea.

The following towns, which lie on the Connecticut River, are so much alike that a description of one will serve for the whole, viz. *Windsor, East Windsor, Glastenbury, Endfield, Suffield, Chatham, Haddam,* and *East Haddam.* Windsor, the best, is cut in two by the river Ett, which wanders from the northward 100 miles, through various meadows, towns, and villages, and resembles Bedford. Township ten miles square, forming three parishes. It was settled in 1637 by the Rev. Mr. Huet and his associates, who fled from religious slavery in Boston, to enjoy the power of depriving others of liberty.

The following towns, lying back of the river towns, being similar in most respects, I shall join also in one class, viz. *Hebron, Colchester, Bolton, Tolland, Stafford,* and *Sommers.*

Hebron is the centre of the province, and it is remarkable that there are thirty-six towns larger and thirty-six less. It is situated between two ponds, about two miles in length and one in breadth, and is intersected by two small rivers, one of which falls into the Connecticut, the other into the Thames. A large meeting stands on the square, where four roads meet. The town resembles Finchley. The township is eight miles square; five parishes, one is episcopal. The number of houses is 400; of inhabitants, 3,200. It pays one part out of seventy-three of the governmental taxes, and is a bed of farmers on their own estates. Frequent suits about the Indian titles have rendered them famous for their knowledge in law and self-preservation. In 1740 Mr. George Whitefield gave them this laconic character: "Hebron," says he, "is the "stronghold of Satan; for its people mightily oppose "the work of the Lord, being more fond of earth than "heaven." This town is honoured by the residence of the Rev. Dr. Benjamin Pomeroy, an excellent scholar, an exemplary gentleman, and a most thundering preacher of the New-Light order. His great abilities procured him the favour and honour of being the instructor of Abimeleck, the present king of Mohegin. He is of a very persevering, sovereign disposition, but just, polite, generous, charitable, and without dissimulation. *Avis alba.* Here also reside some of the descendants of William Peters, Esq. already spoken of, among whom is the Rev. Samuel Peters,[1] an episcopal clergyman, who, by his generosity and zeal for the Church of England, rendered himself famous both in New and Old-

[1] The Rev. Mr. Dean went to England and took orders for the church at Hebron, but died at sea on his return, about the year 1745. The Rev. Mr. Punderson, of Groton, then preached to them, and administered the sacrament, from 1746 to 1752. The people of Hebron were very unfortunate with respect to the gentlemen who went to England for orders in their behalf. A Mr. Cotton, in 1752, received orders for them, but he died, on his passage for New-England, with the small-pox. Mr. Graves, of New-London, served them from 1752 to 1757. In 1757 one Mr. Usher

England, and in some degree made an atonement for the fanaticism and treason of his uncle Hugh, and of his ancestor on his mother's side, Major-General Thomas Harrison, both hanged at Charing-Cross in the last century.

Colchester has to boast of the Rev. John Buckley for its first minister, whose grandfather was the Rev. Peter Buckley, of Woodhill, in Bedfordshire in Old-England; who, after being silenced by the bishop for his misconduct, went to New-England in 1635, and died at Concord in 1658.

John Buckley was a great scholar, and, suffering prudence to govern his hard temper, he conciliated the esteem of all parties, and became the ornament of the *Sober Dissenters* in Connecticut. He was a lawyer, a physician, and divine. He published an ingenious pamphlet to prove that the title of the people to their lands was good, because they had taken them out of the state of nature. His argument satisfied many who thought their titles were neither legal, just, nor scriptural; indeed, it may seem conclusive, if his major proposition be granted, that the English found Connecticut in a state of nature. His son John was a lawyer and physician of great reputation, and was appointed a Judge of the Superior Court very young. He and his father were suspected to be not sound in faith, because

went for orders in their behalf; he was taken by the French, on his passage to England, and died in captivity.

The Rev. Samuel Peters was ordained their priest in August, 1759, and the next year returned to New-England. He continued priest at Hebron until the commencement of the Revolutionary War, when he was driven from his country by the mobs of Windham, instigated by Governor Trumbull.—ED. NOTE.

they used in their prayers, "From battle and murder, "and from sudden death, good Lord deliver us, for the "sake of thine only Son, who commands us thus to pray, "Our Father," &c., &c. Peter Buckley was possessed of a gentleman's estate in Bedfordshire, which he sold, and spent the produce among his servants in Massachusets-Bay. His posterity in Colchester, in Connecticut, are very rich, and, till lately, were held in great esteem, which, however, they lost by conforming to the Church of England.

There is nothing remarkable to be observed of any of the other towns I have classed with Hebron, except *Stafford*, which possesses a mineral spring that has the reputation of curing the gout, sterility, pulmony, hysterics, &c., &c., and therefore is the New-England "Bath," where the sick and rich resort to prolong life and acquire the polite accomplishments.

Herrington, Farmington, and *Symsbury,* lying on the west of Hertford, and on the river Ett, will finish the county of Hertford.

Herrington is ten miles square, and forms two parishes.

Farmington resembles Corydon. The township is fifteen miles square, and forms eight parishes, three of which are episcopal. Here the meadow-land is sold at 50*l.* per acre.

Symsbury, with its meadows and surrounding hills, forms a beautiful landscape, much like Maidstone, in Kent. The township is twenty miles square, and consists of nine parishes, four of which are episcopal. Here are copper mines. In working one, many years ago, the miners bored half a mile through a mountain,

THE CATACOMB OF CONNECTICUT. 143

making large cells, forty yards below the surface, which now serve as a prison, by order of the General Assembly, for such offenders as they choose not to hang. The prisoners are let down on a windlass into this dismal cavern, through a hole which answers the triple purpose of conveying them food, air, and—I was going to say—light, but that scarcely reaches them. In a few months the prisoners are released by death, and the colony rejoices in her great humanity and the mildness of her laws. This conclave of spirits imprisoned may be called with great propriety the Catacomb of Connecticut. The light of the sun and the light of the Gospel are alike shut out from the martyrs, whose resurrection-state will eclipse the wonder of that of Lazarus. It has been remarked by the candid part of this religious colony, that the General Assembly and Consociation have never allowed any prisoners in the whole province a chaplain, though they have spent much of their time and public money in spreading the gospel in the neighbouring colonies among the Indians, Quakers, and episcopalians, and though, at the same time, those religionists preach damnation to all people who neglect to attend public worship twice every Sabbath, fasting, and thanksgiving days, provided they are appointed by themselves, and not by the King and Parliament of Great Britain. This well-founded remark has been treated by the zealots as springing more from malice than policy.

I beg leave to give the following instances of the humanity and mildness the province has always manifested for the episcopal clergy.

About 1746, the Rev. Mr. Gibbs, of Symsbury, refusing to pay a rate imposed for the salary of Mr. Mills, a dissenting minister in the same town, was, by the collector, thrown across a horse, lashed hands and feet under the creature's belly, and carried many miles in that humane manner to gaol. Mr. Gibbs was half dead when he got there; and though he was released by his church wardens, who, to save his life, paid the assessment, yet, having taken cold in addition to his bruises, he became delirious, and has remained in a state of insanity ever since.

In 1772 the Rev. Mr. Moyley, a missionary from the Society for the Propagation of the Gospel, at Litchfield, was presented by the Grand Jury for marrying a couple belonging to his parish, after the banns had been duly published, and consent of parents obtained. The Court mildly fined Mr. Moyley 20*l.* because he could not show any other license to officiate as a clergyman than what he had received from the Bishop of London, whose authority the Court determined did not extend to Connecticut, which was a chartered government. One of the Judges said: " It is high time to put a stop to the " usurpations of the Bishop of London, and to let him " know that, though his license be lawful, and may em- " power one of his curates to marry in England, yet it " is not so in America; and if fines would not curb " them in this point, imprisonment should."

The second county in the Kingdom of Connecticote, and the most mountainous in the whole province, is *Litchfield*, which produces abundance of wheat, butter, cheese, iron ore, &c., and has many iron works, foundries, and furnaces. It contains the following fourteen towns:

Litchfield is watered by two small rivers. An elegant meeting-house and decent court-house, with steeple and bells, ornament the square, where three roads meet. The best street is one mile long. It resembles Dartford. The township is twelve miles square, and forms five parishes, one of which is episcopal.

Though Litchfield is the youngest county of Connecticut, yet in 1766 it set an example to the rest worthy of imitation. The province had always been greatly pestered by a generation of men called "quacks," who, with a few Indian nostrums, a lancet, a glister-pipe, rhubarb, treacle-water mixed with Roman bombast of *vena cava* and *vena porta*, attacked fevers, nervous disorders, and broken bones, and, by the grace of perseverance, subdued Nature, and helped their patients to a passage to the world of spirits before they were ready. The surgeons and physicians who were not quacks formed themselves into a society for the encouragement of literature and a regular and wholesome practice. But their laudable endeavours were discountenanced by the General Assembly, who refused to comply with their solicitations for a charter; because the quacks and the people said, "If the charter were granted, the learned men would "become too rich by an monopoly, as they did in Eng-"land." The answer to this question was, "Would it "not be better to permit a monopoly to preserve the "health and lives of the people, than to suffer quacks "to kill them and ruin the province?" The reply proved decisive in that fanatical Assembly, viz. "No "medicine can be serviceable without the blessing of "God. The quacks never administer any physic with-"out the prayers of the minister." One doctor proposed the trial of a dose of arsenic—whether it would

146   GENERAL HISTORY OF CONNECTICUT.

not kill any one who would take it, though twenty ministers should pray against it. He was called a profane man, the petition was rejected, and quackery remains triumphant.[1]

New-Milford lies on the Osootonoc River. A church and meeting, with steeples and bells, beautify the town, which resembles Fulham. The township, twelve miles square, forms five parishes, of which two are episcopal.

Woodbury lies on the same river, and resembles Kentish-town. The township, twelve miles square, is divided into seven parishes, three of them episcopal. In this town lives the Rev. Dr. Bellamy, who is a good scholar and a great preacher. He has attempted to shew a more excellent way to heaven than was known

---

[1] The following is a portion of a communication to some paper in Connecticut, part of which has been destroyed:

"MR. PRINTER: You have shewn no partiality in your paper among contending parties, but have given all rational systems, at least all popular plans, a chance in the world by your medeocritical channel. What I am desirous of communicating to the public is very popular : It is, to put the Quacks Club in the East upon a reputible footing, as the licensed Physiognomers in the West.

"At a meeting held in Connecticut, October, 1767, it was resolved:

"First: We Etiologists, viz. John Whiggot, Esq. President, Adam Kunenow, Michel Nugnug, Shazael Bulldunce, Committee for said Club of Quackism. That we may serve each other in our Occupation, we have appointed a meeting to be upon the first Tuesday of every month, for the year ensueing, at the house of Mr. Abram Bruntick, in Green Lane, nigh the Crow Market, straight forward from the sign of the Goose, at the sign of the Looking Glass.

"Second : To lay some plan to support Dr. Leaffolds Latina Anatomy.

"Third : To choose a Proluctor, able to defend the high pretensions made by these mercurial sons in the West against your art in Pharmacy, Chemistry, and Physic, in the East.

"Fourth: To make some Laws for admission of young Quacks into this most popular Club."

No doubt the above was a burlesque upon the law that had passed the year before, or rather upon the one the General Assembly refused to pass.—ED. NOTE.

before. He may be called the Athenian of Connecticut, for he has published something new to the christian world. Zuinglius may learn from him.

The following towns lie also on the Osootonoc, viz. *Sharon, Kent, Salisbury, New Fairfield, Cornwall, Goshen,* and *Canaan;* and all of them resemble Finchley. Each township is ten miles square.

Sharon forms three parishes, one of which is episcopal. It is much noted on account of a famous mill, invented and built by a Mr. Joel Harvey upon his own estate; for which he received a compliment of 20*l.* from the Society of Arts in London. The water, by turning one wheel, sets the whole in motion. In two apartments wheat is ground; in two others, bolted; in another, thrashed; in a sixth, winnowed; in the seventh, hemp and flax are beaten; and in the eighth, dressed. Either branch is discontinued at pleasure, without impeding the rest.

The other towns of Litchfield county are: *New-Hertford, Torrington, Hartland,* and *Winchester;* all which lie on the river Ett. The townships are severally about six miles square, and each forms one parish.

The KINGDOM OF QUINNIPIOG constituted the Dominion of Newhaven, divided into two counties, viz. Newhaven and Fairfield; these again divided into seventeen townships, about twelve miles square each. The number of houses is nearly 10,000, and that of the inhabitants 60,000.

The county of *Newhaven* is hilly, and has a thin soil, enriched, however, by the industry of its inhabitants. The chief commodities are flax, rye, barley, white beans, and salt hay. It contains eight towns, four of which lie on the Sound, and the others on the back of them. Newhaven township comprises fourteen parishes, three of them episcopal and one Sandemanian. The town, being the most beautiful in New-England, if not in all America, is entitled to a minute description. It is bounded southly by the bay, into which the river Quinnipiack empties itself; easterly and westerly by two creeks two miles asunder; and northerly by a lofty mountain, that extends even to the river St. Lawrence, and forms a highland between the rivers Hudson and Connecticut, standing in a plain three miles by two in extent. This plain is divided into 300 squares of the size of Bloomsbury Square, with streets twenty yards wide between each division. Forty of these squares are already built upon, having houses of brick and wood on each front, about five yards asunder; every house with a garden that produces vegetables sufficient for the family. Two hundred houses are annually erected. Elms and button-trees surround the centre square, wherein are two meetings, the court-house, the gaol, and Latin school; in the fronts of the adjoining squares are Yale College, the chapel, a meeting, and a church: all these grand buildings with steeples and bells. The market is plentifully supplied with every necessary during the whole year, excepting greens in winter. But the harbour is incommoded by flats near the town for one mile in width, and by ice in winter. The former evil is, in some measure, remedied by long and expensive wharves, but the latter is incurable. The people, however, say their trade is greater than that of Norwich or New-London; and their shipping, of different burthens, consists of nearly 200 sail.

According to Dr. Mather, Newhaven was, about 1646, to have been made a city, the interests of the colony with Cromwell's party being then very great; but a wonderful phenomenon prevented it. As the good Dr. Mather never wanted faith through the whole course of his "Magnalia," and as the New-Englanders to the present time believe his reports, I will here present my readers with the history of this miracle:

"The people of Newhaven fitted out a ship, and sent her
" richly laden for England, to procure a patent for the colony and
" a charter for the city. After the ship had been at sea some
" weeks, there happened in New-England a violent storm, which
" induced the people of Newhaven to fast and pray, to inquire of
" the Lord whether their ship was in that storm or not. This
" was a real fast: for the people neither eat nor drank from sunrise
" to sunset. At five o'clock in the afternoon they came out of
" the meeting, walking softly, heavily, and sadly, homewards. On
" a sudden the air thundered and the lightnings shone abroad.
" They looked up towards the heavens, when they beheld their
" ship in full sail, and the sailors steering her from West to East.
" She came over the meeting, where they had fasted and prayed,
" and there was met by a euroclydon, which rent the sails and
" overset the ship. In a few moments she fell down near the
" weathercock, on the steeple, and instantly vanished. The peo-
" ple all returned to the meeting, when the minister gave thanks
" to God for answering the desires of his servants, and for giving
" them an infallible token of the loss of their ship and charter."

This, and divers other miracles which have happened in New-England, have been and still are useful to the clergy in establishing the people in the belief that there is a great familiarity between God and their ministers. Hence the ministers govern the superstitious; whilst the deacon, the lawyer, and the merchant, for lucre, wink at the imposition. Yet the ministers, in their turn, are governed by their abettors.

Thou genius of adventure, that carriedst Columbus from eastern to western shores, the domain of savage beasts and savage men, now cursed with the demons of superstition and fanaticism, oh, kindle in no other breast the wish to seek new worlds! Africa already mourns, and Europe trembles!

The true character of Davenport and Eaton, the leaders of the first settlers of Newhaven, may be learnt from the following fact: An English gentleman of the name of Grigson, coming on his travels to Newhaven about the year 1644, was greatly pleased with its pleasant situation, and, after purchasing a large settlement, sent to London for his wife and family. But, before their arrival, he found that a charming situation, without the blessings of religious and civil liberty, would not render him and his family happy; he resolved, therefore, to quit the country and return to England as soon as his family should arrive, and accordingly advertised his property for sale; when, lo! agreeable to one of the Bible laws, no one would buy, because he had not, and could not obtain, liberty of the selectmen to sell it. The patriotic virtue of the selectmen thus becoming an insurmountable bar to the sale of his Newhaven estate, Mr. Grigson made his will, and bequeathed part of his lands towards the support of an episcopal clergyman, who should reside in that town, and the residue to his own heirs. Having deposited his will in the hands of a friend, he set sail with his family for England, but died on the passage. This friend proved the will, and had it recorded, but died also soon after. The record was dexterously concealed, by glueing two leaves together; and, after some years, the selectmen sold the whole estate to pay taxes, though the rent of Mr. Grigson's house alone, in one year, would pay taxes for ten. Some persons hardy enough to exclaim against this glaring act of injustice, were soon silenced and expelled the town. In 1750 an episcopal clergyman was settled in Newhaven, and, having been informed of Grigson's will, applied to the town clerk for a copy, who told him there was no such will on record, and withal refused him the liberty of searching. In 1768, Peter Harrison, Esq. of Nottinghamshire in England, the king's collector in Newhaven, claimed his right of searching public records; and, being a stranger, and not supposed to have any knowledge of Grigson's will, obtained his demand. The alphabet contained Grigson's name, and referred to a page which was not to be found in the book. Mr. Harrison supposed it to have been torn out; but, on closer examination, discovered one leaf much thicker than the others. He put a corner of the thick leaf in his mouth, and soon found it was composed of two leaves, which with much difficulty having separated, he found Grigson's will! To make sure of the work, he took a copy of it himself, and then called the clerk to draw and attest another, which was done. Thus furnished, Mr. Harrison instantly applied to the selectmen, and demanded a surrender of the land which belonged to the Church, but which they as promptly refused; whereupon Mr. Harrison took out writs of ejectment against the possessors. As might be expected, Mr. Harrison, from a good man, became, in ten days, the worst man in the world; but, being a generous and brave Englishman, he valued not their clamors and curses, though they terrified the gentlemen of the law. Harrison was obliged to be his own lawyer, and boldly declared he expected to lose his cause in New-England; but after that he would appeal, and try it, at his own expense, in Old-England, where justice reigned. The good people, knowing Harrison did not get his bread by their votes, and that they could not baffle him, resigned the lands to the Church on that gentleman's own terms, which in a few years will support a clergyman in a very genteel manner. The honest selectmen yet possess the other lands, though report says Mr. Grigson has an heir of his own name residing near Holborn, in London, who inherits the virtues of his ancestor, and ought to inherit his estate.

The sad and awful discovery of Mr. Grigson's will, after having been concealed for one hundred years, would have confounded any people but those of Newhaven, who study nothing but religion and liberty. Those pious souls consoled themselves by comparison: "We are no worse," said they, "than the people of "Boston and Windham County." The following will explain this justification of the saints of Newhaven:

In 1740 Mrs. Cursette, an English lady, travelling from New-York to Boston, was obliged to stay some days at Hebron; when, seeing the church not finished, and the people suffering great persecutions, she told them to persevere in their good work, and she would send them a present when she got to Boston. Soon after her arrival there Mrs. Cursette fell sick and died. In her will she gave a legacy of 300*l*. old tenor (then equal to 100*l*. sterling) to the Church of England in

ORIGIN OF THE NAME OF "PUMPKIN-HEADS." 153

Hebron, and appointed John Handcock, Esq. and Nathaniel Glover, her executors. Glover was also her residuary legatee. The will was obliged to be recorded in Windham County, because some of Mrs. Cursette's lands lay there. Glover sent the will to Deacon S. H—, of Canterbury, ordering him to get it recorded, and keep it private, lest the legacy should build up the Church. The Deacon and Registrar were faithful to their trust, and kept Glover's secret twenty-five years. At length the Deacon was taken ill, and his life was supposed in great danger. Among his penitential confessions, he told of his having concealed Mrs. Cursette's will. His confidant went to Hebron, and informed the wardens that for one guinea he would discover a secret of 300*l.* old tenor consequence to the Church. The guinea was paid and the secret disclosed. A demand of the legacy ensued. Mr. Handcock referred to Glover, and Glover said he was neither obliged to publish the will nor pay the legacy: it had lapsed to the heir-at-law. It being difficult for a Connecticut man to recover a debt in the Massachusets-Bay, and *vice versa*, the wardens were obliged to accept from Mr. Glover 30*l.* instead of 300*l.* sterling; which sum, allowing 200*l.* as lawful simple interest at six per cent. for twenty-five years, ought in equity have been paid. This matter, however, Mr. Glover is to settle with Mrs. Cursette in the other world.

Newhaven is celebrated for having given the name of "pumpkin-heads" to all the New-Englanders. It originated from the "Blue Laws," which enjoined every male to have his hair cut round by a cap. When caps were not to be had, they substituted the hard shell of a pumpkin, which being put on the head every Saturday, the hair is cut by the shell all round the head. Whatever religious virtue is supposed to be derived from this custom, I know not; but there is much prudence in it: first, it prevents the hair from snarling; secondly, it saves the use of combs, bags, and ribbons; thirdly, the hair cannot incommode the eyes by falling over them; and fourthly, such persons as have lost their ears for heresy, and other wickedness, cannot conceal their misfortune and disgrace.

Cruelty and godliness were perhaps never so well reconciled by any people as by those of Newhaven, who are alike renounded for both. The unhappy story of Deacon Potter has eternalized the infamy of their Blue Laws, and almost annexed to their town the name of Sodom. The Deacon had borne the best of characters many years; he was the peacemaker, and an enemy to persecution; but he was grown old, was rich, and had a young wife. His young wife had an inclination for a young husband, and had waited with impatience for the death of her old one, till at length, resolving, if possible, to accelerate the attainment of her wishes, she complained to the magistrate that her husband did not render her due benevolence. The Judge took no notice of what she said. She then swore that her husband was an apostate, and that he was fonder of his mare, bitch, and cow, than of her; in which allegation she was joined by her son. The Deacon was brought to trial, condemned, and executed with the beasts, and with them also buried in one common grave. Dr. Mather, with his usual quantity of faith, speaks of the Deacon as very guilty, as having had a fair, legal, and candid trial, and convicted on good and scriptural evidence. I am willing to allow the Doctor as much sincerity as faith. He had his information from the party who condemned the Deacon; but there are manuscripts, which I have seen, that state the matter thus: Deacon Potter was hanged for heresy and apostacy, which consisted in showing hospitality to strangers, who came to his house in the night, among whom were Quakers, Anabaptists, and Adamites. This was forbidden by the Blue Laws, which punished for the first and second offence with fines, and with death for the third. His wife and son betrayed him for hiding the spies and sending them away in peace. The Court was contented with calling his complicated crimes beastiality; his widow with a new husband; and the son with the estate; while the public were deceived by the arts of the wicked junto.

I have related this story to shew the danger of admitting a wife to give evidence against her husband, according to the Blue Laws; and to caution all readers against crediting too much the historians of New-England, who, either from motives of fear or emolument, have in numberless instances designedly disguised or concealed the truth. Such persons whose stubborn principles would not bend to this yoke, were not suffered to search the colonial records; and those who have dared to intimate that all was not right among the first settlers, have been compelled to leave the country with the double loss of character and property.

To Newhaven now belongs Yale College, of which I have promised my readers a particular account. It was originally, as already mentioned, a School, established by the Rev. Thomas Peters at Saybrook, who left it his library at his death. It soon acquired the distinguished appellation of "Schola Illustris," and about 1700 was honoured by the General Assembly with a charter of incorporation, converting it into a college, under the denomination of Yale College, in compliment to a gentleman of that name, governor of one of the West India Islands, and its greatest benefactor. The charter constitutes a president, three tutors, twelve overseers, and a treasurer; and exempts it from any visitation of the Governor or Assembly, in order to secure it against the control of a King's Governor, in case one should ever be appointed. I have already observed that a power of conferring Bachelors' and Masters' degrees was granted by the charter, and that the corporation have thought proper to assume that of conferring Doctors' degrees. By the economical regulations of the College, there are a professor of divinity, mathematics, and natural philosophy; and four classes of students, which were at first attended by the president and the three tutors; but the president has long been excused that laborious task, and a fourth tutor appointed in his stead. Each class has its proper tutor. Once a week the president examines them all in the public hall, superintends their disputations and scientific demonstrations, and, if any student appears to be negligent, orders him under the care of a special tutor—a stigma which seldom fails of producing its intended effect. Greek, Latin, geography, history, and logic, are well taught in this seminary; but it suffers for want of tutors to teach the Hebrew, French, and Spanish languages. Oratory, music, and politeness, are equal-

EVENING AMUSEMENTS. 157

ly neglected here and in the colony. The students attend prayers every morning and evening, at six o'clock. The president, professor, and one of the tutors, reads and expounds a chapter, then a psalm is sung, after which follows a prayer. The hours of study are notified by the College bell, and every scholar seen out of his room is liable to a fine, which is seldom excused. The amusements for the evenings are not cards, dancing, or music, but reading and composition. They are allowed two hours' play with foot-ball every day. Thus cooped up for four years, they understand books better than men or manners. They then are admitted to their Bachelor's degree, having undergone a public examination in the arts and sciences. Three years afterwards they are admitted to their Master's degree, provided they have supported moral characters. The ceremony used by the president upon these occasions is to deliver a book to the intended Master in Arts, saying: "Ad- "mitto te ad secundum Gradum in Artibus, pro more " Acadæmiarum in Anglia; tradoque tibi hunc librum, " una cum protestate publici prælegendi quoties cunque " ad hoc munus evocatus fueris." For Bachelors the same, mutatis mutandis. A diploma in vellum, with the seal of the College, is given to each Master, and signed by the president and six fellows or overseers. The first degrees of Masters were given in 1702. The students in late years have amounted to about 180. They dine in the common hall at four tables, and the tutors and graduates at a fifth. The number of the whole is about 200.

Yale College is built with wood, and painted a sky colour; it is 160 feet long and three stories high, besides garrets. In 1754, another building of brick, 100 feet long and three stories high, exclusive of garrets, with double rooms, and a double front, was added, and called Connecticut Hall. About 1760, a very elegant chapel and library was erected, with brick, under one roof. But it cannot be supposed the latter is to be compared with the Vatican or the Bodleian. It consists of eight or ten thousand volumes in all branches of literature, but wants modern books; though there is a tolerable sufficiency, if the corporation would permit what they call Bishops' and Arminian books to be read. Ames' Medulla is allowed, while Grotius de Veritate Religionis is denied. It was lately presented with a new and valuable apparatus for experimental philosophy. The whole library and apparatus was given by various persons, chiefly English.

The General Assembly have endowed this College with large tracts of land, which, duly cultivated, will soon support the ample establishment of an university; but, even at present, I may truly say, Yale College exceeds the number, and perhaps the learning, of its scholars all over British America. This seminary was in 1717 removed from Saybrook to Newhaven; the extraordinary cause of its transition I shall here lay before the reader.

Saybrook Dominion had been settled by Puritans of some moderation and decency. They had not joined with Massachusets-Bay, Hertford, and Newhaven, in sending home agents to assist in the murder of Charles I. and the subversion of the Lords and Bishops; they had received Hooker's heretics, and sheltered the apostate from Davenport's millenarian system; they had shewn an inclination to be dependent on the Mother Country, and had not wholly anathematized the Church of England. In short, the people of Hertford and Newhaven suspected that Saybrook was not truly protestant; that it had a passion for the leeks and onions of Egypt; and that the youth belonging to them in the "Schola Illustris" were in great danger of imbibing its lukewarmness.

A vote therefore passed at Hertford, to remove the College to Weathersfield, where the leeks and onions of Egypt would not be thought of; and another at Newhaven, that it should be removed to that town, where Christ had established his dominion from sea to sea, and where he was to begin his millenarian reign. About 1715 Hertford, in order to carry its vote into execution, prepared teams, boats, and a mob, and privately set off for Saybrook, and seized upon the College apparatus, library, and students, and carried all to Weathersfield. This redoubled the jealousy of the saints at Newhaven, who thereupon determined to fulfil their vote; and, accordingly, having collected a mob sufficient for the enterprise, they sat out for Weathersfield, where they seized by surprise the students, library, &c. &c. But, on the road to Newhaven, they were overtaken by the Hertford mob, who, however, after an unhappy battle, were obliged to retire with only a part of the library and part of the students. Hence sprung two colleges out of one. The quarrel increased daily, everybody expecting a war more bloody than that of Sassacus; and no doubt such would have been the case, had not the peacemakers of Massachusets-Bay interposed with their usual friendship, and advised their dear friends of Hertford to give up the College to Newhaven. This was accordingly done in 1717, to the great joy of the crafty Massachusets, who always greedily seek their own prosperity, though it ruin their best neighbours.

The College being thus fixed forty miles further west from Boston than it was before, tended greatly to the interest of Harvard College; for Saybrook and Hertford, out of pure grief, sent their sons to Harvard, instead of the College at Newhaven. This quarrel continued until 1764, when it subsided into a grand continental consociation of ministers, which met at Newhaven to consult the spiritual good of the Mohawks and other Indian tribes, the best method of preserving the American Vine, and the protestant, independent liberty of America: a good preparatory to the rebellion against Great Britain.

The Rev. Mr. Naphtali Dagget is the fourth president of Yale College since its removal to Newhaven. He is an excellent Greek and Latin scholar, and reckoned a good Calvinistic divine. Though a stranger to European politeness, yet possessing a mild temper and affable disposition, the exercise of his authority is untinctured with haughtiness. Indeed, he seems to have too much candour and too little bigotry to please the corporation and retain his post many years. The Rev. Mr. Nehemiah Strong, the College professor, is also of an amiable temper, and merits the appointment.

Were the corporation less rigid, and more inclined to tolerate some reasonable amusements and polite accomplishments among the youth, they would greatly add to the fame and increase of the College, and the students would not be known by every stranger to have been educated in Connecticut. The disadvantage under which they at present appear, from the want of address, is much to be regretted.

Beauford, *Guilford*, and *Milford*, are much alike.

Guilford is laid out in squares, after the manner of Newhaven, twenty of which are built upon. The church and two meetings stand in the centre square. One of the meetings is very grand, with a steeple, bell, and clock. The parishes in it are eight, three of them episcopal.

This town gave birth to the Rev. Samuel Johnson, D. D., who was the first episcopal minister in Connecticut, and the first president of King's College in New-York. He was educated and became a tutor in the College at Saybrook, was an ornament to his native country, and much esteemed for his humanity and learning.

The Rev. Mr. George Whitefield, in a sermon he preached in the great meeting, gave the character of the people of Guilford in 1740. His text was, " Anoint " mine eyes with eye-salve." After pointing out what was not the true eye-salve, he said : "I will tell you " what is the true eye-salve : it is faith, it is grace, it " is simplicity, it is virtue. Ah, Lord! where can they " be found? Perhaps not in this grand assembly."

I have frequently quoted the Rev. George Whitefield, without that ludicrous intention which, possibly, the reader may suspect me of. I admire his general character, his good discernment, his knowledge of mankind, his piety, his goodness of heart, his generosity, and hatred of persecution, though I think his zeal was sometimes too fervent. I ever viewed him as an instrument of Heaven, as the greatest Boanerges and blessing America ever knew. He turned the profligate to God; he roused the lukewarm christian ; he tamed the wild fanatic, and made Felix tremble. It is true, he has also made wise men mad; but this is the natural effect of the word, which is the savour of life and the savour of death at one and the same time. New-England before his coming was but the slaughter-house of heretics. He was admired by the oppressed episcopalians, the trembling Quakers, the bleeding Baptists, &c., &c. He was followed by all sects and parties, except the *Sober Dissenters*, who thought their craft in danger. He made peace where was no peace, and even his enemies praised him in the gate. Whitefield did what could not have been done without the aid of an Omnipotent arm : he planted charity in New-England, of which the increase has been a thousand-fold. He is lauded where the wicked cease from troubling ; where his works of faith, love, and charity, clothe him ; and where the glory of eternity blesses him with a welcome ineffably transporting. May his virtues be imitated, his imperfections forgiven, and his happiness obtained by all !

Wallingford, Durham, Waterbury, and *Derby*, finish the County of Newhaven. *Wallingford* is the best of the four : it lies on the Quinnipiack River, and forms eight parishes, two of which are episcopal. The town street is one mile long, and the houses stand pretty thick on both sides. The church and two meetings, one with a steeple, bell, and clock, stand in the middle of the street. The grave-stones point out the characters of the first settlers. An extract from one follows:

"Here lies the body of Corporal Moses Atwater, who left "England in 1660, to enjoy the liberty of conscience in a howling "wilderness."

The second county in the Kingdom of Quinnipiog is *Fairfield*. It is situated west of Osootonoc River, and contains nine townships, five of which lie on the sea, and resemble one another; and on the back of them are situated four others, which also have a mutual resemblance. The soil is rich and uneven; the chief productions, excellent wheat, salt hay, and flax. Those townships which lie out on the sea are *Fairfield, Norwalk, Stamford, Greenwich,* and *Stratford.* This last I shall describe.

Stratford lies on the west bank of the Osootonoc River, having the sea, or Sound, on the south; there are three streets running north and south, and ten east and west. The best is one mile long. On the centre square stands a meeting, with steeple and bell, and a church, with a steeple, bell, clock, and organ. It is a beautiful place, and from the water has an appearance not inferior to Canterbury. Of six parishes contained in it, three are episcopal. The people are said to be the most polite of any in the colony, owing to the singular moderation of the town in admitting latterly Europeans to settle among them. Many persons come also from the Islands and southern provinces for the benefit of their health. Here was erected the first episcopal church in Connecticut. A very extraordinary story is told concerning the occasion of it, which I shall give the reader the particulars of, the people being as sanguine in their belief of it as they are of the ship's sailing over Newhaven.

An ancient religious rite called the Powwow was annually celebrated by the Indians, and commonly lasted several hours every night for two or three weeks. About 1690 they convened to perform it on Stratford Point, near the town. During the nocturnal ceremony, the English saw, or imagined they saw, devils rise out of the sea, wrapped up in sheets of flame, and flying round the Indian camp, while the Indians were screaming, cutting, and prostrating themselves before their supposed fiery gods. In the midst of the tumult, the devils darted in among them, seized several and mounted with them in the air, the cries and groans issuing from whom quieted the rest. In the morning, the limbs of Indians, all shrivelled and covered with sulphur, were found in different parts of the town. Astonished and terrified at these spectacles, the people of Stratford began to think the devils would take up their abode among them, and called together all the ministers in the neighbourhood to exorcise and lay them. The ministers began and carried on their warfare with prayer, hymns, and abjurations; but the powwows continued, and the devils would not obey. The inhabitants were about to quit the town, when Mr. Nell spoke and said, "I would to God Mr. Visey, the episcopal minister " at New-York, was here; for he would expel those evil " spirits." They laughed at his advice; but on his reminding them of the little maid who directed Naaman to cure his leprosy, they voted him their permission to bring Mr. Visey at the next powwow. Mr. Visey attended accordingly; and as the powwow commenced with howling and whoops, Mr. Visey read portions of the holy scriptures, litany, &c. The sea was put into great commotion; the powwow stopped; the Indians dispersed, and never more held a powwow in Stratford. The inhabitants were struck with wonder at this event, and held a conference to discover the reason why the devils and the powwowers had obeyed the prayers of one minister, and had paid no regard to those of fifty. Some thought the reading of the holy scriptures, others thought that the litany and Lord's prayer, some again that the episcopal power of the minister, and others that all united, were the means of obtaining the heavenly blessing they had received.

Those that believed that the holy scriptures and litany were effectual against the devil and his legions, declared for the Church of England; while the majority ascribed their deliverance to complot between the devils and the episcopal minister, with a view to overthrow Christ's vine planted in New-England. Each party acted with more zeal than prudence. The Church, however, increased, though oppressed by more persecutions and calamities than were ever experienced by puritans from bishops and powwowers. Even the use of the Bible, the Lord's prayer, the litany, or any part of the prayer-book was forbidden; nay, ministers taught from their pulpits, according to the Blue Laws, "that the lovers of " Zion had better put their ears to the mouth of hell and " learn from the whispers of the devil, than read the " bishops' books;" while the Churchmen, like Michael the archangel contending with the devil about the body of Moses, dared not bring against them a railing accusation. But this was not all. When the episcopalians had collected timber for a church, they found the devils had not left town, but only changed their habitation—had left the savages, and entered into fanatics and wood. In the night before the church was to be begun, the timber set up a country-dance, skipping about and flying in the air with as much agility and sulphurous stench as ever the devils had exhibited around the camp of the Indian powwowers. This alarming circumstance would have ruined the credit of the Church, had not the episcopalians ventured to look into the phenomena, and found the timber had been bored with augers, charged with gunpowder, and fired off by matches—a discovery, however, of bad consequence in one respect: it prevented the annalists of New-England from publishing this among the rest of their miracles. About 1720, the patience and sufferings of the episcopalians, who were then but a handful, procured them some friends even among their persecutors; and those friends condemned the cruelty exercised over the Churchmen, Quakers, and Anabaptists, in consequence of which they first felt the effects of those gentle weapons, the New-England whisperings and backbitings; at length were openly stigmatized as Armenians, and enemies of the American Vine. The conduct of the *Sober Dissenters* increased the grievous sin of moderation, and nearly twenty of their ministers, at the head of whom was Dr. Cutler, President of Yale College, declared, on a public commencement, for the Church of England. Hereupon the General Assembly and Consociation, finding their comminations likely to blast the American Vine, instantly had recourse to flattery, larded with tears and promises, by which means they recovered all the secessors but four, viz. Dr. Cutler, Dr. Johnson, Mr. Whitemore, and Mr. Brown, who repaired to England for

A NEST OF ZEALOTS.

holy orders. Dr. Cutler had the misfortune to spend his life and great abilities in the fanatical, ungrateful, factious town of Boston, where he went through fiery trials, shining brighter and brighter, till he was delivered from New-England persecution, and landed where the wicked cease from troubling. Dr. Johnson, from his natural disposition, and not for the sake of gain, took pity on the neglected church at Stratford, where for fifty years he fought the beast of Ephesus with great success.[1] The Doctor was under the bountiful protection of the Society for the Propagation of the Gospel in Foreign Parts, incorporated by William III., to save from the rage of republicanism, heathenism, and fanaticism, all such members of the Church of England as were settled in our American colonies, factories, and plantations beyond the sea. To the foresight of that monarch, to the generous care and protection of that society, under God, are owing all the loyalty, decency, christianity undefiled with blood, which glimmer in New-England. Dr. Johnson having settled at Stratford among a nest of zealots, and not being assassinated, other dissenting ministers were induced to join themselves to the Church of England, among whom were Mr. Beach and Mr. Pen-

[1] The episcopal church in Stratford is the oldest of that denomination in the State. But episcopacy made very little progress in Connecticut, until after the declaration of Rector Cutler, Mr. Johnson, Mr. Whitemore, and Mr. Brown, for episcopacy, in 1722. Numbers of Mr. Johnson's and Mr. Whitemore's hearers professed episcopacy with them, and set up the worship of God, according to the manner of the Church of England, in the West and North-Haven. Mr. (afterward Dr.) Johnson was a gentleman distinguished for literature, of popular talents and engaging manners. In 1724, after receiving episcopal ordination in England, he returned to Stratford, and, under his ministry to that and the neighboring churches of that denomination, they were increased.—ED. NOTE.

derson. These gentlemen could not be wheedled off by the Assembly and Consociation; they persevered, and obtained names among the Literate that will never be forgotten.

The four remaining towns of Fairfield County, viz. *Newtown, Reading, Danbury,* and *Ridgfield,* lie behind the towns on the sea. I shall describe the last of them, which is *Danbury.* It has much the appearance of Croydon, and forms five parishes, one of which is episcopal, and another Sandemanian; a third is called Bastard Sandemanian, because the minister refused to put away his wife, who is a second wife. The town was the residence, and is now the tomb, of the learned and ingenious Rev. Mr. Sandeman, well known to the literary world. He was the fairest and most candid Calvinist that ever wrote in the English language, allowing the natural consequences of all his propositions. He taught that a bishop must be the husband of one wife—that is, he must be married before he was ordained—and, if he lost his wife, he could not marry a second; that a bishop might dress with ruffles, a red coat, and sword; that all converted brothers and sisters, at their coming into the Church, ought to salute with an holy kiss; that all true christians would obey their earthly king: for which tenets, especially the last, the *Sober Dissenters* of Connecticut held him to be a heretic.

It is strikingly remarkable, that near one-half of the people of the Dominion of Newhaven are episcopalians, though it was first settled by the most violent of puritans, who claimed so much liberty to themselves that they left none for others. The General Assembly computed that the Church of England professors amounted to one-third of the whole colony in 1770. Hence has arisen a question, how it came to pass that the Church of England increased rapidly in Connecticut, and but slowly in Massachusets-Bay and Rhode-Island? The reason appears obvious to me. It is easier to turn fanatical farmers from their bigotry than to convert fanatical merchants, smugglers, and fishermen. Pride and gain prevent the two first, and ignorance the last, from "worshipping the Lord in the beauty of holiness." The General Assembly of Rhode-Island never supported any religion; nay, lest religion should chance to prevail, they made a law that every one might do what was right in his own eyes, with this proviso, that no one should be holden to pay a note, bond, or vote, made or given to support the Gospel. Thus barbarism, inhumanity, and infidelity, must have overrun the colony, had not its good situation for trade invited Europeans to settle therein. As to the people of Massachusets-Bay, they, indeed, had the highest pretensions to religion; but then it was so impregnated with chicane, mercantile policy, and insincerity, that infidelity got the better of fanaticism, and religion was secretly looked upon as a trick of State. Connecticut was settled by a people who preferred the arts and sciences to the amusements which rendered Europe polite; whence it has happened that their boys and girls are at once amused and improved in reading, writing, and cyphering, every winter's night, whilst those in the neighbouring colonies polish themselves at cards, balls, and masquerades.

In Connecticut, zeal, though erroneous, is sincere; each sect believes religion to be a substantial good; and fanaticism and prejudice have turned it into superstition, which is stronger than reason or the law of humanity. Thus it was very observable, that when any persons conform to the Church of England, they leave neither their superstition nor zeal at the meetings; they retrench only fanaticism and cruelty, put on bowels of mercy, and pity those in error. It should be added, that every town in the colony is by law obliged to support a grammar school, and every parish an English school. From experience, therefore, I judge that superstition with knowledge and sincerity is more favourable to religion than superstition with ignorance and insincerity; and that it was for this reason the Church thrives in Connecticut, and exists only in New-England provinces. In further support of my opinion, I shall recite the words of Mr. George Whitefield, in his first tour through America in 1740. He found the people of Connecticut wise in polemical divinity, and told them much learning had made them mad; that he wished to leave them with "sleep on and take your rest in the "Bible, in Baxter, Gouge, and Bunyan, without the "knowledge of Bishops' books."

Persons who supposed Churchmen in Connecticut possessed of less zeal and sincerity than the various sects among the dissenters, are under a mistake; for they have voluntarily preferred the Church under every human discouragement, and suffered persecution rather than persecute. Conducting themselves upon this truly christian though impolitic principle, they have, in the space of sixty years, humanized above sixty thousand puritans, who had ever been hating and persecuting one another; and though the General Assembly and Consociation are alarmed at the progress of christian moderation, yet many individuals among them, perceiving that persecution declines wherever the Church prevails, bless God for its growth; whilst the rest, more zealous for dominion and the politics of their ancestors the regicides than for the gospel of peace and love, compass sea and land to export and diffuse that intolerant spirit which overthrew the Eastern Church and has cursed the Western. For this purpose they have sent New-England ministers as missionaries to the southern colonies, to rouse them out of their religious and political ignorance; and, what is very astonishing, they succeeded best with the episcopal clergy, whose immorality, vanity, or love of self-government, or some less valuable principle, induced them to join the dissenters of New-England, against an American bishop, from a pure intention, they said, of preserving the Church of England in America. If their reward be not pointed out in the fable of the Fox and Crane, they will be more fortunate than most men. Other missionaries were dispersed among the Six Nations of Indians, who were under the care of the clergy and schoolmasters of the Society for the Propagation of the Gospel. There, for a time, wonders were effected; the Indians were made drunk with zeal. But when their fanaticism was abated, they cursed the protestant religion, and ordered the ministers of all denominations to depart out of their country in a fixed time, on pain of death. Another band of saints went to Nova-Scotia to convert the unconverted, under the clergy appointed by the Bishop of London; among whom, however, meeting with little encouragement, they shook off the dust of their feet against them, and returned home.

These peregrinations, the world was taught to believe, were undertaken solely to advance the interests of religion; but righteousness and peace have not yet kissed each other in New-England; and, besides, the pious pretences of the *Sober Dissenters* ill accord with their bitter revilings of the Society for the Propagation of the Gospel, for sending clergymen to promote the spiritual good of the Churchmen among them.

It is worthy of especial notice, that, among all the episcopal clergy settled in Connecticut, only one of them has been accused, even by their enemies, of a scandalous life, or of any violation of moral law. They have exercised more patience, resignation, and self-denial, under their various trials, fatigues, and oppressions, than can be paralleled elsewhere in the present century. The countenance of the Society for the Propagation of the Gospel in Foreign Parts, and an allowance of 650*l.* per annum between eighteen of them, have proved the means of averting from the professors of the Church of England that rigour which has constantly marked the conduct of the General Assembly and Consociation towards Anabaptists, Quakers, &c. &c. Had the bishops shewn as much concern for the welfare of the Church of England in America as the Society have done, they would have prevented many reproaches being cast upon them by the dissenters as hireling shepherds, and have secured the affections of the American clergy in every province to themselves, to the King, and the British Government. If the religion of the Church of England ought to have been tolerated and supported in America, (which, considering the lukewarmness of the bishops in general, even since the

Restoration of Charles II., seems to have been a dubious point,) policy and justice long ago should have induced the King and Parliament of Great Britain to have sent bishops to America, that Churchmen at least might have been upon an equal footing with dissenters. Against American bishops I have never heard of any objections, either from the dissenters or the episcopal clergy south of the Delaware River, so powerful as the following:

"That the Church of England increases in America, "without bishops, faster than it does in England, where "are bishops to spare." If the dissenters in America err not in advancing, as a fact, that in 1715 the Church of England, under the bishops, had been upon the decline, and the protestant dissenters upon the increase, in England, it may be but natural to suppose that the dissenters in America wish to have the English bishops resident there, and the dissenters in England to retain them, as they appear to be so beneficial towards the growth of the dissenting interests here; and so the dissenters in both countries disputing about the residence of the bishops merely because the absence of them is disadvantageous to the one, and their presence advantageous to the other, would it not be the best way of strengthening the interest of both those parties, and weakening that of the Church of England, to retain half the bishops in England and send the other half to America? Against this plan, surely, no dissenter could object; it will neither add to the national expense nor to the disadvantage of England or America, since it promises to be equally serviceable to the protestant dissenting interest on both sides the Atlantic and will reconcile a difference between the protestant dissenters, that has been supposen in New-England to be the reason of bishops not being sent to about one million episcopalians in America, who are left like sheep in a wilderness without a shepherd, to the great danger of the protestant dissenting religion in those parts. Nor can it be apprehended that this plan of dividing the bishops will meet with the disapprobation of the episcopalians, except a few licentious clergymen in the American southern colonies, who dread their lordships' sober advice and coercive power.

Of all the wonders of the English Church, the greatest is that the rulers of it should hold episcopacy to be an institution of Christ, and that the Gospel should be spread among all nations, and, at the same time, should refuse the American Churchmen a bishop, and the fanatics and heathen all opportunities of enjoying the Gospel dispensation in the purity and lustre with which it shines in the Mother Country. If bishops are necessary, let America have them; if they are not necessary, let them be extirpated from the face of the earth; for no one can be an advocate for their existence merely for the support of pomp, pride, and insolence, either in England or America.

The English and Dutch have always kept their colonies under a state of religious persecution, while the French and Spanish have acted with generosity in that respect towards theirs. The Dutch presbyterians in New-York were held in subordination to the Classis of Amsterdam, till, a few years since, they discovered that subjection to be anti-constitutional and oppressive; upon which a majority of the ministers in their cœtus erected a classis for the ordination of ministers and the government of their churches, in defiance of the ecclesiastical judicatory of Amsterdam. Mr. Smith, in his history of that province, p. 252, justifies the schism upon the following ground: "The expense," says he, " attending the ordination of their candidates in Hol- " land, and the reference of their disputes to the Classis " of Amsterdam, is very considerable; and with what " consequences the interruption of their correspondence " with the European Dutch would be attended, in case " of war, well deserves their consideration." Nevertheless, Mr. Smith agrees with his protestant dissenting neighbours, that the American episcopalians suffered no hardship in being obliged to incur the same expense in crossing the Atlantic for ordination. If the Dutch are justifiable in their schism, I cannot perceive why the American episcopalians might not be justified in a like schism from the bishops of London. Had the episcopalians as little aversion to schism as the protestant dissenters, the clergy north of the Delaware would, in 1765, have got rid of their regard of an English, and accepted of a Greek bishop, whom they could have supported for half the expense their candidates were at in going to England for ordination. But they were said by some to be conscientious men, while others said they were Issachar's sons couching down beneath their burthens.

To proceed in my description of the country:

Connecticut is situated between 41 and 42 degrees of north latitude, and between 72 and 73 degrees 50 minutes west longitude from London. Notwithstanding, from this latitude, New-London lies 600 miles nearer the line than the capital of England, the winter sets in there a month before it does here, and not only continues longer, but is more severe. This extraordinary coldness is said by naturalists to arise from the vast frozen lakes and rivers, and mountains eternally covered with snow, throughout the northernmost parts of America. The mountains may have their share in producing this effect; but I am apt to think the lakes and rivers have a contrary influence. If I ask why lands bordering on them are three weeks earlier in their productions than lands ten miles distant, it will readily be imputed to the warmth of the air, occasioned by the reflection of the sun's rays from the water. On the same principle, I argue that the rays of the sun, multiplied and reflected by ice also, will render the air warmer. But it may be further said, that the cause is perhaps to be ascribed to the soil being more sandy and loose near a lake or river, and, therefore, naturally warmer than that which is remote and not sandy. I reply, that there are loose, sandy plains, twenty miles off from any lake or river, three weeks later in their products, and very perceptibly colder, than lands upon them. It would be to no purpose to urge that the damps and fogs from unfrozen lakes, rivers, &c. &c. affect the distant but not the adjacent country; because I apprehend there are no unfrozen lakes and rivers in the north of America in winter. Besides, if there were, the mists arising from them would naturally be intercepted by the first mountains or forests they approached. But I pretend to little philosophical knowledge in these matters; I write from experience, and can thence, moreover, assert that mountains with snow upon them are not so cold as they would be without it; and that mountains covered with trees are the coldest of all places, but without trees are not so cold as forests or plains. I am clearly of opinion, therefore, that not the lakes or rivers, but the infinite quantity of timber in the immense regions of North-America, whether upon mountains or not, is the grand cause of the coldness of the winters in Connecticut. I will add, moreover, in support of my argument, that beasts, in the coldest weather, are observed to quit the woods and woody mountains for lakes, rivers, and cultivated open country; and that Connecticut, having lost most of its timber, is by no means so intensely cold in winter as it was forty years ago, and as Susquehanna is at present, a wilderness in the same latitude. The snow and ice commonly cover the country, without rains, from Christmas to March; then rains, attended with boisterous winds from the north and east, melt the snow, which converting brooks into rivers and rivers into seas, in four or five days the ice is rent from its groaning banks in such mighty sheets as it shakes the earth for twenty miles. Nature being thus in convulsions, the winds turn her fit into madness, by driving ice upon ice, whose thunders cease not till the ocean swallows up the whole.

It is but natural to suppose that the summers in Connecticut are much hotter than those in England; nevertheless, from the clearness and serenity of the sky, the climate is healthy both to natives and foreigners of all nations. Connecticut is a hospital for invalids of the Islands and southern provinces; but, in general, they no sooner amend their own constitution, than the pestilence, which rages in that province, drives them to Rhode-Island or New-York, where fanaticism is lost in irreligion.

The people of Connecticut reckon time almost five hours later than the English. The longest day consists of fifteen hours, the shortest of nine. The brightness of the sun, moon, and stars, together with the reverberated rays on ice, snow, water, trees, mountains, pebbles, and flat stones, dazzle and weaken the eyes of the New-Englanders to such a degree, that, in general, they are obliged to use glasses before they are fifty years of age. For the most part, also, they have bad teeth, which has been ascribed to the extreme heats and colds of summer and winter; but, as the Indians and negroes in the same climate have remarkably good teeth, it may be said, with great reason, that the many indulgences of the one, and the temperance of the other, and not the heats and colds, are the causes of good and bad teeth.

Soil and Produce.--The soil is various in different parts of the province: in some black, in others brown, and elsewhere red, but all rich. Some plains are sandy and of a whitish colour, and they produce rye, beans, and Indian-corn. The meadows and lowlands are excellent pasturage, and yield great crops of hay. The hills and uplands have a rich, deep soil, but are subject to droughts in July and August, which in many places are relieved by water drawn from rivers, ponds, and brooks, in troughs and ditches. The crops of European grain are always good, when the snow, which in general is the only manure, covers the earth from December to March. One acre generally yields from twenty to thirty bushels of wheat; of Indian-corn, from forty to sixty bushels on even land, and from thirty to forty on hilly land; but it is to be observed, that one bushel of it raised on hilly land weighs thirteen pounds more than a bushel raised on river land. All European grains flourish here, and the grass is as thick, and much longer than in England. Maize, or Indian-corn, is planted in hillocks three feet apart, five kernels and two pumpkin-seeds in a hillock, and between the hills are planted ten beans in a hillock; so that, if the season prove favourable, the beans and the pumpkins are worth as much as the corn. If from an acre the crop of corn be twenty bushels, add the beans and pumpkins, and it will be equal to sixty bushels; so, if there be sixty bushels of corn, a proportionate growth of beans and pumpkins will render the product equal to one hundred and eighty bushels. One man plants an acre in a day; in three days he hoes the same three times; and six days more suffice for plowing and gathering the crop. For these ten days' work the price is thirty shillings; and, allowing ten shillings for the use of the land, the whole expense is two pounds, and no more, while the corn is worth two shillings a bushel. The gain is seldom less than 300, and often 600 per cent. It is thus that the poor man becomes rich in a few years, if prudent and industrious.

The limits of Connecticut are reckoned to comprise 5,000,000 acres, half of which is supposed to be swallowed up in rivers, ponds, creeks, and roads. The inhabitants are estimated at 200,000, so that there remains but twelve and a half acres for each individual. Let it now be considered that the people buy no provisions from other provinces, but, on the contrary, export full as much as they consume, and it will appear that each person has in fact only six and a quarter acres for his own support, two of which must be set apart for the growth of wood, the only fuel of the colony. Should I, then, not be justified in saying that Connecticut is as good and flourishing land as any part of Great Britain?

The face of the country resembles Devonshire, Gloucestershire, Surrey, and Kent. The farmers divide their lands into four, five, and ten acres, with stone walls or post and rails. The roads from north to south are generally level and good; from east to west hilly, and bad for carriages. The various fruits are in greater perfection than in England. The peach and apple are more luscious, beautiful, and large; 1000 peaches are produced from one tree; five or six barrels of cider from one apple tree. Cider is the common drink at table. The inhabitants have a method of purifying cider by frost and separating the watery part from the spirit, which, being secured in proper vessels, and colored by Indian-corn, becomes in three months so much like Madeira wine, that Europeans drink it without perceiving the difference. They make peachy and perry, grape, cherry, and currant wines, and good beer of pumpkin, molasses, bran of wheat, spruce, and malt. The spruce is the leaves and limbs of the fir tree; their malt is made of maize, barley, oats, rye, chets, and wheat. The pumpkin, or pompion, is one of the greatest blessings, and held very sacred in New-England. It is a native of America. From one seed often grow forty pumpkins, each weighing from forty to sixty pounds, and, when ripe, of the colour of a marigold.

Each pumpkin contains about 500 seeds, which, being boiled to a jelly, is the Indian infallible cure for the strangury. Of its meat are made beer, bread, custards, sauce, molasses, vinegar, and, on thanksgiving days, pies, as a substitute for what the Blue Laws brand as antichristian minced pies. Its skin, or shell, serves as a cap to cut the hair by, (as already mentioned,) and very useful lanthorns. There are no trees, grain, or fruits, growing in England but what will grow in Connecticut. The English oak has been thought much superior to the American. Whatever policy may be in this opinion, I will venture to say there is no truth in it in respect to the white oak in Connecticut, which is tough, close, hard, and elastic as the whalebone dried. The red, black, and chestnut oak are, indeed, much inferior to the white oak. The ash, elm, beech, chestnut, walnut, hazel, sassafras, sumach, maple, and butternut, are the chief timber trees of this province, and grow to an amazing bulk. The last is a native of America, and takes its name from a nut it produces, of the shape and size of a pullet's egg, which contains a meat much larger than an English walnut, in taste like fresh butter; it also makes an excellent pickle. The butternut furnishes fine but tender boards; and its bark dyes black, and cures cutaneous disorders. In February this tree yields a sap, of which are made sugar, molasses, and vinegar. The upland maple also affords a sap equally good, and both saps make a pleasant beverage without boiling, and the best punch ever drank in Connecticut.

Here are many iron mines, nay, mountains of iron ore; and, if they had been attended to with the same diligence as the farms, they would have supplied Great

Britain with iron, to the great prejudice of Sweden and other European nations. For this commercial loss the inhabitants are indebted to their own quarrels, jealousy, and religious feuds, together with the intrigues of their neighbours. Some pig and bar iron they send, out of pure spite or folly, to New-York and Boston, to be shipped for England by the merchants there, who always pay so much less for it as the duty on Swedish iron amounts to, so that Connecticut allows a duty to these merchants which they do not pay themselves.

English, Barbary, and Dutch horses abound in this province; they are not so heavy, but more mettlesome and hardy than in England. Here are more sheep than in any two colonies in America; their wool also is better than that of the sheep in any of the other colonies, yet not so fine and good as the English. A common sheep weighs sixty pounds, and sells for a dollar, or 4s. 6d. The horned cattle are not so large as the English; yet there have been a few instances of oxen six years old weighing 1900 pounds each. The fat hogs here excel any in England; many weigh five or six hundred pounds. Connecticut pork is far superior to any other.

There are only two small parks of deer in Connecticut, but plenty of rabbits, hares, grey, black, striped and red squirrels, otters, minks, raccoons, weasels, foxes, whapperknockers, woodchucks, cubas, and skunks. The following description of the four last-mentioned animals may be new to the reader:

The whapperknocker is somewhat larger than a weasel, and of a beautiful brown colour. He lives in the woods on worms and birds; is so wild that no one can tame him, and, as he never quits his harbour in the daytime, is only to be taken by traps in the night. Of the skins of these animals—which are covered with an exceedingly fine fur—are made muffs, at the price of thirty or forty guineas apiece; so that it is not without reason the ladies pride themselves on the possession of this small appurtenance of female habiliment.

The woodchuck, erroneously called the badger by some persons, is of the size of a large raccoon, in form resembles a Guinea pig, and, when eating, makes a noise like a hog, whence he is named woodchuck, or chuck of wood. His legs are short, but his claws sharp, teeth strong, and courage great on occasions of self-defence. He burrows in the earth, feeds on clover and pumpkin during summer, and sleeps all the winter. His flesh is good to eat, and his skin makes excellent leather.

The cuba I suppose to be peculiar to New-England. The male is of the size of a large cat; has four long tushes sharp as a razor; he is very active in defending himself, and, if he has the first blow, will spoil a dog before he yields. His lady is peaceable and harmless, and depends for protection on her spouse, and, as he has more courage than prudence, always attends him to moderate his temper. She sees danger, and he fears it not. She chatters at him while he is preparing for battle, and, if she thinks the danger is too great, she runs to him and clings about his neck, screaming her extreme distress; his wrath abates, and by her advice they fly to their caves. In like manner, when he is chained, and irritated into the greatest rage by an impertinent dog, his lady, who is never chained, will fly about his neck and kiss him, and in half a minute restore him to calmness. He is very tender of his family, and never forsakes them till death dissolves their union. What further shows the magnanimity of this little animal, he never manifests the least anger towards his lady, though I have often seen her extremely loquacious, and, as I guessed, impertinent to him. How happy would the rational part of the creation become if they would follow the example of these irrational beasts! I the more readily suppose the cuba to be peculiar to New-England, not only from my never having yet seen the creature described, but also on account of its perverse observance of carnival and neglect of *carême*.

The skunk is also peculiar to America, and very different from the pole-cat, which he is sometimes called. He is black, striped with white, and of the size of a small raccoon, with a sharp nose. He burrows in the earth like a fox, feeds like a fox on fowls and eggs, and has strong teeth and claws like a fox. He has long hair, and thick, good fur; is the beauty of the wilderness; walks slowly, and cannot run as fast as a man; he is not wild, but very familiar with every creature. His tail, which is shaggy and about one foot in length, he turns over his back at pleasure, to make himself appear larger and higher than he really is. When his tail is thus lying on his back he is prepared for war, and generally conquers every enemy that lives by air, for on this lies his only weapon: about one inch from his body or rump, in a small bladder or bag, which is full of essence, whose tint is of the brightest yellow, and odour somewhat like the smell of garlic, but far more exquisite and piercing than any volatile spirit known to chemists. One drop will scent a house to such a degree that musk, with the help of brimstone and tar burnt, will not expel it in six months. The bladder in which this essence lies is worked by the animal like an engine, pump, or squirt; and when the creature is assaulted, he turns his head from his enemy and discharges from his tail the essence, which fills the neighbouring air with a mist that destroys the possibility of living in it. I have seen a large house-dog, by one discharge of the skunk, retire with shame and sickness; and, at another time, a bullock bellowing as if a dog had held him by the nose. Were it not for man, no creature could kill this animal, which, instead of the lion, ought to be crowned king of animals, as well on account of his virtues and complaisance as his courage. He knows his forte; he fears nothing, he conquers all; yet he is civil to all, and never gives, as he will not take, offence. His virtues are many. The wood of calambac, which cures fainting-fits and strokes of the palsy, and is worth its weight in gold, is far less valuable than the abovementioned essence of this animal. The bag is extracted whole from the tail, and the essence preserved in glass; nothing else will confine it. One drop sufficiently impregnates a quart of spring water, and half a gill of water thus impregnated is a dose. It cures hiccups, asthmatic, hysteric, paralytic, and hectic disorders, and the odour prevents faintness. The flesh of this animal is excellent food, and its oil cures sprains and contractions of the sinews.

The feathered tribe in Connecticut are the turkey, geese, ducks, and all kinds of barn-door poultry; innumerable flocks of pigeons, which fly to the south in the autumn; cormorants of all sizes; hawks, owls, ravens, and crows; partridges, quails, heath-hen, blackbirds, snipes, larks, humilitys, whippoorwills, dew-minks, robins, wrens, swallows, sparrows, the flax, crimson, white, and blue birds, &c. &c.; to which I may add the humming-bird, though it might wantonly be styled the empress of the honey-bees, partaking with them of the pink, tulip, rose, daisy, and other aromatics.

The partridges in New-England are nearly as large as a Dorking fowl, the quail as an English partridge, and the robin twice as big as those in England. The dew-mink, so named from its articulating those syllables, is black and white, and the size of an English robin. Its flesh is delicious. The humility is so called because it speaks the word humility, and seldom mounts high in the air. Its legs are long enough to enable it to outrun a dog for a little way; its wings long and narrow; body maigre and of the size of a blackbird's; plumage variegated with white, black, blue, and red. It lives on tadpoles, spawn, and worms; has an eye more piercing than the falcon, and the swiftness of an eagle; hence it can never be shot, for it sees the sparks of fire even before it enkindles the powder, and by the extreme rapidity of its flight gets out of reach in an instant. It is never known to light upon a tree, but is always seen upon the ground or wing. These birds appear in New-England in summer only; what becomes of them afterwards is not discovered. They are caught in snares, but can never be tamed.

The whippoorwill has so named itself by its nocturnal songs. It is also called the Pope, by reason of its darting with great swiftness from the clouds to the ground and bawling out Pope, which alarms young people and the fanatics very much, especially as they know it to be an ominous bird. However, it has hitherto proved friendly, always giving travellers and others notice of an approaching storm by saluting them every minute by Pope! pope! It flies only a little before sunset, unless for this purpose of giving notice of a storm. It never deceives the people with false news. If the tempest is to continue long, the augurs appear in flocks, and nothing can be heard but Pope! pope! The whippoorwill is about the size of a cuckoo, has a short beak, long and narrow wings, a large head, and mouth enormous, yet is not a bird of prey. Under its throat is a pocket, which it fills with air at pleasure, whereby it sounds forth the fatal word Pope in the day, and Whip-her-I-will in the night. The superstitious inhabitants would have exorcised this harmless bird long ago, as an emissary from Rome and an enemy to the American Vine, had they not found out that it frequents New-England only in the summer, and prefers the wilderness to a palace. Nevertheless, many cannot but believe it a spy from some foreign court, an agent of antichrist, a lover of persecution, and an enemy of protestants, because it sings of whipping, and of the Pope, which they think portends misery and a change of religion.

The principal insects are the hornet, bull-fly, glowbug, humble-bee, and black and yellow wasp.

The bull-fly is armed with a coat of mail, which it can move from one place to another, as sliders to a window are moved. Its body is about an inch long, and its horns half an inch, very sharp and strong. It has six feet, with claws as sharp as needles, and runs fast. In sucking the blood or juice of its prey, the creature holds the same in its claws; otherwise the prey is carried between its horns.

The glow-bug both crawls and flies, and is about half an inch long. These insects fly, in the summer evenings, nearly seven feet from the ground, in such multitudes that they afford sufficient light for the people to walk by. The brightness, however, is interrupted by twinklings; but they are instantaneous and short as those of the eye, so that darkness no sooner takes place than it vanishes.

The humble-bee is almost as large as the humming-bird, but cannot fly near so fast. It builds its nest in the ground, where it makes a honey-comb of the size of a man's hand, and fills it with bees'-bread, wax, and honey, excelling that of the honey-bee in taste. Two or three begun, and having shortly multiplied to about forty, the young ones leave home as soon as they can fly, to begin new settlements. These bees are wrongly named: they are warriors, and only want a quantity of poison to be more fatal than rattle-snakes.

The honey-bees can sting but once, while the humble-bee will sting a thousand times. Their body is black and white; wings of a Doric colour; sight piercing, hearing quick, and temper cruel.

Among the reptiles of Connecticut are the black, the water, milk, and streaked snakes, all harmless. The belled or rattle-snakes are large, and will gorge a common cat. They are seldom seen from their rocky dens. Their bite is mortal if not speedily cured; yet they are generous, and without guile; before they bite they rattle their bells three or four times, but after that their motion is swift and stroke sure. The Indians discovered and informed the English of a weed, common in the country, which, mixed with spittle, will extract the poison.

The toads and frogs are plenty in the spring of the year. The tree-frogs, whippoorwills, and whooping owls, serenade the inhabitants every night with music far excelling the harmony of the trumpet, drum, and jews-harp.

The tree-frog cannot be called an insect, a reptile, or one of the winged host; he has four legs, the two foremost short, with claws as sharp as those of a squirrel; the hind-legs five inches long, and folding by three joints. His body is about as big as the first joint of a man's thumb. Under his throat is a wind-bag, which assists him in singing the word I-sa-ac all the night. When it rains, and is very dark, he sings the loudest. His voice is not so pleasing as that of the nightingale; but this would be a venial imperfection, if he would but keep silence on Saturday nights, and not forever prefer I-sa-ac to Abraham and Jacob. He has more elasticity in his long legs than any other creature yet known. By this means he will leap five yards up a tree, fastening himself to it by his fore-legs, and in a moment will hop or spring as far from one tree to another. It is from the singing of the tree-frog that the Americans have acquired the name of Little Isaac. Indeed, like a certain part of them, the creature appears very devout, noisy, arbitrary, and phlegmatic, and associates with none but what agree with him in his ways.

The oysters, clams, quauhogs, lobsters, crabs, and fish, are innumerable. The shad, bass, and salmon, more than half support the province. The sturgeon is made no use of. From the number of seines employed to catch the fish passing up to the lakes, one might be led to suppose the whole must be stopped; yet, in six months' time they return to the sea with such multitudes of young ones as to fill Connecticut River for many days, and no finite being can number them.

Population and Inhabitants.—Connecticut, in proportion to its extent, exceeds every other colony of English America, as well in the abundance of people as in cultivation of soil. The number of the first settlers at Saybrook, in 1634, was 200; in 1636, at Hertford, 106; in 1637, at Newhaven, 157; in all, 463. In 1670 the residents of these three settlements amounted to 15,000, of whom 2000 were men capable of bearing arms; the rest old men, women, and children. In 1680 the residents were 20,000; in 1770, 200,000. Hence it appears that the people of Connecticut did, during the 90 years, double their number ten times over. Should the 200,000 which existed in Connecticut in 1770 double their number in the same manner for the ensuing 90 years, the province will, in the year 1860, contain 2,000,000; and if the fighting men should then be in the same proportion to the rest of the inhabitants as they were in 1670, they will amount to no less than 266,000. I see no reason in Nature why it may not be so.

Since 1670, emigration from Europe, or elsewhere, to Connecticut, has been trifling, in comparison to the emigration from Connecticut to New-Jersey, Newhampshire, Massachusets-Bay, Nova-Scotia, &c.

Manufactures.—The inhabitants manufacture coarse and fine flannels, linen, cotton and woollen cloths, woollen stockings, mittens, and gloves, for their own use; they spin much cotton and flax, and make common and the best kind of beaver hats. Ship-building is a great branch of business in Connecticut, which is carried on much cheaper than in Europe, by means of saw-mills worked by water. The planks are cut by a gang of ten or twelve saws, more or less, as occasion requires, while the carriage is backed but once. Great part of the ship-timber is also cut by water. Anchor-making is done by water and trip-hammers, without much fatigue to the workmen. Distilling and paper-making increase every year. Here are many rope-walks, which want neither hemp nor flax; and formerly here were rolling and slitting works, but they have been suppressed by an act of Parliament, to the ruin of many families.

Commerce.—The exports of Connecticut consist chiefly of all sorts of provisions, pig and bar iron, pot and pearl ashes, staves, lumber, boards, iron pots and kettles, anchors, planks, hoops, shingles, live cattle, horses, &c. &c. To what amount these articles are annually exported, may be judged from the following very low estimate:

Pork	93,750*l.*
Beef	100,000
Mutton	5,000
Horses	40,000
Wheat	340,000
Butter, cheese, rye, oats, onions, tobacco, cider, maize, beans, fowls, eggs, tallow, and hides.	90,000
Ships' anchors, cables, cordage, pig and bar iron, pots, kettles, pot and pearl ashes, boards, and lumber	250,000
	918,750*l.*

besides hay, fish, &c. &c. The salmon, large and small, are exported both pickled and dried.

In the above statement of exports I have allowed only for horses bred in the colony, and not for those brought for exportation from Canada and other northern parts, which are very numerous. The calculation of the wheat, the common price of which is three shillings sterling per bushel, is founded upon the allowed circumstance of the exportation being equal to the consumption, viz. 2,600,000 bushels among 200,000 persons, according to the acknowledged necessary portion of thirteen bushels to one person. The pork is estimated according to the reputed number of houses in the province, viz. 30,000, allowing one and a quarter barrels for each house, at 2*l*. 10*s*. per barrel.

The imports in 1680, when the number of inhabitants was 20,000, amounted to 10,000*l*., i. e. at the rate of 10*s*. for each individual. Supposing the increase of imports only to keep pace with that of the people, they would, in 1770, when the province contained 200,000 souls, amount to 100,000*l*.; but I believe that to be not above one-quarter of their value.

Boston, New-York, and Newport, have the greatest share of the exports of Connecticut, and pay for them in English or Dutch goods at cent. per cent. profit to themselves, upon a moderate computation. What few of them are sent from the colony to the West Indies, are paid for honourably in rum, molasses, sugar, salt, brandy, cotton, and money.

Consequences very prejudicial attend the commerce of Connecticut, thus principally carried on through the medium of the neighbouring colonies. I will here point out one material instance: Connecticut pork, a considerable article of exportation, excels all others in America, and fetches a halfpenny per pound more. Of this difference in the price the merchants in New-York, Boston, &c. have taken care to avail themselves, by mixing their own inferior pork with that of Connecticut, and then selling the whole at the full price of the latter. This fair dealing was managed thus: The pork of Connecticut was packed up in barrels, each of which, according to statute regulations, must weigh 220 lbs. and contain not more than six legs and three half heads. The packer is to mark the barrel before it is shipped, and is liable to a heavy punishment if there should be found four half heads and seven legs in the barrel when it is delivered for exportation. But of large pork, two legs and half a head will be a sufficient proportion of those parts in a barrel. This gives the New-York and Bostonian merchants an opportunity of taking out the best part of the Connecticut pork, and substituting in its place an equal weight of their own, whereby it often happens that four legs and two half heads are found in a barrel of reputed Connecticut pork. Though it then remains a barrel according to the statute, it cannot but be supposed that the practice must greatly hurt the credit of Connecticut pork with all who are not apprised that it passes through the renounded provinces of Massachusets-Bay and New-York.

 The people of Connecticut have long been sensible of the many great impositions and disadvantages which beset their commercial system; yet, though sufficient power is in their own hands, they have no inclination or resolution to attempt a reformation of it. The reason is, the mutual animosities and rancour subsisting between the dominions of New-London, Hertford, and Newhaven, each of which prefers the general ruin of the province to a coalition upon any terms short of conquest. The seeds of this discord were thus sown by these two insidious neighbours. The port of New-London is by far the best in the province, and extremely well calculated for its capital and grand commercial emporium; and about fifty years since, a number of merchants there began to export and import goods, seemingly to the satisfaction of the whole colony, but to the great displeasure and chagrin of those of New-York and Boston, whom it threatened with ruin. Something was necessary to be done. The poor Bostonians, according to custom, privately sent for their faithful allies at Hertford, to infuse into them an idea that their town ought to be the capital, and not New-London, which belonged to the Dominion of Sassacus, who had murdered so many christians; adding that, if they would engage in such an attempt in favour of Hertford, the Boston merchants would supply them with goods cheaper than they could buy them at New-London. The good people at Hertford, forgetting their river was frozen for five months in the year, remembering how they had obtained their Charter, hating Sassacus, and loving self, immediately gave in to the designing Bostonians' suggestions, and refused to receive any more goods from New-London. The friendly Mynheers of New-York played off a similar trick upon Newhaven, and promised to support that town as the capital of the colony. The plots succeeded. Contentions and quarrels arose among the three parties, the effects of which remain to this day. The merchants of New-London were obliged to quit Connecticut, and the trade of the province was chiefly divided between New-York and Boston, at cent. per cent. disadvantage to an ill-natured colony, and at the same time advantage to its cunning neighbours. When party spirit yields to self-interest, New-London will again become the emporium of Connecticut, where merchants will settle and import goods from foreign countries at 35*l.* per cent. extra profit to the consumers, and 15*l.* per cent. extra profit to themselves, and withal save as much in the exports from Connecticut, by taking the full price and bounty of its goods at foreign markets, instead of yielding the same to the people of New-York and Boston, who have too long kept 200,000 as negroes on their own farms, to support twice 20,000 artful citizens. Thus has Connecticut, by contention and folly, impoverished and kept in obscurity the most fruitful colony in America, to support the fame and grandeur of Boston and New-York among the trading nations of Europe. When I view the less fertile soil of Boston, the conscience of merchants, the pride of the pretended Gospel ministers, the blindness of bigotry, and the mercantile ignorance of farmers, I forgive Boston, New-York, and Rhode-Island, but condemn Connecticut. I will leave a legacy to the people of my native country, which possibly may heal their divisions, and render them partial to their own province, as the Bostonians are to theirs. It consists of two lines :

"But if men knaves and fools will be,
"They'll be ass-ridden by all three."

Revenue and Expenditure.—In 1680 the whole corporation were estimated to be worth 120,000*l.* They had 30 small vessels, 26 churches, and, as above mentioned, 20,000 inhabitants. If their value had increased only in proportion with the inhabitants, who, as I have said, amounted to 200,000 in 1770, the corporation would then have been worth no more than 1,200,000*l.*, a sum not equal to 10*s.* per acre, though in a great measure cultivated, and surrounded with stone walls which alone cost 10*s.* by the rod; but in that year, viz. 1770, land sold in Connecticut from 4*l.* to 50*l.* per acre; their vessels, also, had increased to about 1200, and the churches—least in proportion—to about 300. The true method, therefore, of forming the valuation of Connecticut in 1770, is not by calculating upon this State in 1680, but by estimating the number of its acres, appreciating them by purchases then made, and adding a due allowance for the stock, &c. Now, Connecticut has been reputed to contain 2,500,000 solid acres, which, at the very moderate price of 8*l.* each, are worth 20,000,000*l.* sterling; and 14,000,000*l.* being added as a reasonable allowance for stock, shipping, &c. the whole valuation of Connecticut would amount to 34,000,000*l.* The annual income, supposing the 2,500,000 acres and stock rented at 10*s.* per acre, one with another, would be 1,250,000*l.* A list of rateables, called the General List, is the foundation upon which the revenue is raised in Connecticut, being the valuation of a man's property by the year. It is formed in the following manner :

One acre of land, per annum	0*l.*	10*s.*
One horse	3	00
One house	3	00
One ox	3	00
One swine	1	00
One cow	3	00
One two-year-old heifer	2	00
One yearling do.	1	00
One poll or male, between 16 and 60 years	18	00
One lawyer for his faculty	20	00
One vessel of 100 tons	10	00
	65*l.*	10*s.*

Every person annually gives his list, specifying the property he possesses, to the selectmen, who send the sum total of each town to the General Assembly, when a tax of one shilling, more or less, according to public exigencies, is imposed on each pound.

According to the general list of the colony for 1770, I have underrated its annual worth, which then was fixed at 2,000,000*l.*; for, though that list includes the poll-tax of 18*l.* per head for all males above sixteen and under sixty years of age, the faculty tax, and the tax on shipping, all which may amount to 600,000*l.*, there nevertheless remains a surplus of 150,000*l.* above my calculation. But, supposing a tax of one shilling in the pound (the common colonial assessment) on 1,250,000*l.*, the produce will be 62,500*l.*, exclusive of the poll, faculty, and other taxes. Small, however, as this assessment is, it has never been collected without much difficulty and clamour; yet the people lose, by trading with Boston, New-York, and Newport, in exports and imports, 600,000*l.* annually; and that for nothing but to oblige the traders of those towns, and disoblige one another.

The annual expenditure of the colony is as follows:

Salary of Governor..........................	300*l.*	00*s.*
" Lieutenant-Governor...........	150	00
" Treasurer......................	150	00
" Secretary......................	150	00
" the twelve assistants in Council with the Governor........	800	00
" 146 Representatives...........	2,500	00
" 300 Ministers, 100*l.* each......	30,000	00
Allowance for contingencies.............	28,450	00
Total............................	62,500*l.*	00*s.*

The above-mentioned list of the colony, including the poll-tax, &c. would afford 32,500*l.* more for contingencies.

Religion and Government.—Properly speaking, the Connectitensians have neither, nor ever had; but, in pretence, they excel the whole world, except Boston and Spain. If I could recollect the names of the multifarious religious sects among them, it might afford the reader a pleasant idea of the prolific invention of mankind. I shall mention a few of the most considerable, specifying the number of their congregations:

	CONGREGATIONS.
Episcopalians..................................	73
Scotch presbyterians............................	1
Sandemanians...................................	3
Ditto Bastard...................................	1
Lutherans.......................................	1
Baptists...	6
Seventh-day ditto...............................	1

SECTS PECULIAR TO THE COLONY.

	CONGREGATIONS.
Quakers	4
Davisonians	1
Separatists	40
Rogereens	1
Bowlists	1
Old Lights	80
New Lights	87
	300

An account of some of these sects is to be found in the history of Munster; but the Bowlists, Separatists, and Davisonians are peculiar to the colony. The first allow of neither singing nor prayer; the second permit only the elect to pray; and the third teach universal salvation, and deny the existence of a hell or devils. The presbyterians and episcopalians are held by all to be the enemies of Zion and the American Vine; nay, the former are even worse hated than the Churchmen, because they appear to be dissenters, and are not genuine enemies to episcopacy, but "hold the truth in unright-"eousness." Some travellers have called the fanatical sects of Connecticut by the general name of Legionists, because they are many; and others have called them Pumguntums, Cantums, &c. because they groan and sing with a melancholy voice their prayers, sermons, and hymns. This disgusting tone has utterly excluded oratory from them; and did they not speak the English in greater perfection than any other of the Americans, few strangers would disoblige them with their company. Their various systems are founded upon those of Peters, Hooker, and Davenport, of which I have already spoken; yet the modern teachers have made so many new-fangled refinements in the doctrine and discipline of those patriarchs, and of one another, as render their passions for ecclesiastical innovation and tyranny equally conspicuous. But the whole are enveloped with superstition, which here passes for religion, as much as it does in Spain, France, or among the savages.

I will instance that of an infant, in 1761. Some children were piling sand-heaps in Hertford, when a boy, only four years old, hearing it thunder at a distance, left his companions and ran home to his mother, crying out, "Mother, mother, give me my book, for I heard "God speaking to me!" His mother gave him his book, and he read A, B, C, D, &c.; then gave up his book, saying, "Here, mother, take my book; I must go to my "sand-houses: now I am not afraid of all the thunder "and lightning in the world."

As to their government, we may compare it to the regularity of a mad mob in London, with this exception: the mob acts without law, and the colonists by law. They teach that legal righteousness is not saving grace. Herein they are right; but it appears they believe not their own doctrine, for legal righteousness is their only shield and buckler. In January County Court, at Hertford only, 1768, there were about 3000 suits on the docket; and there are four of these courts in a year, and perhaps never less suits at a court than 2000.

In the course of this work my readers must necessarily have observed, in some degree, the ill effects of the democratical constitution of Connecticut. I would wish them to imagine, for I feel myself unable adequately to describe, the confusion, turbulence, and convulsion arising in a province where not only every civil officer, from the governor to the constables, but also every minister, is appointed as well as paid by the people, and faction and superstition are established. The clergy, lawyers, and merchants or traders, are the three efficient parties which guide the helm of the government. Of these, the most powerful is the clergy, and, when no combinations are formed against them, they may be said to rule the whole province; for they lead the women captive, and the women the men; but when the clergy differ with the lawyers and merchants, the popular tide turns. In like manner, when the clergy and lawyers contend with the merchants, it turns against these; and is the same when the clergy and merchants unite against the lawyers. This fluctuation of power gives a strange appearance to the body politic at large. In Hertford, perhaps, the clergy and merchants are agreed, and prevail; in Weathersfield, the clergy and lawyers; in Middletown, the lawyers and merchants; and so on, again and again, throughout the colony. Thus the General Assembly becomes an assembly of contending factions, whose different interests and pursuits it is generally found necessary mutually to consult in order to produce a sufficient coalition to proceed on the business of the State.— *Vos ipsos pseudo-patres patriæ, veluti in speculo aspicite?*—Sometimes, in quarrels between the merchants and lawyers of a particular parish, the minister is allowed to stand neuter; but, for the most part, he is obliged to declare on the one side or the other; he then, remembering from whence he gets his bread, espouses that which appears to be the strongest, whether it be right or wrong, and his declaration never fails to turn the adverse party.—*En rabies vulgi!*—I must beg leave to refer my readers to their own reflections upon such a system of government as I have here sketched out.

The historians of New-England boast much of the happiness all parties there enjoy in not being subject, as in England, to sacramental test by way of qualification for preferment in the State; on which account, with peculiar propriety, it might be called a free country. The truth is, there never has been occasion for such a test-act. The Assemblies never appointed any, because the magistrates are annually chosen by the people, of whom the far greater part are church members; and this church-membership, in its consequences, destroys all liberty in a communicant, who is necessitated to swear to promote the interests of that church he is a member of, and is duly informed by the minister what that interest is. The minister is the eye of conscience to all freemen in his parish, and tells them that they will perjure themselves if they give their votes to an episcopalian, or any person who is not a member of the Church of the *Sober Dissenters*. Those freemen dare not go counter to the minister's dictate, any more than a true Mussulman dare violate the sacred law of Mahomet. What need, then, is there of a civil test, when a religious test operates much more powerfully, and will ever keep Churchmen, Separatists, Quakers, Baptists, and other denominations from governmental employments in Connecticut, and confine them to the Old and New Lights; whilst the test act in England prevents no dissenter from holding any civil or military commission whatsoever? Upon this subject Mr. Neal has exerted himself in so signal a manner, that he ought to be styled the Champion of New-England. He represents that there were two State factions in New-England: the one out of place he calls spies and malcontents, chiefly because they had no share in the government. He adds, p. 615: "I can assure the world that "religion is no part of the quarrel; for there is no sac-"ramental test for preferment in the State."—Many people in New-England have not been able to assign a reason for Mr. Neal's choosing to hide one truth by telling another, viz. that there was no statute in New-England to oblige a man to receive the sacrament among the *Sober Dissenters* as a qualification for civil office. This assertion is really true; and when Mr. Neal speaks a truth, he, above all men, ought to have credit for it. But Mr. Neal well knew it to be the truth, also, that no man could be chosen a corporal in the train-band unless he was a member of the Church of the *Sober Dissenters*, because then every voter was subject to a religious test of the Synod or Consociation. Mr. Neal, indeed, seems to think that a civil test is heresy itself, but that a religious test is liberty, is gospel, and renders "all parties of christians in New-Eng-"land easy—a happy people." The reason, however, of his muffling truth with truth, was, he wrote for the Old Lights and against the New Lights for hire; the New Lights being the minority, and out of place in the State. Those two sects differed about the coercive power of the civil magistrate. The Old Lights held that the civil magistrate was a creature framed on purpose to support ecclesiastical censure with the sword of severity; but the New Lights maintained that the magistrate had no power or right to concern himself with

Church excommunication, and that excommunication was all the punishment any one could undergo in this world, according to the rules of the Gospel. These were, and always have been, two great articles of faith in New-England; nevertheless, Mr. Neal says he can assure the world that " religion is no part of the quarrel." I hope Mr. Neal did not mean to quibble, as the New-Englanders generally do, by Jesuitism, viz. that religion is peaceable and admits not of quarrels; and yet, if he did not, he meant not a full representation of the matter, for he well knew that the difference in respect to the intent and power of the magistrates was a religious point, and formed the partition wall between the Old and New Lights. The civilians and magistrates were too wise to countenance the New Lights, who promised little good to them; while the Old Lights gave them a power of punishing, even unto death, those whom they had anathematized, and who would not submit to their censures by penitence and confession. The Old Lights, in short, supported the practice of the inquisitors of Spain and Archbishop Laud—the ostensible occasion of their ancestors flying from England to the wilderness of America.

But Mr. Neal contented not himself with one mistake; he added, "that the people of New-England are a "dutiful and loyal people." They never merited this character, and they always had too much honesty and religion to claim it. From the first they have uniformly declared, in Church and State, that America is a new world, subject to the people residing in it, and that none but enemies of the country would appeal from their courts to the King in Council. They never have prayed for any earthly king by name. They have always called themselves republicans, and enemies to kingly government, to temporal and spiritual lords. They hate the idea of a Parliament, consisting of King, Lords, and Commons; they declare that the three branches should be but one, the king having only a single vote with the other members. Upon this point they have always quarrelled with the governors. They never have admitted one law of England to be in force among them till passed by their assemblies. They have sent agents to fight against the kings of England. They deny the jurisdiction of the Bishop of London, which extends over America by a royal patent. They hold Jesus to be the only King, whom if they love and obey they will not submit, because they have not submitted, to the laws of the King of Great Britain.

Mr. Neal, furthermore, professes his want of conception why the Society for the Propagation of the Gospel in Foreign Parts should send missionaries into New-England, when Oliver Cromwell had, in 1640, instituted a society to propagate christian knowledge there. Mr. Neal might have learnt the cause of this phenomenon from the charter granted to the first-mentioned society by King William III., who was a friend to civil and christian liberty, and who endeavoured to suppress the intolerable persecutions in his days prevailing in New-England. But, besides, Mr. Neal could not but know that there were many Churchmen in New-England desirous of the use of the liturgy and discipline of the English Church; and for what reason should they not have ministers of their own persuasion, as well as the sober and conscientious dissenters? I hope my readers will not think me a partial advocate for the Church of England, which, perhaps, has lost the opportunity of civilizing, christianizing, and moderating the burning zeal of the dissenters of New-England, who were honest in their religion merely by the sinful omission of not sending a bishop to that country, who would have effected greater things among them than an army of 50,000 men. I avow myself to be liberal-minded towards all sects and parties; and, if I had power, I would convert all sorts of ministers into popes, cardinals, prelates, dominies, potent presbyters, and rich Quakers, that the world might be excused from hearing again of preaching, defamation, insurrections, and spiritual jurisdictions, which result more from pride, poverty, avarice, and ambition, than the love of peace and christianity.

It has been said by the deists, and other politicians, that ministers, by preaching, have done more hurt than good in the christian world. If the idea will hold in any part it will be in New-England, where each sect preaches, for Gospel, policy and defamation of its neighbour; whence the lower classes think that christianity consists in defending their own peculiar Church and modes, and subverting those of others, at any rate; while the higher ranks value religion and the Gospel as laws of a foreign country, and the merchants powwowers, subtle, cruel, and greedy of riches and dominion over all people. For this reason the savages have taken an aversion to the protestant religion, and they say they would rather follow Hobbomockow and the Roman priests than New-England christians, who persecute one another, and killed their ancestors with a pocky Gospel.

With scorn they cry out: " We value not your Gospel,
" which shews so many roads to Kicktang; some of
" them must be crooked, and lead to Hobbomockow.
" We had, therefore, better continue Indians like our
" ancestors, or be Catholics, who tell us of only one way
" to Kicktang, or the invisible God."

Laws.—A stranger in the colony, upon hearing the inhabitants talk of religion, liberty, and justice, would be induced to believe that the christian and civil virtues were their distinguishing characteristics; but he soon finds his mistake in fixing his abode among them. Their laws grind the poor, and their religion is to oppress the oppressed. The poll-tax is unjust and cruel. The poor man is compelled to pay for his bread eighteen shillings per annum, work four days on the highways, serve in the militia four days, and pay three shillings for his hut, without a window in it. The best house and richest man in the colony pays no more!

The law is pretended to exempt episcopalians, Anabaptists, Quakers, and others, from paying rates to the *Sober Dissenters*, but, at the same time, gives the *Sober Dissenters* power to tax them for minister, school, and town rates, by a general quota; and no law or court can put asunder what the town has joined together. The law also exempts from paying to *Sober Dissenters* all Churchmen " who live so near that they can and do at-" tend Church." But hence, if a man is sick, and does not attend more than twenty-six Sabbaths in a year, he becomes legally a *Sober Dissenter;* and if the meeting lies between him and the Church, he does not live so near the Church that he can attend, because it is more than a Sabbath-day's journey, and therefore unnecessary travel.[1]

The law provides whipping, stocks, and fines, for such as do not attend public worship on the Sabbath. The Grand Jury complains, and the Justice inflicts the punishment. This has been the practice for many years. About 1750, Mr. Pitt, a Churchman, was whipped for not attending meeting. Mr. Pitt was an old man. The episcopal clergy wrote to England, complaining of this cruel law. The Governor and Council immediately

---

[1] An early provision was therefore made by law in Massachusetts and Connecticut for the support of the ministry. In Connecticut all persons were obliged by law to contribute to the support of the Church as well as of the Commonwealth.

All rates respecting the support of ministers, or any ecclesiastical affairs, were to be made and collected in the same manner as the rates of the respective towns.

Special care was taken that all persons should attend the means of public instruction. The law obliged them to be present at public worship on the Lord's-day, and upon all days of public fasting and praying, and of thanksgivings appointed by civil authority, on penalty of a fine of five shillings for every instance of neglect. The Congregational churches were adopted and established by law; but provision was made that all sober, orthodox persons dissenting from them should, upon the manifestation of it to the General Court, be allowed peaceably to worship in their own way.

It was enacted, "That no person within this Colony shall in any wise "embody themselves into Church estate without consent of the General "Court and approbation of neighbouring elders."

The law also prohibited that any ministry or Church administration should be entertained or attended by the inhabitants of any plantation in the Colony, distinct and separate from, and in opposition to, that which was openly and publicly observed and dispensed by the approved minister of the place; except it was by the approbation of the Court and neighboring churches. The penalty for every breach of this act was 5*l*.—Ed. Note.

broke the Justice who punished Mr. Pitt, and wrote to the Bishop of London that they had done so as a mark of their disapprobation of the Justice's conduct, and knew not what more they could do. This apology satisfied the Bishop, and the next year the Governor and Council restored the Justice to his office; however, Quakers and Anabaptists only were whipped afterwards.

Formerly, when a *Sober Dissenter* had a suit in law against a Churchman, every juryman of the latter persuasion was by the Court removed from the jury and replaced by *Sober Dissenters*. The reasons assigned for this extraordinary conduct was, " that justice and impar-" tiality might take place." The episcopalians, Quakers, and other sects not of the *Sober Dissenters*, were not admitted to serve as jurymen in Connecticut till 1750. Such of them whose annual worth is rated at not less than 40*l.* in the general list, have enjoyed the liberty of voting for civil officers a much longer term; but for parish concerns they are still totally excluded.

Other laws I have occasionally animadverted upon in the course of this work; and a specimen of the Blue Laws, and of various courts, is inserted.

Nothing can reflect greater disgrace upon the colony than the number of suits in all the County Courts, amounting in the whole to between 20 and 30,000 annually; the greater part of which are vexatiously commenced from expectations grounded upon the notorious instability of the judges' opinions and decisions.

The spirit of litigation which distracts the province in general is, however, a blessing to the judges and lawyers. The court has one shilling for every action called, and twenty shillings for those that come to trial;

and the fee to each lawyer is twenty shillings, whether the action be tried or not, besides various other expenses. There are as many suits of conscience before the justices of the peace, and ministers, and deacons; so that the sum annually expended in law in the whole colony is amazing. It was not without reason, therefore, that the judges, the lawyers, the ministers and deacons, the sheriffs and constables, opposed the stamp-act with all their might. They told the people that, if this act took place, their liberties would be destroyed, and they would be tried by King's judges without jury.

The singular nature of some of the suits entitles them to particular notice. When the ice and flood prevail in the great river Connecticut, they frequently carry off large pieces of ground on one side, and carry them over to the other. By this means the river is every year changing its bed, to the advantage of some persons and the disadvantage of others. This has proved the source of perplexing lawsuits, and will most likely continue to produce the same effects so long as the demi-annual assemblies remain in the colony; for the judgment of the Assembly in May is rescinded by that in October, and so *vice versa*. Thus a lawsuit in Connecticut is endless, to the ruin of both plaintiff and defendant.

The County and Superior Courts, also, in different years give different judgments; and the reason is the popular constitution of the colony, whereby different parties prevail at different times, each of whom carefully undoes what the others have done. Thus the glorious uncertainty of the law renders the possession of property in Connecticut extremely precarious. The question, however, touching the lands being removed from place to place by the floods and ice, requires the skill of both juries and casuists. The most simple case of the kind that has been communicated to me is the following:

A piece of land belonging to A., in Springfield, with a house, &c. standing upon it, was removed by the flood to another town, and settled on land belonging to W. A. claimed his house and land, and took possession of them; whereupon W. sued A. for a trespass, and the court ejected A. But A. afterward obtained a revision of the judgment; when W. again sued A., and got a decree that A. should remove his own land off from the land of W., or pay W. for his land. Further litigation ensued, both parties pleading that the act of God injured no man according to the English law. The judges said that the act of God in this case equally fell upon A. and W. The dispute rests *in statu quo*, the jurisprudence of Connecticut not having yet taught mankind what is just and legal in this important controversy.

Supposing the flood had carried A.'s ship or raft on W.'s land, the ship or raft would still belong to A., and W. could recover damages; but then A. must take away his ship or raft in a reasonable time. Yet, in the case where an island, or point of land, is removed by the waters, or an earthquake, upon a neighbouring shore, Q. Ought not the islanders to keep possession of the superficies? This may be a new case in Europe.

Manners and Customs.—Gravity and serious deportment, together with shyness and bashfulness, generally attend first communications with the inhabitants of Connecticut; but after a short acquaintance they become very familiar, and inquisitive about news. Who are you? whence come you? where going? what is your business? and what your religion? They do not consider these, and similar questions, impertinent, and consequently expect a civil answer. When the stranger has satisfied their curiosity, they will treat him with all the hospitality in their power, and great caution must be observed to get quit of them and their houses without giving offence. If the stranger has cross and difficult roads to travel, they will go with him till all danger is past, without fee or reward. The stranger has nothing to do but civilly say, "Sir, I thank you, and " will call upon you when I return." He must not say, " God bless you," or " I shall be glad to see you at my " house," unless he is a minister; because they hold that the words " God bless you " should not be spoken by common people; and " I shall be glad to see you at "my house" they look upon as an insincere compliment, paid them for what they do out of duty to the stranger. Their hospitality is highly exemplary; they are sincere in it, and reap great pleasure by reflecting that, perhaps, they have entertained angels.

The Rev. Mr. George Whitefield, in one of his sermons, gave them the following character: "I have " found," said he, " the people of Connecticut the " wisest of any upon the continent; they are the best " friends and the worst enemies; they are hair-brained " bigots on all sides, and they may be compared to the " horse and mule, without bit and bridle. In other " colonies I have paid for food and lodging, but could " never spend one penny in fruitful Connecticut, whose " banks flow with milk and honey, and whose sons and "daughters never fail to feed and refresh the weary "traveller, without money and without price."

On Saturday evenings the people look sour and sad; on the Sabbath they appear to have lost their dearest friends, and are almost speechless; they walk softly; they even observe it with more exactness than did the Jews. A Quaker preacher told them, with much truth, that they worshipped the Sabbath, and not the God of the Sabbath. These hospitable people, without charity, condemned the Quaker as a blasphemer of the holy Sabbath, fined, tarred, and feathered him, put a rope about his neck, and plunged him into the sea; but he escaped with life, though he was about seventy years of age.

In 1750 an episcopal clergyman, born and educated in England, who had been in holy orders above twenty years, once broke their sabbatical law by combing a discomposed lock of hair on the top of his wig; at another time, for making a humming noise, which they called whistling; at a third time, by walking too fast from church; at a fourth, by running into church when it rained; at a fifth, by walking in his garden and picking a bunch of grapes: for which several crimes he was complained of by the Grand Jury, had warrants granted against him, was seized, brought to trial, and paid a considerable sum of money. At last, overwhelmed with persecution and vexation, he cried out: "No Briton, "nay, no Jew, should assume any public character in "Connecticut till he has served an apprenticeship of "ten years in it; for I have been here seven years, and "strictly observed the Jewish law concerning the Sab- "bath, yet find myself remiss in respect to the perfect "law of liberty!"

The people are extremely fond of strangers passing through the colony, but very averse to foreigners settling among them; which few have done without ruin to their characters and fortunes, by detraction and lawsuits, unless recommended as men of grace by some known and revered republican protestant in Europe. The following story may be amusing:

An English gentleman, during a short residence in a certain town, had the good luck to receive some civilities from the Deacon, Minister, and Justice. The Deacon had a daughter, without beauty, but sensible and rich. The Briton (for that was the name he went by), having received a present from the West-Indies of some pineapples and sweetmeats, sent his servant with part of it to the Deacon's daughter, to whom, at the same time, he addressed a complimentary note, begging Miss would accept the pineapples and sweetmeats, and wishing he might be able to make her a better present. Miss, on reading the note, was greatly alarmed, and exclaimed, "Mamma, mamma! Mr. Briton has sent me a love-letter." The mother read the note and shewed it to the Deacon, and, after due consideration, both agreed in pronouncing it a love-letter. The lawyer, justice, and parson were sent for, who in council weighed every word in the note, together with the golden temptation which the lady possessed, and were of opinion that the writer was in love, and that the note was a love-letter, but worded so carefully that the law could not punish Briton for attempting to court Miss without having obtained her parents' consent. The parson wrung his hands, rolled up his eyes, shrugged up his shoulders, groaned out his hypocritical grief, and said, "Deacon, I hope you do not "blame me for having been the innocent cause of your "knowing this imprudent and haughty Briton. There "is something very odd in all the Britons; but I thought "this man had some prudence and modesty. However, "Deacon," putting his hand on his breast, and bowing, with a pale, deceitful face, "I shall in future shun all "Britons, for they are all strange creatures." The lawyer and justice made their apologies, and were sorry that Briton did not consider the quality of the Deacon's daughter before he wrote the letter. Miss, all apprehension and tears, at finding that no punishment could reach Briton in the course of law, cried out to her counsellors, "Who is Briton? Am I not the Deacon's "daughter? What have I done, that he should take "such liberties with me? Is he not the natural son of "some priest, or foundling? Ought he not to be ex"posed for his assurance to the Deacon's daughter?"

Her words took effect. The council voted that they would show their contempt of Briton by neglecting him for the time to come. On his return home, the parson, after many great signs of surprise, informed his wife of the awful event which had happened by the imprudence of Briton. She soon communicated the secret to her sister-gossips, prudently cautioning them not to report it as from her. But, not content with that, the parson himself went among all his acquaintance, shaking his head, and saying, "O sirs! have you heard of "the strange conduct of friend Briton—how he wrote a "love-letter, and sent it, with some pineapples, to the "Deacon's daughter? My wife and I had a great "friendship for Briton, but cannot see him any more."

Thus the affected parson told this important tale to

every one except Briton, who, from his ignorance of the story, conducted himself in his usual manner towards his supposed friends, though he observed they had a show of haste and business whenever he met with any of them. Happily for Briton, he depended not on the Deacon, minister, or colony, for his support. At last a Scotchman heard of the evil tale, and generously told Briton of it, adding that the parson was supposed to be in deep decline merely from grief and fatigue he had endured in spreading it. Briton thanked the Scotchman, and called on the friendly parson to know the particulars of his offence. The parson, with sighs, bows, and solemn smirkings, answered, "Sir, the fact " is, you wrote a love-letter to the Deacon's daughter " without asking her parents' consent; which has given " great offence to that lady, and to all her acquaintance, " of whom I and my wife have the honour to be reck-" oned a part." Briton kept his temper. "So, then," said he, "I have offended you by my insolent note to the " Deacon's daughter! I hope my sin is venial. Pray, " sir, have you seen my note?" "Yes," replied the " parson, "to my grief and sorrow. I could not have " thought you so imprudent, had I not seen and found " the note to be your own handwriting." "How long " have you known of this offence?" "Some months." " Why, sir, did you not seasonably admonish me for " this crime?" "I was so hurt and grieved, and my " friendship so great, I could not bear to tell you." Mr. Briton then told the parson that his friendship was so fine and subtle, it was invisible to an English eye; and the Gospel ministers in England did not prove their friendship by telling calumnious stories to everybody but the person concerned. "But I suppose," added he, "this is genuine New-England friendship, "and merits thanks more than a supple-jack." The parson, with a leering look, sneaked away towards his wife; and Briton left the colony without any civil or ecclesiastical punishment, telling the Scotchman that the Deacon's daughter had money, and the parson faith without eyes, or he should never have been accused of making love to one who was naturally so great an enemy to Cupid. Of such or worse sort being the reception foreign settlers may expect from the inhabitants of Connecticut, it is no wonder that few, or none, choose to venture among them.

The custom of settling and dismissing a sober dissenting minister is very singular. All the parishioners meet and vote to apply to the Association for a candidate, and one is accordingly sent. If he pleases, the people vote to give him a call; if he accepts the call, the actual communicants, and they alone, make the covenant between him and them as Christ's Church, and thus they are married to him. After the candidate is ordained, others, by acknowledging and swearing to support the covenant, become married to him also. (N. B. Baptism is not sufficient to take them out of their natural state.) The call is an invitation from the parishioners to the candidate to take upon him the ministerial office of their Church, on condition that he be allowed 300*l.* or 400*l.* settlement, and perhaps 100*l.* salary, besides wood, &c. &c. during his residence among them in that capacity. The candidate, after looking round him and finding no better terms offered from any other parish, answers in this manner: "Breth-

"ren and friends, I have considered your call, and, after "many fastings and prayers, I find it to be the call of "God, and close with your offer." The Church then appoints a day for his ordination, and the ministers who shall assist in the ceremony, which is as follows: 1. The meeting is opened with a hymn. 2. Some one makes a prayer. 3. Another hymn succeeds. 4. A sermon. 5. Another prayer. 6. The covenant is read. 7. The prayer of consecration, with imposition of hands by the minister. 8. The right hand of fellowship, which conveys that half of ministerial power which I have already spoken of as communicated by the Churches. 9. The charge—that is, to behave well in the office whereto God has called him. 10. Prayer. 11. Another hymn. 12. The young minister dismisses with his benediction. Numerous as the ceremonies are in a minister's ordination, there are but few judged necessary in dismissing him; a majority of the Church is enough to turn the minister from bed and board, or, in their language, "to divorce him"—which happens more frequently than is decent. The minister has no remedy but in appealing to the Association, which step entitles him to his salary till dismissed by that powerful body. Incontinency, intemperance, lying, and idleness, are the common accusations brought against the minister, but seldom founded in truth, and yet always proved by knights of the post. However, the minister carries off his settlement in case he is dismissed for immoralities, but not if he turns Churchman; then his old parishioners are mean enough to sue for the settlement. A recent instance of this kind happened at New-London, where the minister, Doctor Mather Byles, desired a dismission, which was given him; but, finding the Doctor's design was to become a Churchman, the people demanded the settlement given him twelve years before. The Doctor, with a spirit worthy of himself and his venerable ancestors, returned the money, with, "You "are welcome to it, since it proves to the world that "you could not accuse me of anything more agreeable "to ungenerous minds."

The manner of visiting the sick in this province is more terrible than charitable. The minister demands of the sick if he be converted, when, and where. If the answer is conformable to the system of the minister, it is very well; if not, the sick is given over as a non-elect, and no object of prayer. Another minister is then sent for, who asks if the sick be willing to die—if he hates God—if he be willing to be damned, if it please God to damn him? Should he answer No, this minister quits him, as the former. Finally, the sick man dies, and so falls out of their hands into better.

Amidst all the darkness of superstition that surrounds the State, the humanity it shows to poor strangers seized with sickness in the colony, or to such persons as are shipwrecked upon its coasts, shines with distinguished lustre. These unfortunate sufferers are immediately provided with the necessaries of every kind, by order of the selectmen, whose expenses are reimbursed out of the colony Treasury.

Thus is laudably employed a part of the money allowed for contingencies; but another part is consumed in a very different manner. It frequently happens that, whenever the episcopalians become so numerous in a parish as to gain the ascendency over the *Sober*

Dissenters, and the latter cannot, by their own strength, either destroy the episcopal or support their own Church, the Governor and Council, with the advice of the Consociation, kindly relieve them with an annual grant out of the public Treasury, sometimes to the amount of the whole sum paid into it by every denomination of the parish. An act of charity of this kind lately took place at Chelsea, in Norwich, where the *Sober Dissenters* were few and poor, and without a meeting-house or minister, so that they were obliged to walk a mile to a meeting, or go to church. The young people chose the latter, which alarmed the *Sober Dissenters* to such a degree that they applied for and obtained from the generous Governor and his virtuous Council 300*l.* per annum out of the Treasury, besides the duties on the vessels of the Churchmen of that port. This largition enabled them to build a meeting-house and settle a minister. When the Churchmen complained of this abuse of the public money, the Governor answered, "The "Assembly has the same right to support christianity "as the Society for the Propagation of the Gospel in "Foreign Parts, or the Parliament of Great Britain."

The murmurs of the people on the collection of the revenue bespeak embezzlements of another kind. It should seem that they believed the General Assembly to be in the same predicament as the devil thought Job was, when he said, "Doth Job serve God for nought?"

Estates in Connecticut pass from generation to generation by gavelkind; so that there are few persons, except of the labouring class, who have not freeholds of their own to cultivate. A general mediocrity of station being thus constitutionally promoted, it is no wonder that the rich man is despised, and the poor man's blessing is his poverty. In no part of the world are *les petits* and *les grands* so much upon a par as here, where none of the people are destitute of the conveniences of life and the spirit of independence. From infancy, their education as citizens points out no distinction between licentiousness and liberty; and their religion is so muffled with superstition, self-love, and provincial enmity, as not yet to have taught them that humanity and respect for others which from others they demand. Notwithstanding these effects of the levelling plan, there are many exceptions to be found in the province of gentlemen of large estates and generous principles.

The people commonly travel on horseback, and the ladies are capable of teaching their neighbours the art of horsemanship. There are few coaches in the colony, but many chaises and whiskeys. In winter the sleigh is used—a vehicle drawn by two horses, and carrying six persons in its box, which hangs on four posts standing on two steel slides or large skates.

Dancing, fishing, hunting, skating, and riding in sleighs on the ice, are all the amusements allowed in this colony.

Smuggling is rivetted in the constitution and practice of the inhabitants of Connecticut, as much as superstition and religion, and their province is a storehouse for the smugglers of the neighbouring colonies. They conscientiously study to cheat the King of those duties which, they say, God and Nature never intended should be paid. From the Governor down to the tithing-man, who are sworn to support the laws, they will aid smugglers, resist collectors, and mob informers. This being a popular Government, all the officers are appointed by the freeholders. There are very severe laws against bribery. The candidates are not suffered to give a dinner, or a glass of cider, on the day of the election, to a voter. Indeed, bribery is the next greatest crime to a breach of the Sabbath; yet open bribery, as established by custom immemorial in Rhode-Island, is more praiseworthy than the practice of Connecticut. I will give the reader some idea of the mode in which an election is managed in Connecticut.

All the voters in a township convene in the town meeting-house. One of the ministers, after prayers, preaches from some such text as, "Jabez was more "honourable than his brethren." The people keep their seats, while the constables take their votes in a box; and if a voter has not his vote written, the constable gives him one. So Jabez is elected; and the meeting is concluded with a prayer of thanks to the Lord God of Israel for "turning the hearts of his people against " the enemies of Zion, and for uniting them in Jabez, " the man after his own heart." The manner in which the preacher treats his text will more particularly appear from the animadversion of a certain Quaker on one of these occasions. "Friend," said he to the pedagogue, " I do thee no wrong in telling thee that thou hast prayed " and preached against bribery, but forgot to keep thy " tongue from speaking evil against thy neighbour. "Dost thou think the Lord will regard thy preaching "so much as the voters whom thou dost call freemen? " If thou believest it, thou hast bribed not only the peo- "ple, but the Lord also, to reject Ebenezer and Benja- "min." The preacher called upon the constable to take away this babbler and open the meeting; which was done, and Ebenezer and Benjamin were rejected by the voters.

The men in general throughout the province are tall, stout, and robust. The greatest care is taken of the limbs and bodies of infants, which are kept straight by means of a board—a practice learnt from the Indian women, who abhor all crooked people—so that deformity is here a rarity.

Another custom derived from the Indians is, to welcome a new-born infant into the world with urine and honey, the effects of which are wonderful; and hence it is that at groanings there are always a little hog and a rattle-snake's skin, the latter of which prevents numbness and the cramp. The women are fair, handsome, genteel. They have, indeed, adopted various customs of the Indian women, but cannot learn, like them, how to support the pains of child-bearing without a groan. Naturalists and surgeons have not been able to assign the reason why a negro woman should have a hundred pains, a white woman ten, and an Indian none. Some have said that the fatigues and hardships which negroes endure are the cause; but the Indians undergo many more: others have said it was owing to the change of climate; but this is suppletory: while the enthusiastic divines attribute it to the sin of Eve, and to the curse laid on the Canaanites. The deists ask these divines if Eve was not the common mother of the white, black, and copper-coloured women, and how it appears that negroes are the descendants of Canaan? Their answer is, that all Nature is mystery.

The women of Connecticut are strictly virtuous, and

to be compared to the prude rather than the European polite lady. They are not permitted to read plays; cannot converse about whist, quadrille, or operas, but will freely talk upon the subject of history, geography, and mathematics. They are great casuists and polemical divines; and I have known not a few of them so well skilled in Greek and Latin as often to put to the blush learned gentlemen.

Notwithstanding the modesty of the females is such that it would be accounted the greatest rudeness for a gentleman to speak, before a lady, of a garter, knee, or leg, yet it is thought but a piece of civility to ask her to bundle—a custom as old as the first settlement in 1634. It is certainly innocent, virtuous, and prudent, or the puritans would not have permitted it to prevail among their offspring, for whom, in general, they would suffer crucifixion. Children brought up with the chastest ideas, with so much religion as to believe that the omniscient God sees them in the dark, and that angels guard them when absent from their parents, will not—nay, cannot—act a wicked thing. People who are influenced more by lust than a serious faith in God, who is too pure to behold iniquity with approbation, ought never to bundle. If any man, thus a stranger to the love of virtue, of God, and the christian religion, should bundle with a young lady in New-England, and behave himself unseemly towards her, he must first melt her into passion, and expel heaven, death, and hell, from her mind, or he will undergo the chastisement of negroes turned mad; if he escapes with life, it will be owing to the parents flying from their beds to protect him.

The Indians, who had this method of courtship when

the English arrived among them in 1634, are the most chaste set of people in the world.

Concubinage and fornication are vices none of them are addicted to, except such as forsake the laws of Hobbomockow and turn christians. The savages have taken many female prisoners, carried them back three hundred miles into their country, and kept them several years, and yet not a single instance of their violating the laws of chastity has ever been known. This cannot be said of the French, or of the English, whenever Indian or other women have fallen into their hands. I am no advocate for temptation, yet must say that bundling has prevailed 160 years in New-England, and, I verily believe, with ten times more chastity than the sitting on a sofa. About the year 1756, Boston, Salem, Newport, and New York, resolving to be more polite than their ancestors, forbade their daughters bundling on the bed with any young man whatever, and introduced a sofa, to render courtship more palatable and Turkish. Whatever it was owing to, whether to the sofa or any uncommon excess of the *feu d'esprit,* there went abroad a report that the *raffinage* produced more natural consequences than all the bundling among the boors with their *rurales pendantes* through every village in New-England besides.

In 1766, a clergyman from one of the polite towns went into the country and preached against the unchristian custom of young men and maidens lying together upon the same bed. He was no sooner out of the Church, than attacked by a shoal of good old women, with, "Sir, do you think we and our daughters are "naughty because we allow bundling?" "You lead "yourselves into temptation by it." They all replied at once, "Sir, have you been told thus, or has experience "taught you?" The Levite began to lift his eyes and to consider his situation, and, bowing, said, "I have been "told so." The ladies, *una voce*, bawled out, "Your in-"formants, sir, we conclude, are those city ladies who "prefer a sofa to a bed. We advise you to alter your ser-"mon by substituting the word sofa for bundling, and, "on your return home, preach to them: for experience "has told us that city-folks send more children into the "country without father and mother to own them, than "are born among us; therefore, you see, a sofa is more "dangerous than a bed." The poor priest, seemingly convinced of his blunder, exclaimed, "*Nec vitia nostra,* "*nec remedia pati possumus,*" hoping hereby to get rid of his guests; but an old matron pulled off her spectacles, and, looking the priest in the face like a Roman heroine, said, "*Noli putare me hæc auribus tuis dares.*" Others cried out to the priest to explain his Latin. "The English," he said, "is this: Woe to me that I "sojourn in Meseck, and dwell in the tents of Kedar!" One pertly replied, "*Gladii decussati sunt gemina* "*presbytericalvis.*" The priest confessed his error, begged pardon, and promised never more to preach against bundling, or to think amiss of the custom; the ladies generously forgave him, and went away.

It may seem very strange to find this custom of bundling in bed attended with so much innocence in New-England, while in Europe it is thought not safe, or scarcely decent, to permit a young man or maid to be together in private anywhere. But, in this quarter of the Old World, the viciousness of the one and the simplicity of the other are the result merely of education and habit. It seems to be a part of heroism, among the polished nations of it, to sacrifice the virtuous fair one whenever an opportunity offers, and thence it is concluded that the same principles actuate those of the New World. It is egregiously absurd to judge of all countries by one. In Spain, Portugal, and Italy, jealousy reigns; in France, England, and Holland, suspicion; in the West and East-Indies, lust; in New-England, superstition. These four blind deities govern Jews, Turks, christians, infidels, and heathen. Superstition is the most amiable. She sees no vice with approbation, but persecution, and self-preservation is the cause of her seeing that. My insular readers will, I hope, believe me, when I tell them that I have seen in the West-Indies naked boys and girls, some fifteen or sixteen years of age, waiting at table and at tea, even when twenty or thirty virtuous English ladies were in the room; who were under no more embarrassment at such an awful sight in the eyes of English people who have not travelled abroad, than they would have been at the sight of so many servants in livery. Shall we censure the ladies of the West-Indies as vicious above their sex on account of this local custom? By no means; for long experience has taught the world that the West-Indian white ladies are virtuous prudes. Where superstition reigns, fanaticism will be minister of state; and the people, under the taxation of zeal, will shun what is commonly called vice with ten times more care than the polite and civilized christians who know what is right and what is wrong from reason and revelation. Happy would it be for the world, if reason and revelation were suffered to control the minds and passions of the great and wise men of the world, as superstition does that of the simple and less polished! When America shall elect societies for the promotion of chastity in Europe, in return for the establishment of European arts in American capitals, then Europe will discover that there is more christian philosophy in American bundling than can be found in the customs of nations more polite.

I should not have said so much about bundling had not a learned divine (Dr. Burnaby) of the English Church published his Travels through some parts of America, wherein this remarkable custom is represented in an unfavourable light, and as prevailing among the lower class of people. The truth is, the custom prevails among all classes, to the great honour of the country, its religion, and ladies. The virtuous may be tempted; but the tempter is despised. Why it should be thought incredible for a young man and young woman innocently and virtuously to lie down together in a bed with a great part of their clothes on, I cannot conceive. Human passions may be alike in every region; but religion, diversified as it is, operates differently in different countries. Upon the whole, had I daughters now, I would venture to let them bundle upon the bed, or even on the sofa, after a proper education, sooner than adopt the Spanish mode of forcing young people to prattle only before the lady's mother the chit-chat of artless lovers. Could the four quarters of the world produce a more chaste, exemplary, and beautiful company of wives and daughters than are in Connecticut, I should not have remaining one favourable sentiment for the province. But the soil, the rivers, the ponds, the ten thousand landscapes, together with the virtuous and lovely women which now adorn the ancient kingdoms of Connecticut, Sassacus, and Quinnipiog, would tempt me into the highest wonder and admiration of them, could they once be freed of the skunk, the moping-owl, rattle-snake, and fanatic christian.

My readers will naturally be desirous of information in what manner the people of Connecticut conduct themselves in regard to the Stamp Act, which has proved the subject of so much speculation and controversy both in America and Europe. I will, therefore, give a particular account of their proceedings concerning it, which will, perhaps, appear to have been of far greater consequence than is generally supposed in England.

The American colonists were no sooner extricated from all danger of Gallic depredations by the peace of 1763, than they began to manifest symptoms of ingratitude and rebellion against their deliverers. Connecticut, on several accounts, particularly that of its free constitution in Church and State, which prevented every interruption from a King's Governor, was fixed upon as the fittest site for raising the first-fruits of jealousies and disaffection. Nor did the hatred which kept the province at eternal strife within itself on all other occasions, prevent its political coincidence upon this. In 1764, delegates from every dissenting association in America convened at Newhaven and settled the plan of operations. They voted that the American Vine was endangered by the encroachment of the English Parliament and the Society for the Propagation of the Gospel in Foreign Parts; that episcopacy was established in Nova-Scotia, and missionaries maintained by the English

Government, while New-England and other American States were taxed to support that same Government; that a league and covenant ought to be made and signed by all good protestants against the machinations of their enemies, and in defence of their civil and religious liberties; that it was the duty of all good protestants to stand upon their guard, and collect and send every kind of interesting intelligence to the Moderator at Hertford, whose business would be to communicate the same in his circular letters to the true friends of protestant liberty. In my opinion, whoever does not perceive the spirit of civil as well as religious independence in this convention, and these resolutions of dissenting divines, must be politically blind. Whilst Mr. Grenville was exerting his fanatical faculties for the relief of the Mother Country, ready to sink under the load of expense brought upon her by that war which had opened an avenue to highest exaltation for her American offspring, Connecticut was early advertised by merchants, divines, and ladies, in England, that the Parliament was about to give the colonies a specimen of English burthens. The Consociation ordered a fast, to deprecate the threatened judgments. This fast was served up with sermons pointing out the reigns of wicked kings, lords, and bishops, in the last century; and concluded with, "One woe is past, and, behold, there come two woes "more hereafter!"

A requisition having been made, in 1763, that each colony in America should raise a revenue to assist Great Britain in discharging the national debt, which had been partly incurred at their request and for their preservation, the General Assembly was instructed by Dr. Franklin and others how to act. Accordingly, the Assembly resolved not to raise any money towards the national debt, or any national expenses, till the Parliament should remove the Navigation Act, which, they said, was advantageous to Great Britain and disadvantageous to America; and, therefore, Great Britain, in defraying the whole of the national expense, did nothing more than justice required, so long as that act should be continued. Such were the arguments and resolutions of the General Assembly, although their agent in England had informed them that, if they refused to comply with the requisition of the minister, the Parliament would tax them.

The agent's intelligence proved to be well founded. In 1765 the Stamp Act passed, because the colonies had refused to tax themselves. News so important soon arrived in America, and the Consociation of Connecticut appointed another fast, and ordered the angels to sound their trumpets, and great plagues followed. Thomas Fitch, the Governor, shewed some dislike to the proceedings of the Consociation, but was given to understand that Christ's ministers acted by an authority superior to that of the Governor or a king. The episcopalians, and many sects, saw no reason for keeping the fast; but the Governor observed it with a view of securing his election the next year, and was successful. The episcopalians were rewarded for their disobedience with what is called "a new religious comic Liturgy," which was printed and circulated through the colony as the performance of Doctor Franklin, and acted in many towns by the young people on evenings by way of sport and amusement. The litany was altered in many places, especially in the paragraphs respecting the King, nobility, &c.; and instead of "We beseech thee to hear us, "good Lord!" was substituted, "We beseech thee, O "Cromwell, to hear (our prayers) us." "O holy, blessed, "and glorious Trinity!" was altered thus, "O Chatham, "Wilkes, and Franklin, have mercy upon us!" "From "plague, pestilence, famine," &c. was followed by "O "Cromwell, deliver us!" An episcopal clergyman had courage enough to complain of these blasphemous proceedings, and the Grand Jury indicted the comic actors; but the magistrate to whom the complaint was made refused to grant a warrant, using worse maledictions against the King than were contained in the ludicrous litany. Hereupon the Grand Jury indicted the magistrate for high treason; but no magistrate could be found of resolution enough to grant a warrant against the traitor. However, the comic liturgy was acted but privately afterwards, and, upon the repeal of the Stamp Act, was suppressed as far as they could do it.

This second fast was sanctified with preaching on this and similar texts, "And there arose a new king in "Egypt who remembered not Joseph," and with praying God to grant the King a heart of flesh, and to remove popery out of the British Parliament.

The Stamp Act was to take place in November, 1765; some months before which the stamp-master, Jared Ingersoll, Esq. who had been the colony's agent in England, arrived at Newhaven in Connecticut. In September a special Assembly was convened at Hertford, for the purpose of considering what steps to take. As if to avoid the supremacy of the British Parliament, they determined not to apply themselves for the repeal of the act, but secretly encouraged a number of lawyers, merchants, and divines to meet, by their own authority, at New-York, for that purpose. In the mean time three mobs were raised, under Durgy, Leach, and Parsons, who by different routes marched into Newhaven to seize the stamp-master. They succeeded; and, having brought their prisoner before the Assembly-house at Hertford, they gave him the alternative to resign or die. Mr. Ingersoll appealed several times by confidential messengers to the Assembly then sitting, but, finding them inclined to countenance the mob, he was forced to resign, and authenticate the same by whirling first his hat, and next his wig, three times round his head, and then into the air; whilst the General Assembly and Consociation (which last venerable body never fails to be ready with its counsel and assistance on all salutary occasions) shouted with the multitude, from their windows, at the glorious achievement.

This special Assembly, having sufficiently manifested the part they wished the colony to take, broke up, leaving further proceedings to the mob, who continued to act up to the specimen already given, and the Congress of New York, which met then accordingly, agreed upon and transmitted to England a petition for a repeal of the obnoxious act.[1]

[1] The following will show that a Connecticut mob of *Sober Dissenters* is not inferior to a London mob of drunken Conformists, either in point of ingenuity, low humour, or religious mockery. The stamp-master was declared by the mob at Hertford to be dead. The mob at Lebanon undertook to send Ingersoll to his own place. They made their effigies, one to represent Mr. Grenville, another Ingersoll, and a third the devil. The last was dressed with a wig, hat, and black coat, given by parson Solomon Williams, of Lebanon. Mr. Grenville was honoured with a hat, wig, and coat, a present from Mr. Jonathan Trumbull, who was afterwards

The October session of the General Assembly is always holden at Newhaven: there and then they were chosen Governor, (and who afterwards wrote the letter to General Gage, as appears in a preceding note.) Mr. Ingersoll was dressed in red, with a lawyer's wig, a wooden sword, and his hat under his arm, by the generosity of Joseph Trumbull. Thus equipped, the effigies were put into a cart, with ropes about their necks, and drawn towards the gallows. A dialogue ensued between the criminals. Some friendship seemed to subsist between Mr. Grenville and the devil, while nothing but sneers and frowns passed the devil to Ingersoll; and the fawning reverence of the latter gave his infernal Highness such offence, that he turned up his breech and discharged fire, brimstone, and tar in Ingersoll's face, setting him all in a blaze; which, however, Mr. Grenville generously extinguished with a squirt. This was many times repeated. As the procession advanced, the mob exclaimed, "Behold the just reward of our agent, who sold him-"self to Grenville, like Judas, at a price!" In this manner the farce was continued till midnight, at which time they arrived at the gallows; where a person in a long shirt, in derision of the surplice of a Church clergyman, addressed the criminals with republican Atticisms, railleries, &c., concluding thus: "May your deaths be tedious and intolerable, and "may your souls sink quick down to hell, the residence of tyrants, trai-"tors, and devils!" The effigies were then turned off, and, after hanging some time, were hoisted upon a huge pile of wood and burnt, that their bodies might share a similar fate with their souls. This pious transaction exalted the character of Mr. Trumbull, and facilitated his election to the office of Governor; and, what was of further advantage to him, his mob judged that the bones of Ingersoll's effigy merited christian burial according to the rites of the Church of England, though he had been brought up a *Sober Dissenter*, and resolved, therefore, to bury his bones in Hebron. Accordingly, thither they repaired, and, after having made a coffin, dug a grave in a cross-street, and made every other preparation for the interment, they sent for the episcopal clergyman there to attend the funeral of the bones of Ingersoll the traitor.

The clergyman[1] told the messengers that neither his office nor his person were to be sported with, nor was it his business to bury *Sober Dissenters* who abuse the Church while living. The mob, enraged at this answer, ordered a party to bring the clergyman by force, or send him to

[1] The Episcopal clergyman was the Rev. Samuel Peters.—ED. NOTE.

informed by Mr. Dyer,[1] who had made one of the petitioners at New York, that it was recommended by the Congress for the colonial governors to take the oath prescribed by the Stamp Act.

The General Assembly, however, voted that the Governor of Connecticut should not take it; and, moreover, determined to continue Mr. Fitch in his office, notwithstanding the disfranchisement incident on his refusal, if he would be guided by their advice: the Rev. Mr. Ebenezer Devotion, one of the Representatives, and Eliphalet Dyer (above mentioned), one of the Council, offered to pay the imposed fine of 1,000*l*. However, the Governor presented himself before the Council, whose business it was to administer the oath, but which, it is thought, Mr. Fitch presumed would be denied, and therefore artfully devised this means at once of avoiding the oath and shifting the penalties

hell after Ingersoll. This alarmed the people of the town, who instantly loaded their muskets in defence of the clergyman. Thus checked in their mad career, the mob contented themselves with a solemn funeral procession, drums beating and horns blowing, and buried the coffin in the cross-street, one of the pantomimes bawling out, "We commit this "traitor's bones to the earth—ashes to dust and dust to ashes—in sure "and certain hope that his soul is in hell with all tories and enemies in "Zion." Then, having driven a stake through the coffin, and each cast a stone upon the grave, they broke a few windows, cursed such clergymen as rode in chaises and were above the control of God's people, and went off with a witless saying, viz. "It is better to live with the Church mili-"tant than with the Church triumphant."

[1] This Mr. Dyer had been in England, had petitioned for, and, through ·Dr. Franklin's interest, obtained a new office at the port of New-London, viz. that of Comptroller, but afterwards had thought proper to resign that office, in order to be made a Judge of the Superior Court and one of the Council; and, forsooth, that a stranger only might serve the King of Great Britain in the character of a publican in Connecticut.

from himself upon them. Seven out of the twelve, suspecting the Governor's design, put their fingers in their ears, shuffled their feet, and ran groaning out of the house; the other five stayed, and administered the oath, with a view to saving themselves and the Charter and direct the wrath of the people against the Governor; but in this they were mistaken, incurring in common with him the odium of the patriots. The Stamp Act having thus gained footing, the Assembly broke up. Legal proceedings also were discontinued, and the courts of justice shut. The Consociations and Associations kept frequent fasts of their own appointment, prayers, and preaching against Roman Catholic rulers, Arminian governors, and false-hearted councillors and episcopizing curates. Hereupon the mobs became outrageous; sedition was law and rebellion gospel. The stamp-master was called a traitor to his country, and the episcopalians enemies to Zion and liberty.

The fastings, prayers, and riots brought about a revolution in the colony. Fitch, who had taken, and the five assistants who had administered, the oath, as well as many officers, both civil and military, who declined to take a rebellious part, were dismissed from their posts; and a new Governor, other councillors, &c. were chosen, and the people fitted for every kind of mischief—all, however, under the pretence of religion and liberty. The patriotic Mr. Dyer distinguished himself by furnishing the fasting ministers with proper materials to inflame the minds of the people against the just demands of the King. One of his Machiavellian dogmas was, that the King claimed the colonies as his patrimony, and intended to raise a revenue in each province; and that, having gained this point, his purpose was to govern England by America and America by England, and thereby subvert liberty and establish tyranny in both, as the kings of France had done by means of the various parliaments in that country. Mr. Dyer declared he had this information from the best authority in England, and added, that the liberties of both countries depended on America resisting the Stamp Act, even unto blood. These and such like reveries supplied the ministers of the Gospel with a great body of political divinity, and the mob with courage to break Churchmen's windows, and cry out, "No bishops! "no popery! no kings, lords, and tyrants!" Everything but decency and order overran the colony. Indeed, the General Assembly kept up their meetings, but it was only to transact such business as was not affected by the Stamp Act. The mobs of the fasting ministers continued their lawless proceedings, without further interruption and impediment than what they met with from the strenuous exertions of the King's friends, who had repeatedly saved the lives of the stamp-master, Governor Fitch, the five rejected councillors, the episcopal clergy, and many good subjects, at the hazard of their own, though they could not preserve them from daily abuse and insult.

The mob, having been spirited up and trained to violence and outrage for several months, began to make some alarm even to the instigators, especially as they were hitherto disappointed in their expectations of the act being repealed. The Governor and Council, therefore, directing their attention to the dangerous consequences of the lawless state and refractory temper the people were in, and being struck with the foresight of their own perilous situation, resolved, early in 1766, to open the courts of law under the Stamp Act, if the very next packet did not bring certain advices of its repeal; and all parties who had causes depending in any court were to be duly notified by the Governor's proclamation. This determination was no less mortifying to the mob than gratifying to the King's friends, who were convinced that the Stamp Act ought, both in policy and justice, to be enforced, and therefore had risked their lives, fortunes, characters, and colonial honours in its support. The patriots, now apparently sickened with licentiousness, became very complaisant to the loyalists, declaring that, in all their opposition to the Stamp Act, they had meant nothing personal, and desiring to have past animosities buried in oblivion. All things thus settled, tranquillity seemed to be returning; when, lo! the packet arrived with the fatal news of the repeal of the Stamp Act. Then a double portion of madness seized the patriots, who, in their excess of joy "that "victory was gained over the beast, and over his mark," utterly forgot their late penitential and tranquil professions, branding the King's friends with the appellations of tories, Jacobites, and papists. The Gospel ministers left off their fastings, and turned mourning into joy and triumph. "Now we behold," they said in their pulpits, "that Great Britain is afraid of us; for "the Stamp Act is repealed, even upon the petition of an "illegal body of men. If, therefore, we stand fast in "the liberties wherein Christ has made us free, we need "not fear in future the usurpations of the kings, lords, "and bishops of England." The accompanying claim of Parliament to the power of binding America in all cases whatsoever was, indeed, a thorn which galled them much; but they found a salvo in ordering a copy of the repeal to be burnt under the gallows by the common hangman. The General Assembly also stepped forward, and voted the populace several barrels of powder, and puncheons of rum, together with 100*l*. in money, to celebrate the festival. A tremendous mob met together at Hertford and received their present. The powder was placed in a large brick school, and the rum on the common square. While each one was contending for his share, the powder took fire and blew up the school, killing fifteen or sixteen persons, and wounding many. This disaster shook the house where the Consociation was sitting; upon which they resolved that Heaven did not approve of their rejoicings because the repeal was but partial! They therefore ordered a new fast, to do away the iniquities of that day, and to implore the Supreme to direct them in what manner to guard against the machinations of " the locusts who had a king over them, whose name in " the Hebrew tongue is Abaddon, but in the Greek " Apollyon!"

This fast was cooked up with a favourite text in New-England, viz. " He reproved even kings for their " sake." From these words the preachers proved that the King's power lay in his mouth, and in his tail, which, like " a serpent, did hurt for a month and a " year;" and that God would protect his people against "the murderers, the sorceries, the fornication, the thefts" of bishops, popes, and kings, " and make nations angry, " and give them power to judge and destroy those who

240   GENERAL HISTORY OF CONNECTICUT.

" would destroy his prophets and his saints." In this day of great humiliation the prophets entertained the saints with a spice of rejoicing, because "victory was " gotten over the beast, and over his image, and over his " mark, and over the number of his name." " There-" fore," said they, " rejoice, O inhabitants of the earth " and of the sea, because we can get, buy, and sell, with-" out the mark, or the name of the beast, or the num-" ber of his name."

This bombastic declamation against the authority of Great Britain raised the passions of a great portion of this multitude higher than was intended. They had lately been tutored to form high notions of their own consequence, had been intoxicated with a life of confusion in a lawless country, and had now no relish for a government of any kind whatever; accordingly, inflamed by the rhapsodies of the preachers, they set themselves against that of the colony; arguing that if the Lord would reprove kings, lords, and bishops, for their sake, he would also reprove governors, magistrates, and consociations, for their sakes.

This revolt of a part of the people was encouraged and strengthened by the adherents of Governor Fitch, the five discarded councillors, and the loyalists; so that very formidable bodies soon appeared in divers towns, threatening destruction to the General Assembly, Consociation, Associations, executive courts, &c. &c. Colonel Street Hall, of Wallingford, a loyalist, was appointed governor over these supreme multitudes. They soon acquainted the General Assembly and Consociation that, by the authority that England had been reformed, by the same authority should Connecticut be reformed; and Mr. Hall sent a letter to the Judges of the County Court, then sitting at Newhaven, purporting that it was not agreeable to the people for them to continue their proceedings, or that any executions should be granted, and concluding thus: "Ye that have " ears to hear, hear what is said unto you; for we shall " quickly come." The judges, without hesitation or adjournment, ran out of court and went home as privately as possible. The merchants, the Gospel ministers, the lawyers, and judges, who had with great zeal inculcated the divine right of the people to resist kings, found themselves in a starving condition under the exercise of their boasted right. The General Assembly and Association, however, again convened, and, after much fasting and prayer, resolved that the conduct of Street Hall, Esq. and his associates, was seditious and treasonable; and ordered the Attorney-General, Colonel Elihu Hall, to indict his nephew, Street Hall, for treasonable practices. The Attorney-General refused to comply with this mandate, whereupon he was dismissed, and James Hillhouse, Esq. appointed in his place, who indicted Street Hall; but no sheriff dared serve the warrant. Street Hall ordered his people to prepare for battle and to be ready at a minute's warning, and rode about with one servant, in defiance of the General Assembly, who likewise prepared to support their power. It is most likely that Street Hall would have prevailed had an engagement taken place; for the episcopalians, and all the friends of Mr. Fitch and the five dismissed councillors, would have supported Mr. Hall. But a battle was prevented by the interposition of the Consociation, with this curious Gospel axiom,

viz. that it was legal and politic in the people to oppose and resist the foreign power which was unjustly claimed by the King of Great Britain; but it was neither politic nor right to oppose the magistrates and laws made by themselves. They prevailed on Street Hall to condescend to write to the General Assembly to this effect: " That he was a friend to the laws and con-
" stitution of the colony, and wished to support both;
" and should do it, on condition that they would rescind
" their vote, and that no one should be prosecuted for
" what had been done by him and his associates." The Assembly very gladly voted this overture of Street Hall to be satisfactory; and thus peace was re-established between the Assembly and Street Hall. Nevertheless, Mr. Hall was greatly censured by his partisans for this compromise; and he lived in constant expectation of their hanging him, till he softened them by this remarkable address in vindication of his conduct:
" We have done," said he, " everything in our power to
" support the authority of the British Parliament over
" the colonies. We have lost our property, local repu-
" tations, and all colonial offices and respect among our
" countrymen, in defence of that King and Parliament
" who have not shed a tear for our sufferings, nor failed
" to sacrifice their own dignities and their best friends
" to please a party that never will be easy until another
" Oliver arise and extirpate kings, lords, and bishops.
" By heavens!" added Street Hall, with great energy,
" I will rest my life upon this single question, Who
" would stand up in defence of a king who prefers his
" enemies to his friends? If you acquit me, I shall
" more fully declare my principles."

The mob, after much consideration, declared their approbation of Mr. Hall's conduct; upon which he resumed his address nearly as follows:

"Gentlemen, we have once been betrayed and "forsaken by the King and Parliament of Great "Britain; no dependence, then, ought henceforth to "be placed upon either. It is plain to me, that if "we had extirpated the General Assembly and all "the avowed enemies of the constitution of Great "Britain, yet that very Parliament would have been "the first of all the creation to honour us with a gal-"lows for our reward. I therefore swear by Him who "controls the wheels of time, that in future I will sup-"port the laws and dignity of the colony, and never "more put any confidence in princes or British Parlia-"ment. The Saviour of the world trusted Judas but "once; and it is my opinion that those who betray and "forsake their friends ought to experience the wrath "and indignation of friends turned enemies. In this "case, baseness is policy, ingratitude loyalty, and re-"venge heroic virtue!"

Colonel Street Hall spoke with great vehemence, and might be censured for rashness by people who were not in America at the time; but his sentiments reached the hearts of half of the King's friends there; for the repeal of the Stamp Act had fixed in their breasts an everlasting hatred to the fickle temper of Britons.

Few people, hereafter, will advance a sixpence in support of any acts of the Parliament of Great Britain over her colonies. Prior to the year 1766 such a public spirit prevailed in America over private interest as would naturally have led the people to conform to any acts of the British Parliament, from a deep-rooted confidence that the requisitions of Britain would be no other than the requisitions of wisdom and necessity. Two-thirds, I may say with safety, of all the people in America thought there was wisdom and justice in the Stamp Act, and wished to have it continued: first, because they were sensible of being greatly indebted to the generosity and protection of Britain; secondly, because they had rather be subject to the control of Parliament in regard to a revenue, than have it raised by the authority of their own Assemblies, who favour the rich and oppress the poor; and thirdly, because the Stamp Act would have prevented innumerable suits at law, the costs of which, in Connecticut, have during the last forty years amounted to ten times as much as all others for war, gospel, physic, the poor, &c. &c. It is impossible to describe the disappointment and mortification they suffered by the repeal of that act; it exposed them to calumny, derision, and oppression; it disheartened all, and occasioned the defection of many, while their adversaries triumphed in the encouragement it had given them to prosecute their malicious schemes against the Church, King, laws, and commerce of England. However, in regard to the question of raising a revenue in America, I have never met with one American who would not allow (though unwillingly) the reasonableness of it, with certain conditions and provisos.

Thus: 1. The judges and lawyers required the tax to be imposed by the General Assembly of each province. 2. The merchants, whose conscience is gain, and who commonly constitute more than half of the Assembly, declared that, before any revenue was raised, the

Navigation Act should be repealed, and the East India Company, and all the monopolies, dissolved. 3. The Gospel ministers, whose power in New-England is terrible to flesh and spirit, would contribute to a revenue after the King and Parliament had dropped their claim to supreme authority over America, and secured the American Vine against the domination and usurpations of bishops. To these sources may be traced all the objections made against a revenue in America, which sprung from three orders of men of the least real benefit to the country, and whose proportion to all others there is not one to a hundred; though they have had the art and address, by imposition and delusion, to involve them in their tumultuous contentions and ruinous projects and undertakings. Indeed, the clergy, lawyers, and merchants of European countries have been represented as the worst enemies of society—the great promoters of discord, war, insurrections, and rebellions; but the heathen have not yet given us an example how depraved mankind would be without them. However, supposing the crimination to have foundation, there is one good reason to be offered in palliation of it. Most governments are too apt to adopt the maxim of rewarding prosperous opposing zealots, whilst the exertions of oppressed friends are passed over, if not with contempt at least with silent neglect. Hence, men will naturally be induced, in defiance of law and gospel, to head parties, to become consequential in the world.

APPENDIX.

THE preceding sheets bring the "History of Connecticut" to its latest period of amity with Great Britain, agreeable to the plan upon which it was begun. I propose laying before my readers, in an Appendix, a summary account of the proceedings of the people of Connecticut immediately leading to their open hostilities against the Mother Country, not only because some events are not at all, or erroneously, known here, but also because they will form a supplement necessary in several instances to what has been already related. Another reason that induces me to make the proposed addition is, the contradictions that have so frequently appeared regarding the statements made by the author of the "History," as to acts and laws that were in force in the colony of Connecticut during its early settlement, and which had been handed down to their posterity by the *Sober Dissenters*, as they called themselves, many of which laws remained in force up to the beginning of the Revolutionary War.

Mr. James Hammond Trumbull, a descendant of Governor Trumbull, so frequently spoken of in this work and notes, in a book lately published by him, entitled "The True Blue Laws of "Connecticut and Newhaven, and the False Blue Laws invented "by the Rev. Samuel Peters," has taken unnecessary pains to show that the Blue Laws represented in the "History" were never published in the colony, and consequently must be factitious. The author of the "History" himself mentions that they never were published; and had Mr. Trumbull referred to the action of the meeting of the planters in Quinnipiack, the 4th of June, 1639, he would have seen that the general resolutions then and there adopted were to be their laws, and that no laws were enacted. (See Note on pages 44–47.)

Many writers have endeavoured to point out the motive which prompted the Americans to the wish of being independent of Great Britain, who had for a century and a half nursed and protected them with parental tenderness; but they have only touched upon the reasons ostensibly held up by the Americans, but which are merely a veil to the true causes. These, therefore, I shall endeavour to set before the reader.

In the first place: England, as if afraid to venture her Constitution in America, had kept it at an awful distance, and established in many of her colonies republicanism, wherein the democratic absorbs the regal and aristocratic part of the English Constitution. The people naturally imbibed the idea that they were superior to kings and lords, because they controlled their representatives, governors, and councils. This is the infallible consequence of popular governments.

Secondly: The English had, like the Dutch, adopted the errors of ancient Rome, who judged that her colonies could be held in subjection only by natives of Rome; and therefore all emoluments were carefully withheld from all natives of the colonies.

Thirdly: The learned and opulent families in America were not honoured by their King like those born in Britain.

Fourthly: The Americans saw themselves despised by the Britons, "though bone of their bone and flesh of their flesh." They felt and complained of, without redress, the sad effects of convicts, the curses of human society and the disgrace of England, taken from the dungeons, jails, and gibbets, and poured into America as the common sewer of England, to murder, plunder, and commit outrage upon the people "whom the King did not "delight to honour."

Hence the rebellion. Human nature is always such that men will never cease struggling for honour, wealth, and power, at the expense of gratitude, loyalty, and virtue.

Indignation and despair seized the gentlemen in America, who thought, like Haman, that their affluence and ease was nothing worth so long as they lay under the sovereign's contempt. They declared that the insult reached the whole continent, in which were to be found only two Baronets of Great Britain, while all the other inhabitants were held beneath the yeomanry of England. They added: "Let Cæsar tremble! Let wealth and private "property depart, to deliver our country from the injuries of our "elder brethren!" How easily might the rebellion have been averted by the granting of titles! With what reason faction and discontent spring up in South-America, may be learned from the dear-bought wisdom of Spain, who transported to her colonies her own Constitution in Church and State, rewarded merit in whatever part of her territories it appeared, sent bishops to govern and ordain in every church in South-America, and they, together with the native *noblesse*, promoted harmony, the offspring of justice and policy; while North-America abounded with discord, hatred, and rebellion, entirely from want of policy and justice in their party-coloured charters, and of the honours and privileges of natural-born subjects of Great Britain.

It appears that the British Government, in the last century, did not expect New-England to remain under their authority; nor did the New-Englanders consider themselves as subjects, but allies, of Great Britain. It seems that England's intent was to afford an asylum to the republicans, who had been a scourge to the British Constitution; and so, to encourage that restless party to emigrate, republican charters were granted, and privileges and promises given them far beyond what any Englishman in England was entitled to. The emigrants were empowered to make laws in Church and State, agreeable to their own will and pleasure, without the King's approbation; they were excused from all quit-rents, all Government taxes, and promised protection without paying homage to the British King, and their children entitled to the same rights and privileges as if born in England. However hard this bargain was upon the side of England, she had performed her part, except in the last respect—indeed, the most material in policy and in the minds of the principal gentlemen of New-England. The honour of nobility had not been conferred on any of them, and therefore they had never enjoyed the full privileges and liberties of the Britons, but, in a degree, had ever been held in bondage under their chartered republican systems, wherein gentlemen of learning and property attain not to equal power with the peasants. The people of New-England were rightly styled republicans; but a distinction should be made between the learned and the unlearned, the rich and the poor. The latter formed a great majority; therefore the minority were obliged to wear the livery of the majority, in order to secure their election into office. These very republican gentlemen were ambitious, fond of the power of governing, and grudged no money or pains to obtain an annual office. What would they not have given for a dignity depending not on the fickle will of a multitude, but on the steady reason and generosity of a king? The merchants, lawyers, and clergy, to appearance were republicans, but not one of them was really so. The truth is, they found necessity on the one hand, and British neglect on the other, to be so intolerable, that they rather chose to risk their lives and fortunes to bring about a revolution, than continue in the situation they were. As to the multitude, they had no cause of complaint: they were accuser, judge, king, and subjects, only to themselves.

The rebellion sprung not from them, but from the merchants, lawyers, and clergy, who were never inimical to the aristocratic branch of the Government, provided they were admitted to share in it according to their merits. It is true, they, like Calvin, the author of their religion, maintained that no man can merit anything of the Great Eternal; nevertheless, they thought they had merited the aristocratic honours which emanate from earthly kings; while kings and nobles of the earth imagine themselves to have merited more than they yet enjoy—even heaven itself—only because they happen to enjoy the honour of being descendants of heroic ancestors.

England had also been as careful to keep to herself her religion and bishops as her civil constitutions and baronies. A million of Churchmen in America had been considered as not worthy of one bishop, while eight millions in South-Britain were scarcely honoured with enough with twenty-six: an insult on common justice, which would have extinguished every spark of affection in America for the English Church, and created an everlasting schism, like that between Constantinople and Rome, had not the majority of the American episcopal clergy been possessed of less ambition than love and zeal. They had suffered on both sides of the Atlantic in name and property, for their endeavours to keep up a union between the Mother Country and her children; but all their arguments and persuasions were insufficient to convince their brethren that England would in future be more generous towards her colonies. One of the first fruits of the grand continental meeting of dissenting divines at Newhaven was a coalition between the republican and the minor part of the episcopal clergy, who were soon joined by the merchants, lawyers, and planters, with a view of procuring titles, ordination, and government, independent of Great Britain. Such were the real sources of the rebellion in America. The invasion of this or that colonial right, the oppression of this or that act of Parliament, were merely the pretended causes of it, which the ill-humour of a misgoverned people prompted them eagerly to hold up—causes which would never have found existence, whose existence had never been necessary, if a better system of American policy had been adopted; but, being produced, the shadow of complaint was exhibited instead of the substance, pretence instead of reality. Every republican pulpit resounded with invectives against the King, Lords, and Commons, who claimed a power to tax and govern the people of America— a power which their charters and ancestors knew nothing of. " Britons," they said, " call our property theirs; they consider us " as slaves—as hewers of wood and drawers of water to the de- " scendants of those tyrants of Church and State who in the last " century expelled and persecuted our fathers into the wilds of " America. We have charters sacred as Magna Charta and the " Bill of Rights."

They declared that the liberties of America ought to be defended with the blood of millions; that the Attorney-General ought to impeach the Parliament of Great Britain, and all its abettors, of high treason, for daring to tax the freemen of America; that each colony was a palatinate, and the people a palatine; that the people of Connecticut had as much authority to issue a writ of *quo warranto* against Magna Charta, as the King had to order such a writ against the Charter of Connecticut.

By ravings of this kind did the *Sober Dissenters* manifest their discontents, when the various measures for raising a revenue in America were adopted by the British ministry. That of sending tea to America, in 1773, subject to a duty of three pence on the pound, payable in America, particularly excited their clamour, as designed, they said, to establish a precedent of British taxation in this country; and, notwithstanding all the remonstrances of the loyalists, who strenuously exerted themselves in removing vulgar prejudices and procuring a reconciliation with circumstances rendered unavoidable by the necessity of the times, they effectually inflamed the minds of the populace by reading, in the meetings on Sunday, letters said to have been sent by Dr. Franklin, I. Temple, and others, representing the danger of paying any tax imposed by Parliament, and the evil protestantism was threatened with by a Roman Catholic King, by Jacobites, tories, and episcopal clergy in both countries, all enemies to liberty and the American Vine; and adding that, if the Americans paid the tax on tea, there were three hundred other taxes ready to be imposed upon them, one of which was "50*l*. for every son born in wedlock, to "maintain the natural children of the lords and bishops of Eng-" land."

The moderate counsel of the loyalists had formerly been attended with some effect; but it was forced to give place to the ribaldry just mentioned, and an opposition much more resolute was determined upon against the tea-act than had been made to the Stamp Act.

A provincial congress, committee of correspondence, committee of safety, in every town, &c. &c. now started up for the purpose of setting the colony in an uproar against the Parliament of Great Britain. To this end contributed not a little the falsehoods and artifices of Mr. Handcock, and other Boston merchants, who had in their storehouses nearly 40,000 half-boxes of tea, smuggled from the Dutch; which would never have been sold had the Company's teas been once admitted into America, as the latter were not only the better in quality, but, the duty being reduced from one shilling to three pence, would be also the much cheaper commodity. Mr. Handcock and his compatriots, therefore, were by no means wanting in endeavours to procure for the first teas which arrived in New-England the reception they met with in the harbour of Boston.

That famous exploit afforded them an opportunity of clearing their warehouses, which they prudently resolved to do as soon as possible, lest the reception of the Company's tea in other provinces, or other possible circumstances, should afterwards put it out of their power. An idea began to prevail that a non-importation of tea was an advisable measure upon the present occasion; accordingly, they advertised that, after disposing of their present stock, they would not import or have any further dealings in tea for two years. This at once tended to fill their pockets, and exalt their characters as patriots.

The people, ignorant of the extent of such stock, and apprehensive of being deprived of an article they were so passionately fond of, eagerly furnished themselves with quantities sufficient for that time, mostly of about thirty, forty, and fifty pounds, notwithstanding the prices were advanced one shilling per pound, upon the pretence of raising money to pay for the tea destroyed, in order to secure the religion and liberty of America, which, under that idea, it was generally acknowledged ought to be done. When the tea was mostly disposed of, the people found that the extra price they had given for it was designed for the venders, instead of for the East-India Company, whose tea at the bottom of the harbour was not to be paid for. They murmured; whereupon the smugglers voted that they would not drink any more tea, but burn on the Common what they had left. Some tea was disposed of, and the public-spirited transaction blazoned in the newspapers. But this was not all: the smugglers sent letters to the leaders of mobs in the country, enjoining them to wait upon the purchasers of their tea, and compel them to burn it, as a proof of their patriotism. Those honourable instructions were obeyed, to the real grievance of the holders of the tea. "Let Mr. Handcock," said they, "and "the other merchant-smugglers, return us our money, and then "you shall be welcome to burn the tea according to their "orders."

But it signified nothing to dispute the equity of the requisition; the cry was, "Join, or die!" Nor would the Sons of Liberty be satisfied with anything less than that each owner of tea should with his own hands bring forth the same and burn it, and then sign a declaration that he had acted in this affair voluntarily and without any compulsion, and, moreover, pay the printer for inserting it in the newspapers.

An act of Parliament for shutting up the port of Boston was the immediate consequence of the destruction of the East-India Company's tea. It took place in June, 1774, and was considered by the Americans as designed to reduce the Bostonians "to the "most servile and mean compliance ever attempted to be imposed "on a free people, and allowed to be infinitely more alarming "and dangerous to their common liberties than even the hydra, "the Stamp Act."

Due care had been taken to enforce it, by sending General Gage, as Governor, to Boston, where he arrived the preceding month with a number of troops. Determined, however, as Parliament seemed, on compulsion, the colonists were equally bent on resistance, and resolved on a Continental Congress to direct their operations. In the mean time, contributions for relieving the distressed people in Boston were voted by the colonies; and Connecticut, through the officiousness of Jonathan Trumbull, its Governor, had the honour of first setting the example, by having a meeting called in Hebron, the inhabitants of which remained loyal and refused to vote for the collection. Governor Trumbull imputed this to the influence of the Rev. Samuel Peters (of whom more will be said hereafter) and his family. Many were the attempts made to ruin his character, but unsuccessfully; he was too well beloved and befriended in the town.

Falsehoods and seditions had now for some time been every day increasing in the province; and men who were secret propagators of traitorous opinions, pretended in public to look up to the Consociation, the great focus of Divine illumination, for direction. After much fasting and praying, that holy leaven discovered an admirable method of advancing the blessed work of protestant liberty. The doors of prisons were opened, and prisoners became leaders of mobs composed of negroes, vagabonds, and thieves, who had much to gain and nothing to lose. The besom of destruction first cleared away the creditors of the renegades, and then the Sandemanians, presbyterians, and episcopalians. The unfortunate complained to the Governor and magistrates of the outrages of the banditti, begging the protection of the laws. The following was the best answer returned by the magistrates:

"The proceedings of which you complain are like the acts of "Parliament; but be this as it may, we are only servants of the "people, in whom all power centres, and who have assumed their "natural right to judge and act for themselves."

The loyalists armed, to defend themselves and property against the public thieves; but the Liberty Boys were instantly honoured by the ministers, deacons, and justices, who caused the Grand Jury to indict, as tories and rioters, those who presumed to defend their houses, and the courts fined and imprisoned them.

Thus horridly, by night and day, were the mobs driven on by the hopes of plunder and the pleasure of domineering over their superiors. Having sent terror and lamentation through their own colony, the incarnate fiends paid a visit to the episcopalians of Great Barrington, whose numbers exceeded that of the *Sober Dissenters*. Their wrath chiefly fell upon the Rev. Mr. Bostwick and David Ingersoll, Esq. The former was lashed with his back to a tree, and almost killed; but on account of the fits of his wife and mother, and the screamings of the women and children, the mob released him upon his signing the eighteen articles, or their League or Covenant, as they called it, (which without doubt was the same as that drawn up and written by Governor Trumbull, which will be referred to hereafter.) As to Mr. Ingersoll, after demolishing his house and stealing his goods, they brought him almost naked into Connecticut upon the bare back of a horse, in spite of the distresses of his mother and sister, which were enough to melt the heart of a savage, though producing in the *Sober Dissenters* but peals of laughter that rent the skies.

Treatment so extremely barbarous did Mr. Ingersoll receive

at their hands, that the sheriff of Litchfield County could not withhold his interposition, by which means he was set at liberty, after signing the league and covenant. The Grand Jury indicted some of the leaders in this riot, but the Court dismissed them, upon receiving information from Boston that Ingersoll had seceded from the House of Representatives, and declared for the King of England.

What caused this irruption of the mob into Great Barrington, follows: The laws of Massachusets-Bay gave each town a power to vote a tax for the support of the ministry, schools, poor, &c. The money, when collected, was deposited with the town treasurer, who is obliged to pay it according to the determination of the majority of the voters. The *Sober Dissenters*, for many years, had been the majority in Barrington, and had annually voted about two hundred pounds sterling for the ministry, above half of which was taken from the Churchmen and Lutherans, whose ministers could have no part of it, because separately the greatest number of voters were *Sober Dissenters*, who gave the whole to their minister. This was deemed liberty and gospel in New-England; but mark the sequel. The Lutherans and some other sects having joined the Church party, the Church gained the majority. Next year the town voted the money, as usual, for the ministry, &c.; but the majority voted that the treasurer should pay the share appointed for the ministry to the Church clergyman, which was accordingly done; whereupon the *Sober Dissenters* cried out, "Tyranny and persecution!" and applied to Governor Hutchinson, then the idol and protector of the Independents, for relief. His Excellency, ever willing to leave "Paul bound," found a method of reversing the vote of the majority of the freemen of Barrington in favour of the Churchmen, calling it "a vote obtained by wrong "and fraud." The Governor, by law or without law, appointed Mayor Hawley, of Northampton, to be Moderator of the town-meeting in Barrington. The Mayor accordingly attended, but, after exerting himself for three days in behalf of his oppressed brethren, was obliged to declare that the episcopalians had a great majority of legal voters; he then went home, leaving matters as he found them.

The *Sober Dissenters* were always so poor in Barrington that they could not have supported their minister without taxing their neighbours; and when they lost that power, their minister departed from them, "because," as he said, "the Lord "had called him to Rhode-Island." To overthrow the majority of the Church, and to establish the American Vine upon its old foundation, was the main intention of the *Sober Dissenters* of Connecticut in visiting Great Barrington at this time.

The warlike preparations throughout the colonies, and the intelligence obtained from certain credible refugees of a secret design, formed in Connecticut and Massachusets-Bay, to attack the royal army, induced General Gage to make some fortifications upon Boston-Neck for their security. These, of course, gave offence; but much more the excursion of a body of troops, on the 19th of April, 1775, to destroy a magazine of stores at Concord, and the skirmishes which ensued. In a letter of the 28th of April from Mr. Trumbull, the Governor of Connecticut, to General Gage, after speaking of the "very just and general alarm" given the "good people" of that province by his arrival at Boston with troops, and subsequent fortifications, he tells the General that "the late hostile and secret inroads of some of the "troops under his command into the heart of the country, and "the violence they had committed, had driven them almost into "a state of desperation." Certain it is, that the populace were then so maddened by false representations and aggravations of events, unfortunate and lamentable enough in themselves, as to be quite ripe for the rebellion the Governor and Assembly were on the point of commencing, though they had the effrontery to remonstrate against the defensive proceedings of the General, in order to conceal their own treachery. Further on, in the same letter, Mr. Trumbull writes thus: "The people of this colony, "you may rely upon it, abhor the idea of taking up arms against "the troops of their sovereign, and dread nothing so much as the "horrors of civil war; but, at the same time, we beg leave to assure "your Excellency that, as they apprehend themselves justified "by the principles of self-defence, so they are most firmly re- "solved to defend their rights and privileges to the last extremity;

APPENDIX. 257

"nor will they be restrained from giving aid to their brethren,
"if an unjustifiable attack is made upon them. Is there no way
"to prevent this unhappy dispute from coming to extremities?
"Is there no alternative but absolute submission or the desola-
"tions of war? By that humanity which constitutes so amiable
"a part of your character, for the honour of our sovereign, and
"by the glory of the British empire, we entreat you to prevent it,
"if it be possible. Surely, it is to be hoped that the temperate
"wisdom of the empire might, even yet, find expedients to restore
"peace, that so all parts of the empire may enjoy their particular
"rights, honours, and immunities. Certainly this is an event
"most devoutly to be wished for; and will it not be consistent
"with your duty to suspend the operations of war, on your part,
"and enable us, on ours, to quiet the minds of the people, at
"least till the result of some further deliberations may be
"known?" &c. &c.

From this letter, written, as it was, from the Governor of a province at the desire of its General Assembly, the people of England might have learned to think of the American as they did of the French sincerity. It is almost past credit that, amidst the earnest protestations it contains of a peaceable disposition in Mr. Trumbull and the rest of his coadjutors in the Government of Connecticut, they were meditating and actually taking measures for the capture of certain of the King's forts, and the destruction of General Gage and his whole army, instead of quieting the minds of the people! Yet such was the fact. They had commissioned Motte and Phelps to draft men from the militia, if volunteers should not readily appear, for a secret expedition, which proved to be against Ticonderoga and Crown Point; and the treasurer of the colony, by order of the Governor and Council, had paid 1500*l.* to bear their expenses. Nay, even before the date of the above amiable epistle, Motte and Phelps had left Hertford on that trea-sonable undertaking, in which they were joined on the way by Colonels Allen and Easton. Nor was this the only insidious enter-prise that they had to cover. The "good people" throughout the province, to the number of nearly 20,000, were secretly arming themselves, and filing off, to avoid suspicion, in small parties of ten and a dozen, to meet "their brethren" the Massachusets; not, however, with the view of "giving aid, should any unjustifi- "able attack be made upon them," but to "surprise" Boston by storm. In addition to the Governor's letter, the mock-peacemakers, the General Assembly, had deputed Dr. Samuel Johnson, son of the Rev. Dr. Johnson, spoken of in this work, and Oliver Wolcott, Esq. both of the Council, which had ordered the 1500*l.* for the adventurers to Ticonderoga, to wait upon General Gage, the more effectually to amuse and deceive him into confidence and inaction. But happily, at a critical time, just before the intended storm and slaughter at Boston, the news of the success of the secret expedition reached the town, which fully discovered the true character and business of the two Connecticut ambassadors, and rendered it necessary for them, *sans cérémonie,* to retire from Boston, and General Gage immediately to render the fortifications at the Neck impregnable.

The *Sober Dissenters,* chagrined at being disappointed in their hostile project against Boston, readily embraced the opportunities which afforded of wreaking their vengeance upon New-York. At the instance of the rebel party there, who found themselves too weak to effect their purpose of subverting the Constitution of the province, a large body immediately posted to their assistance, delivered "their brethren" from the slavery of regal government, and invested them with the liberty of doing that which was fit in their own eyes, under the democratic administration of the immaculate Livingstons, Morris, Schuyler, &c. As seemed necessary to the furtherance of their pacific views, frequent irruptions were made afterwards, in which many loyalists were disarmed and plundered, and some of them taken prisoners. Among these last were the Rev. Dr. Seabury and the Mayor of New-York. Governor Tryon happily escaped their fury; as also did the Rev. Miles Cooper, LL.D., who was leaving his house through a back window when a party of ruffians burst into his chamber and thrust their bayonets into the bed he had just quitted. Mr. Rivington was one of the sufferers by the loss of his property.

These "good people" of Governor Trumbull's, who dreaded nothing so much as a civil war, with the reverse of reluctance,

APPENDIX. 259

plundered his house of all printing materials and furniture, and carried the type to Newhaven, where they were used in the service of Congress.

The King's statue, however, maintained its ground till after General Washington, with the Continental army, had taken possession of the city; when it was indicted for high treason against the Dominions of America, found guilty, and received a quaint sentence of this kind, viz. That it should undergo the act of decollation; and, inasmuch as it had no bowels, its legs should be broken, and that the lead of it should be run into bullets, for the destruction of the English bloody-backs, and the refuse cast into the sea. The sentence was immediately carried into execution, amidst the huzzas and vociferations of "Praise ye the "Lord!"

This insult upon his Majesty, General Washington, to his credit, thought proper thus to notice in his general orders of the next day. He was sorry, he said, that his soldiers should in a riotous manner pull down the statue of the King of Great Britain.

While General Washington remained in possession of New-York, Connecticut served as a prison for those persons who had the misfortune to fall under his suspicion as disaffected to the cause of freedom. He was himself, however, at length obliged to evacuate it by General Howe, to the great relief of such royalists as remained.

In April, 1777, some magazines having been formed by the Americans at Danbury and Ridgfield, Major-General Tryon was sent with 1800 men to carry off or destroy them.

They reached the places of their destination with little opposition; but the whole force of the country being collected to obstruct their return, the General was obliged to set the stores on fire, by which means those towns were unavoidably burnt. David Wooster, the rebel general, Benedict Arnold's old friend and acquaintance, and mobbing confederate, received a fatal ball through his bladder as he was harassing the rear of the royal troops, of which, after being carried forty miles to Newhaven, he died, and was buried by the side of the grave of David Dixwell, one of the Judges of Charles the First.

In the summer of 1779 Sir Henry Clinton sent General Tryon, with a large party of soldiers, for the relief of the loyalists in Connecticut. They landed at Newhaven after much opposition, and, having accomplished their object, sailed to Fairfield, which town they were necessitated, by the opposition of the rebels, to set fire to, before the loyalists could be released from prison. General Tryon then repaired to Norwalk, where, having by proclamation enjoined the inhabitants to keep within their houses, he ordered sentinels to be stationed at every door to prevent disorders—a tenderness, however, they insulted, by firing upon the very men thus appointed to guard them. The consequence was, destruction to themselves, and the whole town, which was laid in ashes.

I have now mentioned the principal proceedings by which the people of Connecticut had distinguished themselves in bringing on and supporting the rebellion in America, and that, I believe, in a manner sufficiently particular to show their violence and deceit.

It is very observable that a peculiar characteristic resolution appeared to possess the people of Connecticut. As, on the one hand, rebellion had erected her crest in that province with more insolence and vigour than in the rest, so, on the other hand, loyalty had there exhibited proofs of zeal, attachment, perseverance, and fortitude, far beyond example elsewhere to be found in America. In particular, the episcopal clergy had acquired immortal honour by their steady adherence to their oaths and firmness under the " assaults of their enemies ; " not a man among them all, in this fiery trial, having dishonoured either the King or Church of England by apostacy. The sufferings of some of them I cannot pass over in silence.

Among the greatest enemies to the cause of the *Sober Dissenters*, and among the greatest friends to that of the Church of England, the Rev. Samuel Peters stood conspicuous. A descendant of one of the first settlers in the colony, greatly venerated and beloved by the inhabitants of Hebron, where he was born in 1735, and being a man of such truth and integrity as to command great weight in all that concerned the benefits of the colony, it may not be out of place to give a slight sketch of the treatment he received at the commencement of the war, and the cause that drove him from his native country.[1]

In the year 1758 Dr. Peters went to England for the purpose of being ordained. He had been in ill health for some time previous to this, but was most anxious for his ordination on account of the church in Hebron being vacant. He remained in England, very feeble, for some time, and refused a living there because he wished to return to his numerous relations and friends in New-England, and especially to Hebron, where he had left his mother, whom he highly loved and venerated for her maternal tenderness, wisdom, and piety, and for the sake of the episcopal church in that town, erected in 1735, which never had a resident clergyman, though they had sent four candidates to London for holy orders, and all perished in going or returning, viz. The Rev. B. Dean, in returning, the ship and crew were lost in a storm; the Rev. Jonathan Cotton, returning, died at sea with the smallpox; the Rev. —— Feveryear, died on returning in the West-Indies; Mr. James Usher, A. M., in going out, was taken by the French and carried into Bayonne, dying there with the smallpox.

These four deaths manifested the want of a bishop in North-America, which was owing to bad policy, and not religion, and was one great reason of the separation of the two countries, as clearly now appears by bishops being now established in many States without any offence to other protestant sects of christians.

His Grace the Archbishop of Canterbury and the Lord-Bishop of London willingly gratified the wish of Dr. Peters, appointing him Rector of Hebron and Hertford. The Society for the Propagation of the Gospel in Foreign Parts appointed him their itinerant missionary in New-England, and his Majesty George the Second granted him his letters-patent of protection to all governors, admirals, generals, and officers by sea and land, to protect him against all insults and abuse, and to support him at all times in his sacred office.

[1] Which is taken from a manuscript written by the Doctor himself, and using his own language. This manuscript came into my hands only a few weeks ago, with many other documents relating to the Revolutionary War.—ED. NOTE.

Dr. Peters returned to Hebron in 1760, and was received with much joy and gratitude by the people of all denominations, with whom he had lived fourteen years in love, peace, and harmony, without knowing an enemy, until the tea belonging to the East-India Company was destroyed in Boston. The news, reaching Hertford, caused great surprise and sorrow, and the people condemned the illegal and violent action of the mob in Boston.

The news soon reached England, and the Government sent General Gage and Admiral Graves to block up the harbour of Boston and demand payment for the teas destroyed. Soon after their arrival at Boston a report was spread through the country that General Gage had shut up the town of Boston, and the people must perish with hunger; whereupon Jonathan Trumbull, Governor of Connecticut, pretending to credit the report, sent his circular letter to every clergyman in the colony, requiring it to be read on the Sabbath-day to their respective congregations, and to urge the selectmen to warn town-meetings to appoint a general contribution for the support of the poor people in Boston, shut up to starve by General Gage and Admiral Graves.

The Governor's letter was obeyed. Hebron held the first meeting. Deacon John Phelps was chosen Moderator, and explained the business of the meeting, giving leave to all persons to speak their minds on the subject. Capt. Ben. Buell was the first who spoke in favour of passing a vote for a general collection. Col. Alex. Phelps next spoke against having any collection. The Rev. Elijah Lathrop made the third speech, in favour of a general collection. The Rev. Dr. Samuel Peters made the fourth speech, against having any vote or collection, for the reasons following:

"First: Because Boston is not, and has not been, shut up by
" order of General Gage, and all people pass out of and into Boston
" as usual, and the citizens want not our charitable help; of con-
" sequence, Governor Trumbull's letter was premature, occasioned,
" perhaps, by false information from some friend to the destroy-
" ers of the teas, or an enemy to America.

"Secondly: Governor Trumbull, in his letter, has not assigned
" any proof of the fact that Boston is, or has been, shut up by
" General Gage.

"Thirdly: The teas destroyed in the harbour of Boston ought "to be paid for by the author of that horrible crime; for which "deed the King and Parliament have ordered Admiral Graves to "blockade the harbour of Boston, until the teas wickedly de-"stroyed are paid for; when the blockade will cease, or I will "give my last shilling to help the poor of Boston."

The question was then called for.

The Moderator commanded silence, and said: "Will not more "of this Assembly speak on the subject?"

The answer was a general cry of "No! no!"

The Moderator then put the question: "Will you vote for the "general collection for the support of the poor, said to be shut up "in Boston to perish with hunger, by the order of General Gage? "You that are for the affirmative, hold up your right hands."

Only four hands were held up.

The Moderator said: "You that are for the negative, hold "up your right hands."

Every hand but the four was held up.

The Moderator proclaimed that the negatives, by a vast majority, had determined the question. "Therefore, I dissolve this "town-meeting."

Hertford, the capital of Connecticut colony, held the next town-meeting, and, after due consideration of Governor Trumbull's letter, unanimously negatived to vote for a general collection, and the Moderator dissolved the town-meeting.

The doings of Hertford and Hebron were soon spread, and put a stop to all other town-meetings in Connecticut, to the disappointment and mortification of Governor Trumbull, who laid the blame on the influence of Dr. Peters, the episcopal clergyman of these two towns.

Hence the Governor spread the report that Dr. Peters was a dangerous enemy to America, by his correspondence with Lord North and the bishops of England, and ought to be driven out of his native country for the safety of it. Governor Trumbull began and effected this by his Windham mobs, and the mobs of the tea-destroyers in Boston harbour.

This is the true cause of Dr. Peters leaving America, and not because he was an enemy; for he was never an enemy to any man in his life.

This statement Governor Trumbull spread by his letters to the ministers in Windham, where he resided, and added that it could be proved by copies of letters in the Doctor's house, if sought for suddenly. This letter was read at the meeting on Sunday, the 14th of August, 1774, which caused a large number of the hearers to unite in the afternoon and ride to Hebron, and, after midnight, to surround the house of Dr. Peters, awaking him and his family in great surprise.

Dr. Peters opened the window, and desired to be informed what was the occasion of such a multitude assembling? The answer was, "To search your house! Open your doors!"

Dr. Peters said: "I know you not, but will open my doors "very soon."

Having put on his clothes, he opened his doors and gate, when ten men came into his house. Dr. Peters begged them to be seated, and they sat down. They then said: "We have waited "upon you, sir, to search your house from top to bottom, to find "your correspondence with the English bishops, Lord North, "and other people in Great Britain."

Dr. Peters replied: "Your demand is new and extraordinary; "but here are my keys and library, and you can search my house, "but I hope you will not destroy my papers."

They searched, and read all his correspondence with the bishops and people in England and Europe, and on Monday, before noon, reported to the multitude that they had "seen and read "the correspondence held by Dr. Peters with the people of Eng-"land, and found nothing against the liberty and rights of Amer-"ica; and, as we have been misinformed, let us return home;" and off they went.

This did not satisfy Governor Trumbull. He therefore sent another mob from Windham, armed with guns, swords, and staves, to visit Dr. Peters, and require his signature to eighteen articles which he (the Governor) had written, and his son David, one of the commanders of the mob, presented to Dr. Peters, who read and returned it, saying: "Sir, I cannot sign it without "violating my conscience, the laws of my God, and my oath to "my King."

David Trumbull replied: "My father told me you might sign "it with safety, and it would save you and your house."

Dr. Peters replied he would not sign it to save his life, and all the world, from destruction.

David Trumbull said: "Then you must take the conse- "quences."

His mob then fired balls into the house, and with stones, bricks, and clubs broke the doors, windows, and furniture, wounding his mother, the nurse of his infant son, and his two brothers, and seizing him, tore off his hat, wig, gown, and cassock, stripping off his shirt, made him naked, (except his breeches, stockings, and shoes,) struck him with their staves and spat in his face, and then placed him upon a horse and carried him more than a mile to their liberty-pole, where they threatened to tar and feather him, and hang him up by the hands, unless he would sign the eighteen articles.

Dr. Peters said: "I am in your power; you can soon finish "my mortal existence, but you cannot destroy my immortal "soul; and, to save it, I refuse to sign any one of those articles."

The mob now cried: "Send for the Rev. Dr. Pomeroy to "pray for this stubborn old tory, before we send him to his own "place."

A sergeant and twelve men were ordered to call on Dr. Pomeroy and desire him to attend and pray for this wicked old tory Peters.

Dr. Pomeroy answered: "I will not attend, nor give any "countenance in murdering the best man in Hebron."

The sergeant reported Dr. Pomeroy's answer. Then an order was given to the mob to go and bring Dr. Pomeroy to the liberty-pole, to be dealt with according to his demerits. The mob went, but could not find Dr. Pomeroy.

By this time the mob had drunk sufficiently, and the two commanders (David Trumbull and Major Wright) stood near Dr. Peters. The Hebron people had now collected, and were prepared to take Dr. Peters out of the hands of the mob. Three bold troopers rode up to the commander, and said: "We have "come to kill you, or deliver Dr. Peters. Resign him, or die!" —placing their pistols at the commanders' breasts. They said: "Take him away, and be silent." They then instantly led him away.

Major Wright mounted his horse, and cried to his mob, "Silence! We have done enough to this old tory priest for "one day, and in four days we will return and subdue his obsti-"nate temper and finish this day's work. Make ready and follow "me to Lebanon."

The mob obeyed, and on their way they saw the wife of John Manee, Esq. sister to Dr. Peters, at whom they discharged three musket-balls, which missed her. The mob huzzaed, and cried out, "We are dam'd sorry!"

The troopers carried Dr. Peters into the house of David Barber, Esq. where they put on his clothes, and conducted him home to his half-ruined house.

The next day Dr. Peters went in his carriage and called on Governor Trumbull, and demanded his protection against the Windham mobs.

The Governor replied: "I was once Governor of the people, "but they have taken all power out of my hands into their own; "and you must apply to them for protection, and it is in your "power to gain it."

Dr. Peters asked his Honour to tell him by what means.

The Governor said: "By signing the paper they presented to "you yesterday, which you refused to sign, and so brought on "you their just resentment."

Dr. Peters replied: "Sir, do you think it my duty to sign "the eighteen articles your son David, at the head of a mob, de-"manded me to sign?"

The Governor answered: "Yes, by all means."

Dr. Peters: "Do you wish to have me justify the outrageous "action of casting into the sea the teas, the property of English "merchants?"

The Governor replied: "Yes; and all friends of America will "do it."

APPENDIX. 267

Dr. Peters: "Did your Honour mean to have me guilty of per-"jury and high treason, by signing those eighteen articles, which "you wrote and gave to your son David for me to sign?"

The Governor replied: "Why do you say I wrote those eigh-"teen articles?"

Dr. Peters answered: "Because I read them, and well know "your handwriting; and your son David, Major Wright, and Mr. "Croker, told me so, and that you had sent them to demand my "signature to the paper. I told them I dare not and could not "sign them without committing perjury and high treason, and "violating my own conscience and God's laws."

The Governor replied: "There is no treason in saying that "George the Third, King of England, is a 'Roman Catholic,' a "'tyrant,' and an 'idiot,' and has forfeited the crown; that no "true friend of America ought to obey him, or any of his laws."

Dr. Peters here arose and took leave of the Governor, with the Hon. William Hillhouse and Capt. David Tarbox, who had been present during the interview, and, when out of the house, declared they were astonished at the words and conduct of the Governor.

Dr. Peters then rode to the Judges of the Supreme Court sitting at Hertford, Col. Eliphalet Dyer being one of the Judges, and desired the Court to protect him from the mob at Windham, who had ill-used him, and threatened to take his life in four days if he did not sign his name to a paper containing eighteen treasonable articles.

The Court replied: "We are ready to do our duty, when the "King's Attorney shall exhibit an indictment against the rioters."

The Attorney arose, and told the Court that it was the duty of the Grand Jury to exhibit the indictment, and not his.

Thus ended the protection of the Supreme Court of Connecticut.

From thence Dr. Peters drove in his carriage to Newhaven, forty miles west from Hertford, and so shunned a third visit of the Windham mob. Here the Doctor applied to the Hon. James Hillhouse for protection, who said: "My house is your "protection; yet I want protection myself against the mobs of "Colonel Wooster and Dr. Benedict Arnold, who are mobbing "the Sandemanians for having spoken against the outrageous "conduct of the destroyers of the teas in Boston harbour. But "as you decline my offer, I advise you to put up at the house of "the Rev. Dr. Hubbard, and, if any disturb you, warn them to "keep out of the yard and house upon pain of death; and if they "break the gate, shoot them, and kill as many as enter the yard. "I will raise men, and come to your assistance."

The Rev. Dr. Hubbard gave up his house to Dr. Peters, and, on hearing that Arnold and Wooster had said they would visit Peters and Hubbard as soon as they had finished with the Sandemanians, Dr. Hubbard removed his wife and children to a neighbour's house, and Dr. Peters told him he would pay for all the damage that might be done to his house. Dr. Peters fastened the gate, and obtained twenty muskets, powder, and balls, and, loading the muskets, with his servants and a friend waited for the mob's coming.

At ten o'clock in the evening Dr. Arnold and his mob came to the gate, and found it shut and barred. He called out to open the gate, and Dr. Peters answered: "The gate shall not be opened "this night but on pain of death!"—holding a musket in his hand.

The mob cried: "Dr. Arnold, break down the gate, and we "will follow you, and punish that tory Peters!"

Arnold replied: "Bring an axe, and split down the gate!"

Dr. Peters said: "Arnold, so sure as you split the gate, I will "blow your brains out, and all that enter this yard to-night!"

Arnold retired from the gate, and told one of his fellows to go forward and split the gate. The mob then cried out: "Dr. Ar"nold is a coward!"

Arnold replied: "I am no coward; but I know Dr. Peters' "disposition and temper, and he will fulfill every promise he "makes; and I have no wish for death at present."

The mob then cried: "Let us depart from this tory house!"

In half an hour after appeared another mob, under the command of Col. David Wooster, and ordered the gate to be opened.

Dr. Peters told Wooster not to open that gate unless he was ready to die, and whoever came this night into the yard, or house, he would shoot, at the same time showing his musket.

Wooster then said to his mob: "Let us go on, and leave this "episcopal tory, who has madness enough to kill any man, and "we will see him to-morrow."

The mobs raised a liberty-pole, and kept watch all night over Dr. Peters; but some friends took his horses over the water to Branford, where Dr. Peters and his servant went the next day in disguise, and from there to Saybrook, and thence to Hebron, where they arrived at midnight on Saturday, and found ten men watching his return; who soon informed the Windham mobs, who prepared on Sunday to pay a visit to Dr. Peters on Sunday night.

The Doctor preached in the church to a numerous congregation in the morning. At 11 o'clock a friend arrived from Windham and informed the Doctor that a large mob would be at his house by midnight, and advised him to abscond, and not attend church in the afternoon.

Dr. Peters desired him to be silent, and attended church in the afternoon, when the assembly was much increased, and the Doctor preached an affectionate sermon from these words: "O that my "head was water, and my eyes fountains of tears. I would weep "day and night for the transgressions of my people." The discourse drew tears from every eye, and the congregation was dismissed, after a most excellent prayer. Many people attended the Doctor to his house, and quietness remained till darkness came on, when several persons were observed around the house as spies.

The Doctor then ordered a servant to take a valuable horse and ride to the west two miles, and then turn and ride to the east until he reached Carter's tree, and there abide until the Doctor came to him.

Dr. Peters then told his mother, to prevent a civil war between the Windham mob coming and the people of Hebron, he must leave her, and go to Boston for protection. He then walked out into his garden in the dark, and thence, unsuspected, across the fields to his servant and horse. Mounting, he told his servant to go home, and tell no person where he saw him last. He then rode off for Boston, 100 miles, and reached there at 5 P. M. the next day, and had an interview with General Gage and Admiral Graves, who gave him ample protection.

The Windham mob went to the east border of Hebron, and three spies met them, and told them Dr. Peters had gone off to the west—likely to New-York. The mob therefore returned home.

Dr. Peters remained in Boston some weeks, and hearing that the ship Fox was soon to sail for England, he went off in the night and walked ten miles, when the stage-coach overtook him and carried him to Portsmouth.

Sir John Wentworth, Governor of Newhampshire, and the Hon. Col. Atkinson, called upon him and invited him to dine, and begged him to preach on Sunday, as their church was vacant by the death of Dr. Browne. Dr. Peters replied: "I " would readily comply with your request, but for fear of letting " the tea-destroyers of Boston know where I am; and you know " their malice against me by the newspapers."

Sir John replied: "They have no influence in Portsmouth, and " we can and will protect you against those public enemies."

Dr. Peters consented, and preached in their church on the following Sunday.

All was quiet till Wednesday, at noon, when a man rode up to the door and called the hostler to take his horse and feed him. He then came in and called for dinner. He saw Dr. Peters, but did not know him, and asked him if he belonged to the house.

The Doctor said "Yes." He then gave him a Boston newspaper, in which was an advertisement, signed John Hancock, promising 200*l*. to any person taking up the Rev. Samuel Peters and delivering him to a Committee of Safety, he having "re-" treated from Boston in the night, and will do mischief wherever " he goes, being a most bitter enemy to the rights and liberty of " America."

The man asked the Doctor: "Have you seen that wicked old priest?"

The Doctor replied: "The landlord was at church, and a " stranger preached last Sunday; perhaps he can tell his name. " I will go and call him."

The Doctor went and told the landlord what the stranger was in pursuit of, and wished to see him.

The landlord told his servant to run and tell the ferryman

APPENDIX. 271

to say to any one inquiring after a clergyman, that he had carried over a man in black clothes last Monday, who looked like a clergyman, and who said he was going to Casco Bay, and from thence to London in a mast-ship. The servant soon did his errand, and the landlord went with the Doctor to the stranger at dinner, who wished to know if he could inform him whether Priest Peters had been in Portsmouth.

The landlord replied: "Yes; he preached in our church last "Sunday, and it was said he was going to Casco Bay, to take "passage to London in a mast-ship."

The stranger said: "I am in pursuit of him, and four other "men coming from Boston will be here soon, and we will have "him in custody. I will follow him to Casco Bay, or hell, to take "him. Tell my friends so when they arrive."

He then mounted his horse and rode to the ferry. Asking the ferryman if he had carried over Priest Peters, he answered: "I cannot tell. I carried over a man in black clothes last Mon-"day, who was going to Casco Bay."

The stranger said: "Mr. Ferryman, shoot me over quick, and "I will give you five shillings." The ferryman soon got his five shillings, and the stranger rode off with speed seventy miles, and returned without his prize.

His four companions arrived in the evening, and caused the bells to be rung and the mobs to assemble, who searched the Governor's house and the town to find Dr. Peters, and gain Hancock's reward of 200*l*., but found not the Doctor, who was well secured in a cave on the seashore, where he remained fourteen days.

The Casco Bay news enraged the mob, and they again searched the Governor's house, the town, and Captain Norman's ship, the Fox, placing a guard on board to prevent him taking passengers or sailing for London. They searched the fort three times for the Doctor, but found him not, and placed sentinels in every part of the town, by day and night, to discover him.

The news of the situation of Dr. Peters reached Boston. General Gage and Admiral Graves sent an armed ship of sixteen guns to take him from the cave and carry him to Boston, or any other place he might select. The ship arrived in the night, and took the Doctor on board.

The captain asked him if he should carry him to Boston, or Halifax?

The Doctor said he preferred London, in the ship Fox, Commander Norman, lying in the river Piscataqua, but that the mob would not permit him, or the ship, to sail.

The captain replied: "I will see to that!" and sailed into the river, hailed the ship Fox, and asked if she was ready to sail. The answer was, "Yes." The captain then said: "Let down a "chair." It was done, and he and his men went on board the ship Fox, and called for the master. He appeared, and the captain asked: "What men are those on your decks?"

The master replied: "The committee of safety sent on board "by the mob of the town of Portsmouth."

The captain said: "I commit to your care this worthy and "venerable clergyman, Dr. Samuel Peters; conduct him to your "cabin, and carry him safe to England;" and then, turning to the Committee of Safety, he ordered them to quit the ship in five minutes, or he would throw them overboard into the river. "Your company is not wanted here. I will guard the "ship."

The committee of safety instantly fled into their boats, and went on shore.

The captain ordered the master to hoist his anchors and sails and go to sea. The master obeyed the order, and, October 27, 1774, sailed down the river, the captain following with his ship. The mob on shore, behind some rocks, fired three cannon at the war-ship, who returned their shots, which silenced the mob, and they ran away.

The captain guarded the ship Fox out to sea, clear of the land, and then took leave of her and returned to Boston.

Captain Norman arrived in Portsmouth, December 21, 1774, and carefully executed his orders—put Dr. Peters on shore, who next day reached London, where he was graciously received by the Lord-Archbishop of Canterbury, Dr. Cornwallis, and the Lord-Bishop of London, Dr. Terrick, and the Ministry. He had

APPENDIX.   273

also the honour of kissing the hand of his Majesty, King George the Third.

General Gage and Admiral Graves, two years after, sent, in the Somerset man-of-war, the only daughter of Dr. Peters to England, who was at boarding-school at Boston, (she having seen the battle of Bunker's Hill,) to save her from future evils, and comfort her father in his retreat from the tyranny of the mobs in his native country.

Thus suffered the venerable and exemplary Dr. Samuel Peters, only for obeying his conscience, his God, his king, and the laws of his native country, by censuring the rioters and destroyers of the teas, the property of the East-India Company.

He was highly respected, in England as well as in America, by all pious, benevolent, scientific, and moral christians of all denominations; and he never knew he had an enemy, (until Gov. Jonathan Trumbull, of Connecticut, vouchsafed to support the atrocities of the mobs,) as appears by his benevolent conduct in England to his enemies of New-England, who had ill-treated him two years before the rebellion was commenced.

After the war began many of the Windham mob, who spat in the Doctor's face and grossly insulted him otherwise, were brought prisoners into England, and were in great distress. They then applied to the Doctor for help, (knowing his character in America,) and they never applied in vain; he always helped them, and in many instances obtained their release. They returned home and reported that Dr. Peters was like Joseph in Egypt, and had delivered them out of all their troubles. "Dr. Peters," they said, "fed us when we were hungry, clothed us when naked, visited us "in prison, and delivered us out of our distress. He never "reproached us for what we had done to him and his family. "When we confessed to having abused him, he replied, 'God "'hath sent me here before you to save your lives; it was not "'you that sent me here. Haste ye; go home, and sin no "'more.'"

Notwithstanding such reports were spread through New-England by the redeemed captives, the destroyers of the teas, and their mobs, continued their malicious and false sayings in the newspapers against the Doctor, of whom no man in New or Old-England ever knew one crime of his from his birth; but, on the contrary, was known for his actions of charity, goodwill, and kindness, to all of the human family.

In June, 1806, the Doctor paid a visit to Hebron, his native town, and was received with acclamations of great joy by the inhabitants, the children of his contemporaries, who were all dead in thirty-one years during his absence (except ten persons). He remained in Hebron six weeks, and then paid a visit to Hertford, the capital of Connecticut State, once his faithful parish, and now the seat of bishops. He was kindly and joyfully received by the inhabitants, with whom he spent some time with great pleasure, and from thence returned to New-York, which he made his home.

The Rev. Messrs. Mansfield and Veits were cast into gaol, and afterwards tried for high treason against America. Their real offence was charitably giving victuals and blankets to loyalists flying from the rage of drunken mobs. They were fined and imprisoned, to the ruin of themselves and families. The Rev. Messrs. Graves, Scovil, Debble, Nichols, Leaming, Beach, and divers others, were cruelly dragged through mire and dirt. In short, all the clergy of the Church were infamously insulted, abused, and obliged to seek refuge in the mountains, till the popular frenzy was somewhat abated.

In July, 1776, the Congress, having declared the independence of America, ordered the Commonwealth to be prayed for, instead of the King and royal family. All the loyal episcopal churches north of the Delaware were shut up, except those under the protection of the British army, and one in Newtown, in Connecticut, of which last the Rev. Mr. John Beach was the rector, whose gray hairs, adorned with loyal and christian virtues, overcame even the madness of the *Sober Dissenters*.

This faithful disciple disregarded the congressional mandate, and, praying for the King as usual, they pulled him out of his desk, put a rope about his neck, and drew him across the Osootonoc River at the tail of a boat, to cool his loyal zeal, as they called it; after which the old confessor was permitted to depart, though not without prohibition to pray longer for the King. But his loyal zeal was insuperable. He went to church and prayed again for the King, upon which the *Sober Dissenters* again seized him, and resolved upon cutting out his tongue; when the heroic veteran said: "If my blood must be shed, let it not be done in "the house of God." The pious mob then dragged him out of the church, laid his neck upon a block, and swore they would cut off his head, and insolently cried out: "Now, you old devil, "say your last prayer!" He prayed thus: "God bless King "George, and forgive all his and my enemies." At this unexpected and exalted display of christian patience and charity the mob so far relented as to discharge him, and never molest him afterwards for adhering to the liturgy of the Church of England and his ordination-oath; but they relaxed not their severities towards the other clergymen, because, they said, younger consciences are more flexible.

I cannot conclude this work without remarking what a contrast to the episcopal clergy of Connecticut, and especially the illustrious examples of the venerable Beach and Peters, was offered to many of those that were in the provinces south of the Delaware! In Connecticut, where they suffered everything but death for tenaciously adhering to their ordination-oaths, there some of them, with more enlarged consciences, were not ashamed to commit perjury in prayer and rebellion in preaching. Though, be it remembered, these expressions were decent when compared with those of the fanatics in New-England.

The following prayer, used by them before Congress after the declaration of independence, is likely to gratify the curiosity of my readers. It brought the clergymen into disgrace merely by its moderation:

"O Lord, our heavenly Father, King of Kings and Lord of "Lords, who dost from Thy throne behold all the dwellers of the "earth, and reignest with power supreme and uncontrolled over "all kingdoms, empires, and governments: look down in mercy, "we beseech Thee, upon these our American States, who have "fled to Thee from the rod of the oppressor, and thrown them- "selves upon Thy gracious protection, desiring henceforth to be "dependent only on Thee. To Thee have they appealed for the

" righteousness of their cause; to Thee do they look up for that
" countenance and support which Thou alone canst give. Take
" them, therefore, heavenly Father, under Thy nurturing care;
" give them wisdom in council and valour in the field. Defeat the
" malicious designs of our cruel adversaries; convince them of the
" unrighteousness of their cause, and, if they still persist in their
" sanguinary purposes, O let the voice of Thy unerring justice,
" sounding in their hearts, constrain them to drop the weapons of
" war from their enervated hands in the day of battle. Be Thou
" present, O God of wisdom, and direct the councils of this hon-
" ourable Assembly. Enable them to settle things upon the best
" and surest foundation; that the scenes of blood may soon be
" closed; that order, harmony, and peace may effectually be re-
" stored, and truth and justice, religion and piety, prevail and
" flourish amongst Thy people. Preserve the health of their
" bodies and the vigor of their minds; shower down upon them,
" and the millions they represent, such temporal blessings as
" Thou seest expedient for them in this world, and crown them
" with everlasting glory in the world to come. All this we ask
" in the name, and through the merits, of Jesus Christ Thy Son,
" our Saviour. Amen."

INDEX.

A

Allen, Ethan, origin of his fame, 106; joins in the secret expedition against Ticonderoga, 257.
Amusements, 221.
Argal, Sir Samuel, compels the Dutch at Manhattan to submit, 12.
Arnold, Dr. Benedict, attacks Dr. Peters, 268.
Arran, Earl of, claims part of Connecticut, 27.
Ashford, 133.
Assembly, General, chosen by the people, 82; times of meeting, 83; their laws not to be repealed but by their own authority, 85; resolved to settle their lands on Susquehanna River, 96; hold a special meeting to consider the Stamp-act, 232; vote that the Governor do not take the oath required by it, 235; and treat the populace on its repeal, 239; conduct of, in regard to Colonel Street Hall and the revolters, 240-243.

B

Bays, two principal, 119.
Beach, the Rev. Mr., joins the Church of England, 167; ignominiously and most cruelly treated, his heroism, 274.
Bear, a she, and her cubs, killed by General Putnam, 133, 134.
Beauford, 161.
Bellamy, the Rev. Dr., some account of, 146.
Birds, 185, 186.
Bishop of London's authority derided by an American judge, 144.
Bishops, their neglectful conduct in regard to America, 172; animadversions upon, 173; notices concerning, 61, 171, 172.
Blaxton, the Rev. Mr., particulars relating to, 51, *Note.*
Blue Laws, specimens of, 58.
Bolton, 139.
Boston, peninsula of, obtained and occupied by the Rev. Mr. Blaxton, 51, *Note;* town of, founded, 16; its port shut up, 256; attack meditated against it, 258; Neck fortified by General Gage, 258.
Bostwick, the Rev. Mr., attacked by the mob, 254.
Boundaries, disputes concerning, 99; of Connecticut, as at present allowed, 114.
Bribery disallowed, 222.
Briton, Mr., humourous story concerning him and a deacon's daughter, 214.
Brown, the Rev. Mr., declares for the Church of England, 166.
Brownists set sail for America, and found Plymouth, 16.

INDEX.

Buckley, the Rev. John, some account of, 141.
Buckley, the Rev. Peter, character of, 142.
Bull-fly, description of, 187.
Bundling, singular custom of, justified, 224–229.
Byles, Dr. Mather, disingenuous treatment, 218.

C

Canaan, 147.
Cansey American Indians enjoy liberty in perfection, 110.
Canterbury, 135.
Caterpillars ravage the border of Connecticut River, 131.
Chandler, the Rev. Thomas Bradbury, where born, 133.
Charter, petitioned for privately, 66; obtained, 68; claim founded upon, and prevarications concerning it, 36; powers conferred by, 83, 84; strengthens notions of independence, 86; formally surrendered by the colony to Sir Edmund Andros, 89; regained by a mob, hid in a tree, and reassumed, 90; violated by George II., 102.
Chatham, 139.
Church of England, the first erected in Connecticut, 163; professors of the, number of, in 1770, 168, 169; reason of their great increase, 166; their zeal, 170; measures adverse to, 171.
Clergy, Episcopal, in Connecticut, morality of, 171; one punished for not observing the Sabbath agreeably to the notions of Sober Dissenters, 213; acquire immortal honour by adhering to their ordination-oaths, 260; immoral, anti-episcopal, and rebellious conduct of some of them in the southern provinces, 172–174.

Colchester, 141.
Colden, Lieutenant-Governor, of New-York, grants lands in Verdmont, 105.
Coldness of the winter in Connecticut accounted for, 176.
Comic Liturgy, acted in Connecticut on occasion of the Stamp-act, 231.
Commerce of Connecticut, 191.
Company for Propagating the Gospel in New-England, charter obtained for the, and abuse of it, 52, *Note.*
Connecticote, his kingdom, 135; his conduct toward the settlers, 53; his death, 57.
Connecticut, its latitude and longitude, 175; whence named, 15; three parties of English adventurers arrive in, 16; right to the soil of, considered, 31–35; civil and religious establishments and proceedings of the first English settlers, 37; forms a confederacy with New-Plymouth and Massachusets-Bay, 62; obtains a charter of incorporation, 68; divided into counties, townships, &c., 83; sketch of its religious-political free system since the Charter, 97–100; half the territory of, granted to the Duke of York, 75; its consequent loss of territory, 77, 101; dimensions of, as at present allowed, 114; description of, at large, 115; treatment English travelers met with then from landlords, 111; proceedings of, in regard to the Stamp-act, 229–245; to the Tea-act, 251; to that for shutting the port of Boston, 253; commits the first overt act of high treason, 254.
Connecticut River, description of, 115; astonishing narrows in it, 115, 116.
Contingencies, extraordinary allow-

INDEX.   279

ance for, 198; of what sort some are, 220.
Convention, grand continental, of dissenting ministers at Newhaven, notices concerning, 160.
Cooper, the Rev. Miles, LL.D., narrowly escapes the fury of the mob in New-York, 258.
Cornwall, 147.
Cotton, the Rev. Mr., notices relating to, 50; *Note*, 138.
Council of Plymouth, their grant, 12.
Courts, instituted in Connecticut, 83, 84; cruelty of the ecclesiastical, in New-England, 128.
Coventry, 132.
Cuba, description of an animal so called, and extraordinary qualities of male and female, 183.
Cursette, Mrs., surprising discovery of her will, 153.
Customs of the people, 211; borrowed of the Indians, 223.
Cutler, the Rev. Dr., joins the Church of England, 166.

D

Dagget, the Rev. Mr. Naphthali, character of, 160.
Danbury, 168; burnt, 258.
Davenport, the Rev. John, arrives at Newhaven, 20; his church-system, 42, 43.
Dead, buried with their feet to the west, 123.
Debble, the Rev. Mr., cruelly treated, 274.
Derby, 162.
Dixwell, buried at Newhaven, 63, *Note*.
Douglas, Dr., some account of, 101.
Durham, 162.
Dutch, get footing on Manhattan Island, but are compelled to submit by Argal, 12; revolt, 15.

Dyer, Mr., takes active part in Stamp-act, 236.

E

East Haddam, 139.
East Windsor. *See* Windsor, 139.
Eaton, Mr. Theophilus, arrives at Newhaven, 20; chosen Governor, 42; his true character, 150.
Election, management of, in Connecticut, 222.
Elliot, the Rev. Mr., some mention of, 129.
Endfield, 139.
Expenditure of Connecticut, 196.
Exports of Connecticut, 191.

F

Fairfield, 163; burnt, 260.
Farmington, 142.
Fenwick, George, Esq., first arrival at Saybrook, 17; his and associates' right to settle in Connecticut discussed and disproved, 24—28; disposes of his property in America and returns to England, 49.
Fish of Connecticut, 189.
Fitch, Governor, his conduct on occasion of Stamp-act, 231, 235, 237, 240.
Franklin, Dr., notices concerning, 231, 232, 251.
Frogs, an amazing multitude, humourous story, 129.

G

Gage, General, arrives at Boston, 253; fortifies Boston Neck, 256; in danger of being surprised, 257.
Gates, Sir Thomas, and associates, account of their patent, 11.

Gavelkind, custom of, prevails in Connecticut, 220.
General Assembly. *See* Assembly, 82.
General List, account and specimen of, 206.
Gibbs, the Rev. Mr., inhuman treatment of, 143.
Glastonbury, 149.
Glover, Mr., his concealment of Mrs. Cursette's will, 152.
Glow-bug described, 188.
Goshen, 147.
Government, some account of, 198; the Clergy, Merchants, and Lawyers, the three grand parties in the State, 201.
Governments, bad policy of most, 245.
Graves, the Rev. Mr., cruel treatment of, 274.
Great Barrington, why obnoxious to the mob, 255.
Greensmith, Mrs., the first person executed as a witch in America, 136.
Greenwich, 163.
Grenville, George, Esq., mobbed, hung and burnt in effigy, 234, *Note.*
Grigson, Mr., extraordinary concealment of his will, 150.
Groton, 122.
Guilford described, 161.

H

Haddam, 139.
Hall, Colonel Street, chosen commander of the mob of revolters against the General Assembly, his conduct, and extraordinary speech, 240–243.
Hamilton, Marquis of, his title to part of Connecticut proved, 26.
Hancock, Mr., his opposition to the Tea-act, and artifice in disposing of his own stock, 251.

Hancock, John, Esq., his dishonourable conduct in regard to Mrs. Cursette's will, 152, 153.
Harrington, 142.
Harrison, Peter, Esq., his spirited and honourable conduct in discovering Mr. Grigson's will, 151.
Harrison, Major-General Thomas, hanged at Charing Cross, 141.
Hartland, 147.
Harvey, Mr. Joel, receives a premium from the Society of Arts in London, 147.
Haynes, John, settled at Hertford, 18; chosen Governor, 38, 39.
Hebron, description of, 139; refuses to contribute to the relief of the Bostonians, on the shutting up of their port, 262; town-meeting for collecting money, 263.
Hertford, first settlement there by the English, 16, 17; by what authority, 30; description of, 136; curiosities in, 137.
Hillhouse, William, present at interview with Governor Jonathan Trumbull, 267.
Hooker, Rev. Thomas, settles at Hertford, 18; his motive for quitting Massachusets-Bay, 29; Church-system, 39.
Howling wilderness, Connecticut improperly so called, 107.
Huet, the Rev. Mr., some mention of, 139.
Humble-bee, description of, 188.
Humility, a bird so called, described, 186.

I

Imports, 192.
Independence, idea of, strengthened by Charter, 86; symptoms of, manifested by the colonies, 229; not the wish of the common

INDEX. 281

people, 260; formally declared by Congress, 274.
Indians, their mode of counting, 35, *Note*; number of them killed in Hispaniola, Porto Rico, and South America, and in Connecticut and Massachusets-Bay, 107; in the whole of North America and West Indies, 108; their aversion to the Protestant religion, 206.
Ingersoll, David, barbarously treated, 254.
Ingersoll, Jared, Esq., mobbed, and forced to resign his post of Stamp-master, 233; hung and burnt in effigy, 233, *Note.*
Inhabitants in Connecticut, 190; their hospitality to strangers, 211; of the men, 223; of the women, 224.
Insects, 187.

J

Johnson, Dr. Samuel, character of, 161; declares for the Church of England, 167; treacherous embassy of his son, 258.
Joshua, a pretended sachem, 32.

K

Kent, 147.
Killingsley, 133.
Killingsworth, 129.
King's statue, at New-York, destroyed, 259.

L

Latitude and longitude of Connecticut, 175.
Laws, Blue, specimen of, 58–60; other laws, 85.
Law-suits, amazing number of, 200;

remarkable nature of some of them, 211.
Leaming, the Rev. Mr., cruelly treated, 274.
Lebanon, 132.
Litchfield described, 144.
Little Isaac, a nickname given to Americans, 189.
Lyme, 124.

M

Manners of the people, 211.
Mansfield, the Rev. Mr., tried for high treason, 274.
Mansfield, town, 132.
Manufactures of Connecticut, 190.
Mason, his claim to land in Connecticut, 33.
Massachusets-Bay, settled by Puritans, 16; loses part of its territory, 103.
Merret, his singular treatment, charged with incest, 127.
Middletown described, 138.
Milford, 161.
Mill, curious invention of Joel Harvey, 147.
Minister, Sober Dissenting, manner of settling and dismissing, 217.
Moodus, a pretended sachem, 32.
More, Sir Henry, begins to regrant Verdmont, 105.
Motte treacherously sent against Ticonderoga and Crown Point, 257.
Moyley, the Rev. Mr., fined for marrying a couple of his own parishioners, 144.

N

Neal, the Rev. Mr., his representation about Sunksquaw, Uncas, Joshua, Moodus, &c., exploded, 32–34, 56; refutation of his

doctrine concerning synods, 125; a sacramental test, 202; the loyalty of New-Englanders, 204; his enmity against the Society for the Propagation of the Gospel exposed, 205; notice concerning, 33, 107.
Negro tried for castration, 85; negro slaves, 108.
Nell, Mr., 164.
New-England, the Massachusets county, first so called by Charles, Prince of Wales, 11; divisions of, 13; cause of its first settlement discussed, 107.
New-Fairfield, 147.
Newhampshire deprived of territory, 103.
Newhaven, first settled by the English, 20; totally without authority, 31; early proceedings, 56; Blue Laws, 58; state of, after the death of Cromwell, 62; accedes to the Charter, 69; particular description of, 147; a ship fitted out to secure a patent, and wonderful consequences, 149.
New-Hertford, 147.
New Lights, notices concerning, 99, 202-204.
New-London, described, 120; port of, well calculated for the grand emporium of Connecticut, 194.
New-Milford, 146.
Newtown, 168.
New-York, gains land from Connecticut, 77, 101; from Massachusets-Bay and Newhampshire, 103, 104; constitution of, subverted by the Sober Dissenters, 258.
Nichols, Colonel, deprives Connecticut of Long Island, 77.
Nichols, the Rev. Mr., cruelly treated, 274.
Norwalk, 163; burnt, 260.
Norwich, description of, 123.

O

Old Lights, notices concerning, 99, 202-205.
Oneko, King of Mohegan, 32.
Onions, vast quantity raised in Weathersfield, 138; beds of, weeded by the females, 138.
Osootonoc River, description of, 119.

P

Parsons, Hugh, found guilty of witchcraft, 137.
Penderson, Rev. Mr., joins the Church of England, 167.
Peters, the Rev. Hugh, account of himself and family, 50.
Peters, the Rev. Samuel, account of, 140; interview with Governor Trumbull, 266; escape from Portsmouth and Boston, 270; reward offered by John Hancock for his capture, 270.
Peters, Rev. Thomas, his arrival at Saybrook, 17; Church-system, 37; school, 49; character, 50; some particulars of his life, 50, *Note.*
Peters, William, particulars relating to, 50-52, *Note.*
Phelps, treacherously sent upon an expedition against Ticonderoga and Croton Point, 257.
Pitt, Mr., a Churchman, whipped for not attending meeting, 208.
Plainfield, 135.
Plymouth, New, founded, 16.
Pomeroy, Rev. Dr., character, 140; sent for by the Windham mob, 265.
Pomfret, 133.
Population, 190.
Pork, unfair dealing in, 193.
Potter, Deacon, unjustly convicted of bestiality, 154.
Poultry of Connecticut, 185.
Powwow, ancient Indian rite, cele-

INDEX. 283

bration of, at Stratford described, 164.
Prayer of some of the Episcopal clergy in the southern provinces before Congress, 275.
Presbyterians, disliked and ill-treated by Sober Dissenters, 135, 199.
Preston, 123.
Produce of Connecticut, 178.
Pumpkin, hair cut by the shell, 153, 154.
Pumpkin-heads, a name given to New-Englanders, 153.
Putnam, General, curious anecdotes of, 133; kills a bear and cubs, 134; his narrow escape from Indians, 134; terrible to them, 135; alarms the country in a letter concerning Admiral Graves and General Gage, 262.

Q

Quackery triumphant, 145.
Quaker, shrewd retort of one upon his judges, 99.
Quinnipiog, kingdom, 147; refuses to grant land to the settlers, and is murdered, 56.

R

Rattlesnake, some account of, 188; use of skin, 223.
Reading, 168.
Rebellion, true sources of, in America, 247.
Religion, the established, 84, 85.
Reptiles, 188.
Revenue, 196; objections against raising, in America, 244.
Rhode-Island, infamous law of the General Assembly, 169.
Ridgfield, 168; burnt, 259.
Rivers, the three principal, described, 114–118.

Rivington, Mr., plundered, 258.

S

Sabbath, rigidly observed, 213; how broken by an Episcopal clergyman, 213.
Salary of the Governor, Lieutenant-Governor, Treasurer, &c., 198.
Salisbury, 147.
Sandeman, Rev. Mr., doctrine of, 168.
Sassacus, Sachem of the Pequods, his kingdom and character, 119, 120.
Saybrook, founded, 16; described, 124; its civil and religious establishments, 37; early proceedings, 46; enters the confederacy, 62; refuses to send agents to England to oppose the king, 49; forms an alliance with Hertford, 49; and joins in a secret application for a Charter, 64.
Saybrook platforms, some account of the, 155.
Scovil, the Rev. Mr., cruel treatment of, 274.
Sealbury, Rev. Dr., taken prisoner, 258.
Sects, religious, in Connecticut, some account of the, 198.
Sharon, famous for a mill, 147.
Ship, wonderful story of one fitted out in Newhaven, 149.
Sick, horrid mode of visiting, 219.
Skunk, description and wonderful property of the, 184.
Smith, Rev. Mr., notices of, 53, 138.
Smith, William, notices concerning, 100–102, 105, 113, 175.
Sober Dissenters, religion of, in Connecticut, 85; their uncandid conduct toward Episcopalians, Anabaptists, Quakers, &c., in regard to parish rates, 207; and their severe treatment of

Mr. Gibbs for refusing to pay them, 143; their humanity to sick strangers and persons shipwrecked, 219; partial support, 219.
Society for the Propagation of the Gospel in Foreign Parts, notices concerning, 52, *Note*, 105, 167, 170–175, 205.
Soil, 178.
Sommers, 139.
Stafford, the New-England "Bath," 142.
Stamp-Act, proceedings and opinions relating to, in Connecticut, 229.
Stirling, Earl of, his claim in Connecticut, 25.
Stonington, 122.
Stratford, description of, 163.
Stratford River, 118.
Strong, Rev. Nehemiah, 160.
Suffield, 139.
Sunksquaw, a pretended sachem, 32.
Superstition, striking instance, 200.
Symsbury mines, account of, 142.

T

Tarbox, Capt. David, remark on leaving Governor Trumbull's house, 267.
Tea, act of sending, to America opposed, 251.
Temple, Mr., seditious letters imputed to, 251.
Test, sacramental, unnecessary in New-England, 202.
Thames River described, 114.
Ticonderoga, secret expedition against, 258.
Tolland, 139.
Torrington, 147.
Travellers, English, how treated by landlords, 111.
Tree-frog, agility of, 189.
Trumbull, Governor, furnishes a dress for the effigy of Mr. Grenville, 233, *Note;* writes an insidious letter to General Gage, 256; adds to an alarming one of General Putnam's, 262; and spirits up the mob against the loyalists, 264; writes the eighteen articles for Dr. Peters to sign, 264; his reply to Dr. Peters when asking protection from the Windham mob, 266.
Trumbull, David, in command of the Windham mob, 264; handing Dr. Peters the document containing high treason, to sign, 264; his remark upon Dr. Peters refusing to sign it, 265.
Tryon, Governor, his character, 113; escapes the mob at New-York, 258; leaves Danbury, 258; Ridgfield, 259; releases the prisoners at Newhaven, 260; leaves Fairfield and Norwalk, 260.

U

Uncas, a pretended sachem, 32.
Union, 132.

V

Verdmont, account of, 106.
Viets, Rev. Mr., tried for high treason, 274.
Visey, Rev. Mr., suppresses the powwow at Stratford, 164.
Voluntown, 135.

W

Wallingford, description of, 162.
Warwick, Earl of, his title to the soil of any part of Connecticut disproved, 23–26.
Waterbury, 162.
Weathersfield, description of, 138; singular industry of the females there, 138.

INDEX.

Wentworth, Benning, Esq., grants townships in Verdmont, 104.
Whapperknocker, description of, 182.
Wheelock, Dr. Eleazer, notices concerning, 53, *Note*, 132.
Whippoorwill, description of, 186.
Whitefield, Rev. George, anecdote of, 121; and character, 161; attempts to work a miracle at Saybrook, 128; his character of the people of Norwich, 124; of those of Hebron, 140; of Guilford, 161; of Connecticut in general, 170, 212.
Whitemore, Rev. Mr., joins Church of England, 166.
Will, scandalous concealment of Mr. Grigson's, 151; of Mrs. Cursette's, 152.
Willington, 132.

Winchester, 147.
Windham, 129; inhabitants alarmed by frogs, 130.
Windsor described, 139.
Wolcott, Oliver, treacherous embassy of, 258.
Woodbury, 146.
Woodchuck, 183.
Woodstock, 133.
Wooster, General, attacks Dr. Peters, 268; mortally wounded, 259.
Wright, Major, his actions with the Windham mob, 266.

Y

Yale College, account of, 155–161.
York, Duke of, obtains a grant including half of Connecticut, 75.

THE END.